Economics, Entrepreneurship and Utopia

T0298716

In the early 1800s, Robert Owen was a mill owner, a political figure, and an advocate for social reform, and his publications attained considerable circulation. He believed that people need good working conditions in order to be encouraged to work and to be motivated to learn. Despite the higher costs associated with this kind of operation, compared to the traditional ones, Owen's management resulted in increased productivity and profit. His results caught the attention of men of wealth who were interested in social reform. In particular, at a similar time, Jeremy Bentham was developing his own theories. Owen and Bentham seemed to be based on some similar ideas that the greatest happiness creates the greatest results. Their ideas developed against the backdrop of the Industrial Revolution, and growing social and economic problems in England.

Owen and Bentham were forerunners of highly relevant current theories of economics – marginalism, entrepreneurship, personnel management, and constructivism. They were acquainted with such important authors as James Mill, Malthus, Ricardo and John Stuart Mill. However, their economic theories were ruled out by classical economists, who actively tried to silence perspectives different from the orthodoxy. This book presents an innovative study of these two social thinkers and reformers, who have rarely, if ever, been studied together. This comparative study provides new context both on the social debate taking place during the Industrial Revolution, and on the development of modern social thought, in particular, the relationship between socialism and utilitarianism.

Economics, Entrepreneurship and Utopia will be of great relevance to scholars with an interest in the history of economic ideas, the history of entrepreneurship, and social reform in both historical and contemporary contexts.

Estrella Trincado is Tenured Professor in History of Economic Thought at the Complutense University of Madrid, Spain. Visiting Post-Doctoral Fellow at the Department of Economics in Harvard University, she was awarded the History of Economic Analysis Award in 2005 by the ESHET and the ESHET Young Scholar of the Year Prize for 2011.

Manuel Santos-Redondo is Associate Professor of History of Economic Thought and Business History at the Complutense University of Madrid, Spain. He has published many articles on entrepreneurship and innovation, and cultural industries.

Routledge Studies in the History of Economics

Economics, Entrepreneurship and Utopia

The Economics of Jeremy Bentham
and Robert Owen

**Estrella Trincado and
Manuel Santos-Redondo**

LONDON AND NEW YORK

First published 2018 by Routledge

2 Park Square, Milton Park, Abingdon, Oxfordshire OX14 4RN
52 Vanderbilt Avenue, New York, NY 10017

Routledge is an imprint of the Taylor & Francis Group, an informa business

First issued in paperback 2019

British Library Cataloguing-in-Publication Data
A catalogue record for this book is available from the British Library

Library of Congress Cataloging-in-Publication Data
Names: Trincado, Estrella, author. | Santos Redondo, Manuel, author.
Title: Economics, entrepreneurship and utopia : the economics of Jeremy Bentham and Robert Owen / Estrella Trincado and Manuel Santos-Redondo.
Description: Abingdon, Oxon ; New York, NY : Routledge, 2017. | Includes index.
Identifiers: LCCN 2017008259| ISBN 9781138186132 (hardback) | ISBN 9781315644011 (ebook)
Subjects: LCSH: Bentham, Jeremy, 1748-1832. | Owen, Robert, 1771-1858. | Economics–Great Britain–History–19th century. | Entrepreneurship–Great Britain–History–19th century. | Utopian socialism–Great Britain–History–19th century.
Classification: LCC HB103.A2 T75 2017 | DDC 330.15–dc23
LC record available at https://lccn.loc.gov/2017008259

ISBN: 978-1-138-18613-2 (hbk)
ISBN: 978-0-367-87642-5 (pbk)

Typeset in Times New Roman
by Cenveo Publisher Services

Contents

Illustrations

Part I

Bentham, Owen

Utopians and entrepreneurs

1 Introduction

The story of this book begins during a business visit to Glasgow by Robert Owen (May 1771 – November 1858), a young and successful Manchester industrial manager. He met David Dale, a prosperous Scottish businessman, the owner of New Lanark mills. It was the biggest factory in Great Britain. The meeting seemed to be a part of the love story of Owen with David Dale's daughter, Caroline, finally Owen's wife, but actually it was something quite different. Owen and his partners bought the estate from David Dale, and he became manager, as well as part owner, of the mills in January 1810.

Being an Englishman among Scottish people, at first Owen was regarded with suspicion as a stranger. It took him six years to win the confidence of employees, even after continuing Dale's policy of treating the workforce much better than workers were treated in any other factory.

Some of Owen's schemes entailed considerable expense and this displeased his partners. The expenditure they most objected to was the establishment of new education methods in schools instituted for children in New Lanark. After 1809, Owen frequently sought new partners.

By that time, Owen had become a political figure and an advocate for social reform and his publications attained considerable circulation. They caught the attention of men of wealth who were really interested in social reform. Among other intellectuals with whom Owen associated was James Mill (1773–1836), a philosopher and he was a close friend of the philosopher Jeremy Bentham (February 1748 – June 1832).

After some persuasion, Bentham and other philanthropists, such as the Quaker William Allen, invested some money in New Lanark's cotton mills a remarkable business not only from the humanitarian point of view but also in a strict business sense. In particular, according to Bentham's nephew, George Bentham, Jeremy invested some 10,000 pounds in January 1814 when he was 65 (Bentham, 1997, pp. 184–188).[1] It was a considerable amount of money.[2] New Lanark's shares paid Bentham 500 pounds annually, and in 1814 he rented a large place, Ford Abbey, outside London, for which he paid £315 a year. Years later he had to give the place up because it was too expensive for his income. So, at the time, a £10,000 investment and a £500 return were substantial sums. This investment yielded Bentham at least 5% a year on capital for many years.

Owen said that "his friends have stated that it was the only successful enterprise in which he [Bentham] ever engaged. He, like Mr. Walker, never saw New Lanark" (Owen, 1857, pp. 95–96, 129; see Cole, 1953, p. 169). Indeed, Bentham's own investments were something of a failure. An inheritance received in 1796 provided him with financial stability and, with that acquired money, Bentham invested in the bankrupt James Grellier and Co., a manufacturer of Roman Cement; and in September 1800, he tried to build a 'frigidarium' or ice-house for the preservation of fish, fruits, and vegetables (Bentham, 1838, vol. x, p. 346; see Cohen, 1997). At the same time, Bentham was writing his papers on the Panopticon (Bentham, 1791). For some 20 years Bentham pursued – fruitlessly and at great expense – the Panopticon idea (Bentham, 1838–1843, vol. x, p. 9, p. 144, Griffiths, 1884). Another of Bentham's plans was devised in 1815 for a 'Chrestomathic school'. The scheme never came to fruition. He also devoted a lot of time and effort trying to interest the Treasury in currency schemes, he suggested to the Americans that they should build a canal through Panama and he told the Bank of England how to create an unforgeable banknote. Finally, he also invested in real estate (Bentham, 1838, vol. 10, p. 479, p. 573). As Hazlitt (1969) says, "Mr. Bentham... is a little romantic or so, and has dissipated part of a handsome fortune on impractical speculations".

Robert Owen ran the New Lanark's cotton mills until December 1824, when he went to America to start a new colony, after a long period of friction with Allen and some of his other partners. In 1828, another Quaker, John Walker and his family bought the shares of Robert Owen and his sons William and Robert Dale. He began to run the business, which continued being a successful company and a model social system.

It looks evident that New Lanark seemed to fit Bentham's ideas of the business entrepreneur and his ideals of social reform. Actually, at the moment of the investment, Bentham had developed a clear theory of entrepreneurship. He gave a definition of "business managers" and "entrepreneurs" ("projectors"), presented in his first works, in particular in 1787's *Defence of Usury*.[3] Owen's experiment could have reinforced Bentham's theory, as well as proving in some way the importance of innovation, which is a central idea in *Defence of Usury* (see Bentham, 1818). Owen had made some important innovations in management practice. As he did not wish to conduct the business along ordinary lines, since he believed that people need good laboring conditions to be encouraged to work, he supported education and labor reform, and housing of his employees.

Actually, the conditions at New Lanark for the workers and their families were idyllic for the time. In Owen's time, some 2,500 people lived at New Lanark, many from the poorhouses of Glasgow and Edinburgh. Of those 2,500, 500 were children for whom there was no room in overcrowded poorhouses and charities in Glasgow and Edinburgh. Many of these children worked in the mills and had been well provided for by David Dale, but Owen extended Dale's precedent and in 1816 opened at New Lanark the first infant school in Great Britain. Owen also improved the housing at New Lanark, encouraged the people in personal order, cleanliness, and thrift, and opened a store with fair prices and limited sales of alcoholic beverages. Even given the much higher costs associated with this kind of operation, compared to the traditional ones, Owen's management, based on the wellbeing of the workforce, resulted in increased productivity and profit.

Based largely on his successes at New Lanark, Owen emerged as a leader of social reform, although his successes in New Lanark would contrast with later failures in New Colonies.[4] New Lanark became one of the best known industries of the time and was a place of pilgrimage for social reformers, statesmen and royal personages, including Nicholas, the future emperor of Russia.[5]

However, in his works, Bentham never quoted New Lanark as an example of business. He never visited New Lanark. The fact that an investor so interested in education who was also interested in entrepreneurship took no serious intellectual interest in New Lanark is a strange circumstance. Was there any contradiction between both Bentham's and Owen's management theories, or was the problem a question of Robert Owen and Bentham not getting along?

It is true that Bentham had an odd relationship with Owen; however, after 1824, although New Lanark was then run by Walker's family, Bentham still took no interest in the business. For everybody, New Lanark continued to be linked to Owen's name, but Bentham´s lack of curiosity is somewhat baffling. Maybe Bentham failed to recognize Owen's importance because he disregarded Owen's role as successful entrepreneur, misguided by Owen's messianic personality, and his relevance as an advocate of social reform and communism. However, this public image was not so strange to Bentham as both Owen and Bentham were seen with hostility by the general public at their suggestions for greater sexual and religious freedom. By the time of his business success, Robert Owen was an open atheist, not a socialist. His views on religion and philosophy were presented in *A New View of Society* (1813).

Bentham's mistake has been a common mistake, or bias, among historians ever since: there are plenty of books and articles about "Owen the socialist and the social reformer"; but just a few papers on Owen as a successful manager and entrepreneur in the textile sector during the industrial revolution, in Manchester and New Lanark.[6] And the problem is that this is still true for historians today.

This book is a theoretical and factual explanation of these riddles that compares the theories and practices of these two leading figures, Robert Owen and Jeremy Bentham, trying to understand their influences in the political economy circles and the lessons that we may draw from them for our present society. Although in their living period Owen and Bentham were considered similar in their reformation aims and in their readiness to defend the principle of the greatest happiness to the greatest number, as Semple (1993, p. 307) points out, too much weight should not be put on the similarities between them; the differences between them are more substantial. Those differences are the basis for two different views of institutions and two different philosophies of life, which nowadays are also a part of the different theories of the social phenomena that economists use in their economic models and explanations. Differences are also part of the contemporary debates, which may shed some light on twenty first century worries. As Leavis says talking about Bentham and Coleridge, both men, dissimilar in almost everything, renewed a lesson given to mankind by every age. Bentham's and Owen's theories seem more similar than those of Bentham and Coleridge; and for that very same reason, lessons taken from their differences are much more interesting and go into the farthest depths of human understanding.

So, in the first part of this book we will study personal and intellectual connections between Owen and Bentham, and also their mutual distrust and fundamental differences, which lead us to talk about different philosophies of life. In a second part, we are going to study the performance of Owen and Bentham as entrepreneurs or projectors, and their contribution to the theory of entrepreneurship, which is quite important for both authors. Part III will deal with their proposals of social reform, one put into practice in Owen's New Lanark; and the other constituting the basis for the modern social and economic theory. In this case, main differences are seen in their theory of education, although both may be considered forerunners of present theories such as constructivism and behaviourism. In the last section of this part we will deal with social circles of the time and personal and theoretical links of Owen and Bentham with James Mill, Malthus, Ricardo, Mill, utopian socialism and others. In this very relevant section we see that Owen was being cornered by political economist circles and prominent figures such as David Ricardo more for his image as an extreme communist who put the status quo in jeopardy than for his proposals. Finally, some concluding remarks will be presented that show the importance of having compared such relevant leaders of entrepreneurship and thought.

Notes

1   These figures are not clear. Owen wrote (much later, in 1857), that he told Walker, his leading partner, "to form a partnership of thirteen shares, each share to be ten thousand pounds; and I intend to hold five of those shares". Walker took three shares, and the other 6 partners – Bentham, Foster, Allen, Fox, and Gibbs – took £ 10,000 each. By 4th July 1820, Bentham had £5,491 invested in New Lanark (Letter from Jeremy Bentham to Samuel Bentham, 4 July 1820, Bentham 1994, pp. 5–8).
2   A craftsman's annual salary at the time was no more than 50 pounds (Harte, 2005), and an established doctor or lawyer may have received about 600 pounds.
3   In *Defence of Usury* Bentham talks about managers in modern Schumpeterian terms, as "the prudent and well grounded projector, if the existence of such a being were to be supposed", probably the sober people in Adam Smith's terms. Bentham talks about entrepreneurs (projectors) as "all such persons as, in the pursuit of wealth, strike out into any new channel and, more especially, into any channel of invention'", actually "prodigals and projectors" in Smith's terms. See Pesciarelli (1989), Hébert and Link (2006) and Trincado (2004b).
4   Obviously, it was not only Owen's control of the firm that had influence in its success, but also some economies of localization. However, his success in Manchester and New Lanark was mainly due to personal leadership, technical expertise in cotton spinning and textile marketing, and self-confidence. And we know this because his failure in later enterprise and experiment was also due to some excesses of the same virtues: excess of self-confidence and extreme individual leadership in the field for which Owen lacked the "technical" expertise: intellectual and political training.
5   Even quite recently, in December 2001, New Lanark's importance was recognized by UNESCO (2001).
6   On Owen as an industrial manager and entrepreneur, see Chaloner, 1954, Chatterji, 2009, Cooke, 1979, Gorb, 1951, Robertson, A. J., 1971.

2 The connection between Bentham and Owen

2.1. The meeting between two personalities

Around 1800, both the Enlightenment and the Industrial Revolution had led to new labour relations and social proposals. Debates on poor laws and unemployment were in fashion after the Napoleonic wars (see Lees, 1998, Quigley, 1996). The new social reformers and utopian socialists were usually far away from industrialists and businessmen, in terms of ideas, lives and characters (see Taylor, 2013). But some of them do mix. That was the case with Saint-Simon and Saint-Simonianism in France with the Suez Canal Company and the bank Credit Mobilier (see McWilliam, 1993) and with Robert Owen and Jeremy Bentham in England and Scotland. We start then with a particular and documented confluence of Owen and Bentham, who were both innovators and reformers of the new labour relations, one by a practical man – Owen – and the other by a man of books – Bentham – but close to a real entrepreneur, his brother Samuel. Then, in this chapter we describe the meeting between both philosophers and we try to assess if similarities may lead us to talk about the same philosophies.

We have started the story of the relationship of these great thinkers during a business visit to Glasgow by a young businessman, Robert Owen (see Trincado and Santos, 2014). Owen courted Caroline, the eldest daughter of David Dale. Owen (1857, pp. 51–52) explains that his meeting with David Dale was arranged by Caroline. He met David Dale, owner of the biggest factory in Great Britain, New Lanark mills. Then in 1784 he started a partnership with Richard Arkwright on the Clyde River. Owen at once asked Dale if New Lanark was for sale. Dale was astonished, as Owen was only 28 years old and looked even younger, but he nodded and let him explore the factory. Dale was eager to sell his business, and Owen tried to convince his partners to buy it.

Owen was successful in all these projects: he and his partners bought the estate from David Dale, and soon after he married Caroline, in September 1799. So he set up home there and became manager, as well as part owner, of the mills in January 1810 (Owen, 1857).

At first Owen was regarded with suspicion, especially because some of Owen's schemes entailed considerable expense. In particular, the establishment of new education methods in schools instituted for children in New Lanark. This circumstance displeased his partners, who brought some of his projects to a standstill. In 1809 Owen's partners rebelled against the 'extravagant expenditures', education being Owen's main concern. Owen frequently sought new partners thereafter, but he became tired of finding investors eager to gain high short-term profits. Indeed, Owen was thinking as a businessman, not as a philanthropist (as shown in Owen, 1857, p. 122), but investors did not take into account the implications of continually introducing technical changes, either for the firm's facilities or to motivate the worker. So, financial differences between Owen and his partners were the reason for their discrepancy (Donnachie and Hewitt, 1993, pp. 81–87). Until 1814, Owen definitely sought the greatest possible profit but he sought it within a "cooperative economy" in Keynes' words, as opposed to an entrepreneur economy (Keynes, 1936).

Morton's (1962, p. 78) statement that Owen wanted partners who did not want to obtain the greatest possible profit is not based on evidence. Morton's biography, one of the best available, is an example of the way in which socialist intellectuals tend to deal with the study of Owen (see Santos, 2002). They usually base their claims on an Owen complaint in his autobiography, "I was completely tired of partners who were merely trained to buy cheap and sell dear". But until 1812, Robert Owen was only famed as a businessman (Cooke, 1979). When he wrote his autobiography, he already was a social reformer, not a businessman (Owen, 1857, p. 89). Actually, Owen talked in those days about capitalism as a system that rewards those "who can best succeed in deceiving others by buying the cheapest and selling the dearest... under this system to support life you must be tyrant or slave. If you do not eat the food of others, they will of necessity under this system eat yours".[1]

So, two Owens need to be distinguished. Sometimes we will call them Owen 1 and Owen 2, the successful entrepreneur and the social reformer. Owen 1, the successful entrepreneur, underwent a transformation when he realized that, at that time, working force did not really understand his own interests, and that an education of "false conscienciousness" was needed. In his industrialist period, according to Owen (1957, p. 86), "the workpeople were systematically opposed to every change which I proposed, and did whatever they could to frustrate my object". Owen did not gain his workers' trust until 1812, when a diplomatic crisis made the US cut cotton exports. Then, Owen decided to stop production, but to go ahead with the wage payments, making workers maintain the machinery ready to start up once again. "This procedure won the confidence and the hearts of the whole population" (Owen, 1857, p. 88). Apparently, David Dale did something similar when a fire destroyed part of the factory (Morton, 1962, p. 77). It was in New Lanark, 1788, when a first mill was destroyed by a fire, at the moment the building for the second mill was almost finished (McLaren, 1983).

But by the time of the American diplomatic crisis, due to the success of New Lanark business and the model social scheme, Owen became a political figure and an advocate for social reform. In 1812 he wrote and published a pamphlet called *A Statement Regarding the New Lanark Establishment* (Owen, 1812), and the following year published the first two essays in *A New View of Society;*

or, Essays on the Principle of the Formation of the Human Character. The second of those contains a full account of his methods, purposes and achievements at New Lanark. He expounded on the principles on which his new system of educational philanthropy was based. The non-responsibility of man and the effect of early influences were the hallmarks of Owen's entire system of education and social amelioration. Owen firmly believed that people were the product of their environment, something that increased his support for labour reform (Owen, 1813, Essay 1), see Harrison (1969). From the influences of environment, Owen thought that religion was the greatest obstacle to progress and advocated a natural religion (Herrick, 1985, p. 157).

Owen's publications attained considerable circulation even as far away as London, and, as we have previously said, he caught the attention of men of wealth who were very interested in social reform. Among other intellectuals with whom Owen associated was James Mill. Although Owen never acknowledged the fact, it was probably Mill (and Francis Place) who edited A *New View of Society* and gave the essays the clarity that is missing from some of his later works.[2] Shortly before this, not later than 1810, James Mill had become acquainted with the Quaker William Allen.

It is to be remembered that Quakers are a Christian religious movement generally united in a belief in the ability of each human being to experientially access God, and therefore they profess the priesthood of all believers. Described as natural capitalists, Quakers founded financial institutions, such as Barclays or Lloyds, manufacturing companies, such as Clarks or Cadbury, and philanthropic efforts, including abolition of slavery, prison reform and social justice projects (see Dandelion, 1996 and Reay, 1985). The Quaker Allen was a businessman who secured Owen's active cooperation in a literary enterprise – a quarterly journal, the *Philanthropist*, published for seven years from 1811 at Allen's own risk. Among others, the magazine published articles by James Mill and Jeremy Bentham. Actually, Allen and other Quakers, the same as Jeremy Bentham, were especially interested in prison reform, an interest generally coupled with an opposition to capital punishment (Cooper, 1979).

In 1813, Owen became acquainted by chance with Bentham via Mill and Allen (Cole, 1953, p. 65). Bentham had told Mill to ask Allen for financial advice about investing some money received in compensation for his monetary loss for the Panopticon – £23,000 awarded in 1813 (Bentham 1997, p. 184). In particular, Bentham asked if he should invest in mines. At a dinner in Allen's house, which Allen had arranged in order for Mill and Owen to meet, Allen told Mill to dissuade Bentham from investing in mines as he had lost money some years before in a Cornish mine.[3]

Owen being present during the discussion of these investments, interrupted Allen by saying that if Bentham wished to gain maximum return from an investment, he should buy a share of the Lanark mills. Owen proposed that 5% should be paid on capital and the whole surplus devoted to general education and an improvement in workers' conditions. A building 'at present unoccupied', which ultimately became the Institute for the Formation of Character, was to be equipped with a store cellar, a public kitchen, an eating and exercise room, a school, a lecture room and a church (Donnachie and Hewitt, 1993, p. 96). All in all, he said, he would set a price for New Lanark that did not exceed £100,000 for the whole – and he himself would buy one half. However, after the meeting with Allen and Owen, James Mill did not recommend the investment.[4] Allen would be the one to convince Bentham.

By 1813, Owen's management was under discussion due to his current partners' thinking that the expenses in child education and wellbeing were unnecessary. Owen's partners made him sell New Lanark in a public auction and tried to get the full stake, but Owen made a higher bid with the financial support of his new London partners, and bought New Lanark. Owen bought the business for £114,100. It must have been a well-run business as Owen had bought it for £60,000 in 1799, and in the four-year period from 1809 and 1813 profits rose to £160,000, that is to say £40,000 a year (Owen, 1857, p. 98).

> In a letter to Bentham dated 21 February 1821 Owen explained that the profits to be divided on the last year's business amounted to £15,000, in addition to 5 per cent interest on the capital of each partner (BM Add. MSS. 33545. f. 392, quoted from Harrison 1969, p. 155).

Note that the first figure, £40,000 a year, is recorded in Owen's autobiography, probably to indulge his vanity; but the second, £15,000 a year, is written to a partner in order to pay his part. Anyway, both reflect a remarkable success in business.

On 31 December 1813, six men had joined Owen in this new partnership. The first five were William Allen; Joseph Foster, also a leading Quaker philanthropist; Joseph Fox, a Dissenter; Michael Gibbs, a prestigious Churchman of the City; and John Walker of Arnos Grove, a distinguished amateur of both art and science. These were members of different Christian denominations and the partnership was described as "a mixture of pietistic philanthropy and shrewd, rational calculating Quaker acquisitiveness" (Donnachie and Hewitt, 1993, p. 81). Given their religious inclinations, the five philanthropists seemed strange allies for Owen. The other investor, however, was Jeremy Bentham, who apparently came in after the purchase by Allen, Walker and Fox had actually been completed (Podmore, 1906, p. 98).

There was an element of clear contact between these investors: their interest in education and social reform. Actually, the philanthropists established as a condition for the agreement that they had to create schools "according to the best models of the British system, or any other system that the associates could approve" (Gordon, 1994). According to John Bowring (Bentham's literary executor):

> On the whole it was a fortunate investment; and his [Bentham] influence was always used to keep up the cheerful character of the manufacture, and to administer, as much as possible, to the felicity of the inhabitants, and especially of the younger portion. It was there [at New Lanark] that the first

experiments were made of infant school education – that music and dancing were taught to the children – and that corporal punishment and coercive discipline were wholly excluded [...]. Bentham was attracted by Owen's proposals – who had desired to get rid of his partners, inasmuch as they thwarted his plans of improvement. His theory was, that while he made a manufacturing population more virtuous and happy, he could also render them more productive to their employers: and in this respect he certainly fulfilled his engagements; and Bentham had every reason to be satisfied with the pecuniary results of his investments of money in the New Lanark Mills. (Bowring, in Bentham, 1838–1843, vol. x, pp. 476–477)

2.2. Bentham does not pay a visit to New Lanark

In 1815, Bentham tells Owen: "You heard, I suppose, at the time [of the investment], how it was that the pleasure I had so long been promising myself of paying you a visit at Lanark, was lost to me" (Letter to Owen, 1815, Bentham, 1988, pp. 452–3). But he never visited New Lanark at a time when it was one of the best known factories in Britain. Although Bentham was very circumspect in what he said publicly in association with his own name (Himes, 1936), a trip by Bentham to New Lanark would have been important news. Owen himself was shocked by his partner's lack of interest, and wrote: "He, like Mr. Walker, never saw the New Lanark establishment" (Owen, 1857, p. 96). Owen reckoned that between 1814 and 1824 there were about 2,000 visitors a year (Owen, 1857, p. 114; see also Royle 1998, p. 22). The mill was included in most of the tourist visits of the Falls of the Clyde (Beeho and Prentice, 1997).

Cole (1853, p. 67) puts this lack of motivation to see New Lanark down to Bentham's shyness and reclusive tendency and to the myth that Bentham was a 'mere theorist'.[5] Actually, before Owen could meet with Bentham, he had to be vetted by James Mill and Francis Place, and careful arrangements had to be made for the meeting. Owen said in his autobiography that Bentham "in great trepidation, met me, and taking my hand, while his whole frame was agitated with the excitement, he hastily said – 'Well! Well! It is all over. We are introduced. Come into my study!' And when I was fairly in, and he had requested me to be seated, he appeared to be released from an arduous and formidable undertaking" (Owen, 1857, p. 95). In 1825 he wrote "Before dinner, I never see anybody I can help seeing" (Bentham, 2006, p. 184, Letter to Galloway 3231).

But the fact that Bentham did not pay a visit to New Lanark is not so strange as at the time of the Lanark investment, Bentham was already 65 years old and he, and all Owen's new partners, were located far away in London, while the rail link between Edinburgh and London was not completed until 1848.[6] The journey from London to Glasgow took at least five days by stagecoach (Bentham, 1997, p. 298). Bentham's nephew and heir, the botanist George Bentham, says that for Bentham "it was a severe penance thus riding in a carriage" ([George] Bentham, 1997, p. 268).

Actually George did visit New Lanark in 1823. George wrote an account of his visit in his autobiography, saying that he did not manage to see either Owen or his sons, who were in London, but he did not make any effort to have an interview with them the next day.[7] George affirmed that New Lanark was a remarkable mill, but not as good as Strutt's mills in Derby, which both Benthams must have known well. According to George, Strutt's mill was more focused on business, New Lanark on visitors (Bentham, George, 1997, pp. 199–200). The most remarkable aspect of Strutt's mill was the Round Mill, built between 1803 and 1813 and running since 1816, influenced by the ideas of Jeremy and Samuel for an octagonal building with a central overseer.[8] William Strutt corresponded with the Bentham brothers, particularly with Samuel, on engineering matters (Elliott, 2000, p. 70) and Samuel visited Strutt's mill several times as it was located some 450 km nearer London than New Lanark, even when he was 69 (Bentham, 1997, pp. 184–188, 239–240). Really, he was used to making exploratory tours through the manufacturing districts of England (Bentham, 1862, pp. 97–98).

However, Jeremy Bentham neither mentions New Lanark nor Owen. Maybe he thought that citing Owen would give Owenism, which by that time meant Communism, a lot of undesirable publicity. However, as Steven (1996–2014) says, "New Lanark was not, properly speaking, a socialist experiment. Owen and his partners owned it and he directed it personally with very little democratic input or participation from the workers. Private ownership and the profit motive remained in spite of the more humanistic measures that Owen certainly adopted."

With regard to religious matters, Bentham probably aligned with Owen's atheism, although he was much more discreet. Indeed, Allen and the other partners' conflicts with Owen on religion might have been a good reason for Bentham not mentioning the Mills.

However, Bentham kept up his acquaintance with Owen, and in later years, when his son, Robert Dale Owen, who was his great admirer, begged his father for an introduction, Bentham not only granted it but invited the young man to his seven o'clock 'symposium', i.e., dinner, in 1827.[9] He talked to him, and, according to Owen junior, parted from him with the very characteristic words, "God bless you, if there be such a being; and at all events, my young friend, take care of yourself" (Owen, 1874, p. 67).

2.3. Similarities between Owen and Bentham

Sometime before, in 1818, Owen wrote to Bentham: "However we may differ on some points you may be sure I wish well to whatever is calculated to remove the gross errors which now exist throughout every part of society and which alone keep the population of the world in misery".[10] According to Cole, for all the slighting phrases with which Owen refers to Bentham, he is ready to say that his basic principle of society was the same (Cole, 1953, p. 72). In the *New View of Society,* at the beginning of the fourth essay, he expresses the Hutcheson's – and Bentham's – famous maxim (quite widespread at that time): "That government, then, is the best, which in practice produces the greatest happiness to the greatest number, including those who govern and those who obey".

According to Owen "I am come to this country, to introduce an entire new state of society; to change it from the ignorant, selfish system, to an enlightened social system, which shall gradually unite all interests into one, and remove all cause for contest between individuals" (cited in Lockwood, 1905, p. 83). Although Owen could have accepted, as Bentham typically claimed, the idea that public good was no different from the addition of the parts (as in Owen, 1813, pp 22–23, 27), Bentham's idea of the whole seems to be more individualistic, as norms are performed not from a desire to contribute to the unity of which the individual is part, but from a desire to avoid pain in the most utilitarian sense. However, despite the fact that Bentham measured economic welfare as the addition of individual pleasures and pains (Bentham 1789, p. 30), he added to the four factors of pleasure for the individual (intensity, duration, certainty or uncertainty, propinquity or remoteness) three not primary nor individual factors, in which the individual calculator pays interest to the consequences of his act in terms of pleasures and pains not only for himself but also for others. These are the fecundity of the pleasure, or the chance it has of being followed by sensations of the same kind; its purity, or the chance it has of not being followed by sensations of the opposite kind; and its extent, or the number of people who are affected by it. Bentham recognized that the fifth and sixth circumstances are not inherent properties of pain or pleasure itself but only of the act that produces pleasure or pain – they are not a priori to the individual action and, so, they depend less on the individual choice itself (see Warke, 2000).

Like Owen, Bentham thought that education was a basic element for social reform. Bentham devised in 1815 a 'Chrestomathic school'. The project encountered the opposition of the church; however, Bentham wrote a series of papers on the theory of education, published as Chrestomathia (1816–1817) (Bentham, 1983b). Bentham's 'Chrestomathic school' was a system of schooling based on utilitarian tendencies free of religious instruction and physical punishment, as was the case with Owen's scheme.[11] As mentioned above, their religious ideas were not so different, Owen's being more open and Bentham's more discreet. However, Bentham did nothing to stop his partners putting Owen in a predicament on religious grounds, and finally managing to force his resignation.

Also the relentless surveillance of Bentham's Panopticon, 'a mill for grinding rogues honest, and idle men industrious', in Bentham words, anticipates the disciplinary regimes of New Lanark (Ignatieff, 1978, pp. 214–215).[12] Foucauldians describe New Lanark as a Panopticon, 'an automatic functioning of power where the individual is now the principle of his own subjection... – prevention rather than punishment' (Walsh and Stewart, 1993, p. 797). As McKinlay (2006) argues he was fundamental to understanding the basic infrastructure of a specific deployment of power/knowledge and the new disciplinary institutions and practices of the early nineteenth century are important. These new institutional forms generate new bodies of knowledge that in turn legitimize and 'perfect' the organizing principles of the clinic, the prison and the factory. These institutions and practices become familiar so the operation of disciplinary power becomes increasingly intimate, ever more refined, and ever more opaque to the subjects of the gaze (Levin, 1997, pp. 443–444). In the Panopticon, to increase efficiency and eliminate waste, a standard administrative and cost system was applied; labour discipline became a matter of prior managerial analysis, rather than wasteful ex post facto punishment (Ashworth, 1994, p. 409, p. 435). As Guidi (2004) points out, most of Bentham's arguments amount to the modern economic notions of market policies and principal-agent relationships.[13]

Actually, the Panopticon design was devised by Samuel Bentham to serve for the supervision of a large workshop. Each workman, believing that he might be seen at any time, would be more inclined to stick to his work and the consequence would be a considerable improvement in productivity. Bentham immediately saw the potential of the design for supervision in a prison but to it he added the idea of contract management by private entrepreneurs as being more economical than government management. The details of such projects always fascinated Bentham, in some occasions much to his brother's distress.[14] Bentham hoped that he might be the person to operate such a prison under contract from the government. He saw such a model prison as an ideal place for developing methods of what today would be called behavioural modification in reforming the prisoners, and in preventing crime by using the prisoners as examples of the consequences of ill behaviour. But, as it has been argued, the objective of Robert Owen's parallelogram housing scheme proposed in 1820 (Owen, 1821) was also moral regeneration through collective visibility (Halévy, 1928, p. 251; Harrison, 1969, p. 158).

Finally, as late as 1819, Stephen Bourne seems to be unaware in a letter sent to Bentham of the differences between both authors[15]:

> My Bookseller says that your Papers on Codification cannot be easily obtained – for the Book is very Scarce – might I beg the favour of your allowing me a sight of one of your copies, as well as of any of those of your unpublished works, which will enable me to discover wherein your principles differ from those, which form the basis of Mr. Owen's practice and which his Committee wish to bring the public mind to experiment on?[16]

So, we may conclude, that Owen 1 activity was not seen as based on a much different philosophy than the one that public opinion had about Bentham's theory.

Notes

1 Dialogue between Robert Owen and one of his old friends with regard to writing his life", "Introduction"; Owen, 1857, p. xxiii
2 Donnachie and Hewitt, 1993, p. 115 and Taylor, 1987, pp. 61–65.
3 Letter 2256, from James Mill to Bentham 3 December 1813, in Podmore, 1906, p. 98; and McCabe, 1920, p. 20.
4 James Mill to Bentham, Letter 2256, 3 December 1813 (Bentham, 1988, pp. 361–362).
5 However, Bentham's is considered by some a practical mind (see Mill, 1838, p. 44; Blamires 2008, p. 20): he devised projects and tried to implement them and he repeatedly attempted to legislate in Europe and America.

6 So for Owen, they were unlikely to interfere much in day-to-day management (Donnachie, 2003).
7 [George] Bentham, 1997, pp. 184–189. See also Fitton and Wadsworth 1958, p. 182 and Stevens, 2003.
8 See Fitton and Wadsworth, 1958, p. 221 and Biernacki, 1995, p. 151.
9 Letter from Frances Wright to Jeremy Bentham, 4 November 1827.
10 Letter 2458, 8 February 1818, Bentham (1989, p.160).
11 Bentham's followers founded the University College School, and Bentham was influential in getting UCL established (where his body is preserved). Also, James Mill was a great defender of widespread education (Mill, 1823) and practised utilitarian education with his son John Stuart, publishing various essays on education (Burston, 1969).
12 As defined by its inventor to Brissot, the Panopticon was a model prison where all prisoners would be observable by (unseen) guards at all times (Bowring, 1838–1843, vol. X, p. 226, chap. x, as cited in Mitchell, 1918, p. 194). The Panopticon is based on the 'geometry of thought', a structure organized by the simulation of optical space for a surveillance mechanism (Bentham, 1838, vol. 9, p. 144: and Griffiths, 1884).
13 Bentham's panoptic principle of 'inspectability' was fundamental to mid-nineteenth century factory, hospital and social reform (Elliott, 2000; O'Hagan, 2005; McKinlay, 2006).
14 See Samuel's criticism, particularly directed at *A view of the Hard-Labour Bill*, in his letter to Jeremy (2–13 August 1782), Correspondence, III, pp. 136–137.
15 Probably Stephen Bourne (1791–1868), *the latter* that latter went to Jamaica, 1834, as Special Magistrate, was a settler in South Africa, originally leader of a party from Frome (Mackay, 1820).
16 Letter 2562, 13 September 1819, vol. 9, p. 352. We don't have any record of Bentham answering by mail. The aforementioned Committee had been formed in June 1819 to put into practice Owen's ideas on relieving the distress prevalent after the Napoleonic wars.

3 Friction areas between Bentham and Owen

3.1. Distrust between Bentham and Owen

Although Bentham was then in 1819 the leader of the utilitarians and the acknowledged spokesman of the radical philosophers, Owen did not really appreciate this fact. Of Bentham, Owen wrote in later years that "He had little knowledge of the world, except through books" and "he spent a long life in endeavouring to amend laws, all based on a fundamental error, without ever discovering that error" (Owen, 1957). And he goes on to say that Bentham attempted "to remedy the evils of individual laws, but never attempting to dive to the foundation of all laws, and thus ascertain the cause of the errors and evils of them", showing his basic disagreement with legal punishment. But Owen felt the same contempt for many other people. As Cole (1953, p. 169) says, Owen used to say that he knew better than others and if they remained unconvinced at the end, he had to act against them, because he was right and time would prove it quite soon.

According to Bowring, Bentham also spoke contemptuously of Owen. In his private conversations Bentham said that Owen "began in vapour, and ends in smoke. He is a great braggadocio [empty or pretentious bragging]. His mind is a maze of confusion, and he avoids coming to particulars. He is always the same – says the same things over and over again. He built some small houses; and people, who had no houses of their own, went to live in those houses: – and he calls this success" (quoted by Bowring in Bentham, 1838, vol x, p. 570). The mocking tone of the phrase (in Bowring's quotation), the houses being described as "small", seems to show that Bentham did not consider the building of a house for every working man – and still being able to make profits from the firm – as an achievement.

Is this a personal conflict or maybe some important differences between them were underlying this looking down on each other?

Although Bentham may have trusted Allen's advice, it appears that he was at first distrustful of Owen's investment. The law reformer Samuel Romilly had advised Bentham not to become involved in New Lanark venture (quoted in Harvey, 1949, p. 27 from Romilly, 1840, pp. 135–137). And apparently, Bentham delayed the payment of a sum until the Partnership Deed was set out definitively because he was suspicious of the alterations to which he saw it so frequently subjected and he was afraid that "I might not think it advisable to accede to it".[1] In 1815, Bentham was in the dark about the whole state of the concern and, besides, "Mr Walker was to have his partnership Share, without any such obligation of lending other money at common interest as was imposed upon me". He expresses his desire "to receive from the Lanark Mill concern on the 1st of July" (letter to Owen, 25 March 1815, Bentham, 1988, pp. 451–452). After Bentham's warning, Owen kept Bentham punctually informed of his investment at New Lanark – although, curiously enough, Bentham never answered Owen. From January 1817 to June 1820, Owen sent at least nine letters to Bentham[2] – and Bentham none to Owen. Owen basically accounted for his expenses to Bentham via Allen.

Owen always asked Bentham for some creditor to send the money invested and Bentham counted on the New Lanark money. As late as 1820, Jeremy informed his "short of money brother" (Samuel Bentham) that, when Jeremy mentioned to Samuel some money he could lend him, Jeremy had before him an account from Lanark. "When the time comes I shall pay it off [to the Banker] by so much drawn out of Lanark. If I die before then you will pay my ghost if he demands it: if I live I shall not want it: even should there be no more profit from Lanark: which is not to be apprehended" (Bentham, 1994, pp. 6–7). Bentham was in no doubt of New Lanark's profitability at the time. Eventually, in July 1820, Owen informed Bentham that he had given orders for Bentham's interest due for the last quarter to be remitted.[3] He also pointed out that he had sent two newspapers that contained letters from Owen preparatory to the development of the details of a social system which "will probably soon supersede the present". After that, there is no other letter from or to Owen, as far as we know (although, to date, 3,418 letters have been published from and to Bentham).

From Allen's diary we learn that Allen also had to overcome serious doubts before he finally decided to invest in New Lanark (Allen, 1847, I, pp. 35, 136). He was concerned about two points – the solidity of the business, and whether – having heard some tales of Owen's peculiar religious views – he might find himself contributing funds to the active propagation of atheism. These tales were spread by a committee of factory owners set up when Owen was fighting to improve a Factory Bill which was before Parliament in 1819. They tried to discredit Owen and the New Lanark clergyman, Mr. Menzies, was ordered to keep a watch over him and report to the factory owners in London. In 1819, Allen and Foster visited New Lanark to investigate the claim that dancing and music were taking precedence over religion (Gordon, 1994, p. 8). In July 1822, the London proprietors seem to have become uneasy again; Foster and Gibb went to investigate the state of New Lanark (Podmore, 1906, p. 156). They wrote a long reply describing what Owen had done as "temporal comfort", and setting forth their interest for the "eternal well-being" of the people.[4]

As Gordon (1994, p. 7) says "Although Owen brushed these charges aside, he was eventually, in January 1824, forced to sign an agreement which ended his connection with the school. Weekly readings of the scriptures were instituted and dancing became a paying subject only. The wearing of kilts for boys over 6 was banned, as was singing. Many of the teachers were dismissed and one of the new appointments was a master trained in the Lancasterian system. One redeeming feature was that Allen introduced lectures in chemistry, mechanics and other scientific subjects into the curriculum. Owen now resigned from the management of the institution and thus this valuable experiment came to an end" (also in Robert Owen, Cotton Spinner: New Lanark, 1800–1825, by J. Robertson, ch. 7 of Pollard and Salt, 1971, p. 160).

Allen wrote in his diary when he visited New Lanark in 1824: "Want of subordination and proper instruction" (Allen, 1847, II, p. 141).

Finally, Owen, his efforts concentrated now in founding new colonies in United States, signed an agreement which ended his connection with the school, resigned as managing director in 1825 and, after a long period of friction, resigned all connection with New Lanark in 1828. His actual words to William Allen at the time (attributed 1828) are often quoted as being: "All the world is queer save thee and me, and even thou art a little queer".

In 1824 he had gone to the US and shortly after he opened New Harmony in May 1825. He returned to England, but went back to America in January 1826, and he refounded New Harmony, based on absolute equality. Already in spring 1827, New Harmony had shown itself to be an absolute failure. In 1828, Owen sold off his share in New Lanark. Most of his means having been sunk in the New Harmony experiment, he was no longer a flourishing capitalist but he began to be the head of a vigorous propaganda campaign, in which socialism and secularism were combined.

3.2. Differences between Bentham and Owen

As Steintrager (1977, p. 13) says, the Industrial Revolution, along with other factors, had a devastating effect on England, and successive governments seemed unwilling or unable to deal with the growing economic and social problems. People no longer knew how to deal with one another: the absence of a sense of corporate existence made it very difficult for men to conceive of one another as anything but potential enemies. In this sense, for many people Owen showed it was possible to live in a corporate utopia. It is true that before 1824 New Lanark was not a corporation in a modern sense of the term (it was a family owned, controlled and managed firm). Neither was it a utopia, because it was a profitable capitalist company, more humane than most others but not the only humane one (that is the case with Strutt's mills in Derby). However, Owen's messianic personality nourished the myth of factories being corporate machines producing vice or virtue, what we would now call moral institutions.

In this, we see a clear difference between Owen and Bentham. Bentham would go through individualism to the utilitarian solution promising the greatest happiness for the greatest number. Unfortunately, Bentham was devoid of practical experience, a fault made worse by his unwillingness to learn from others and his considerable disdain for history (Steintrager, 1977, p. 14). Besides, in the early years, Bentham was a crude reductionist in psychology. According to John Stuart

Mill, Bentham was not a great philosopher, but he brought into philosophy something which is greatly needed, his method, that taught the means of organizing and regulating the merely business part of the social arrangements. Owen was to compensate for Bentham's lack of practical experience but, on the other hand, he was not provided with Bentham's method.

The differences between Bentham's and Owen's theories are important and twofold: firstly, they dissented about the nature of personal identity and, so, the rate at which social change could take place and the importance of the part education in a paternalistic sense could play in promoting such a change; then, they disagreed about private property and Owen's communism – although Owen was not in sympathy with any political party.

In terms of the first difference, Owen considered personal identity as a part of a greater reality that includes otherness and circumstances; whereas Bentham considered it to be individual, clearly distinguished, and that individual to be absolutely responsible for his acts. In Bentham the question of determining responsibility is one of the most important elements of moral, social and political order, especially in terms of punishment, adjudication and publicity. Imitation and empathy are not as important for him as is the case with Owen. Bentham remained dubious of the basic goodness of men and his project aimed at punishment and constraint. The control devices in the Panopticon are not only exercised through central surveillance, but through seven ways of authority that aim to reform paupers or convicts: rules, look, classification, word, tradition, sanction and education, which means an idea of community or "communities" of individuals with conflict of interests. Education is part of the art of government, and is a relation of command on the one side and subjection on the other.

Although the objective of Robert Owen's parallelogram housing scheme proposed in 1820 was also moral regeneration through collective visibility and the Panopticon is also based on the geometry of thought, in New Lanark the workers did mind what the guards thought. The practical value of the registers derived from Owen's tours of the mill was a personal, paternalistic power, something like a cottage system. In New Lanark the guards were supposed to be admired by the workers. Workers empathized with the guards and were led by their actions, lessening their responsibility. Houses at New Lanark should always be ready for inspection, the masters being seen as "bug hunters" (Owen, 1967, pp. 72–73; Podmore, 1906, p. 89). Owen's famous disciplinary innovation was the "silent monitor" (Owen, 1857). Each day's individual scores of behaviour and performance were recorded in a permanent register – "the book of character". Such registers were not unique to New Lanark (Williams, 1997, p. 111). But in none of them is there evidence that the numerical codes were aggregated, far less analyzed, although it was a significant innovation to render the individual visible and so calculable (Miller and O'Leary, 1987). Owen's purpose was not solely surveillance of worker behaviour and morals but also to check his supervisors' eagerness to flog the mill children (Butt, 1971, p. 189).

Actually, Owen thought that his paternalistic authoritarian figure (as a manager, an owner and a benefactor) was not important; and that New Lanark's success could easily occur in any self-managed community. Wilson (1940, p. 93) wrote that Owen never considered his own character to be especially noble or his personal control responsible for the exemplary character of New Lanark. According to Owen, the responsibility fell on the natural goodness of the working men, and Owen was surprised by the fact that other masters that he had trained did not achieve the same results in other places as in New Lanark. Wilson (1940, p. 116) is also very illustrative when he interprets Owen's paternalistic outlook as the more meaningful idea of the scheme. Although Owen thought it to be an objective supervision, he recognizes that when workers observed him watch the silent monitor and it was black, Owen looked to the employee and to the colour, but he never said a word of reproach (Morton, 1962, p. 77). Admiration for Owen did the rest. The absence of business records makes it difficult to calculate the impact of Owen's experiment; however, if share selling prices are a good indicator, those that Owen recollects in detail in his autobiography make their constant increase evident.

So, he jumped to the conclusion that all mankind might be governed with the same ease (Southey, 1929, p. 259; Storey, 1997, pp. 275–276).[5]

Then, Owen became a utopian who believed that a perfect society could be, and should be, attained in a very short space of time. Owen seems to have a deterministic view of institutions, and he understood capitalism as an evolutionary process, *à la* Schumpeter (Pesciarelli, 1990). He wanted to introduce changes in the management process so as to change people in an adaptive sense and make them more creative and less stagnant (Owen, 1813, p. 76). Owen set an example for the workers and provided admiration, that is to say, imitation and empathy; and, being aware of this fact, when he realized that his entrepreneurial success could be read in a revolutionary way, he preached a social harmony that could and would be created easily and quickly on the basis of cooperation.[6]

A point to be made here is that, as we see, Owen was paternalistic: so, he did not believe in democracy although he was in direct connection with the people.

As we said before, there is a second main difference between Owen and Bentham which has to do more with fair and efficient social arrangements. According to Owen "the introduction of private property was the introduction of one of the three great curses to humanity [along with religion and marriage], and all laws made to support it and give it a character of sacredness are a continuance of the same erroneous crime against the happiness of our race" (Owen, 1857, introduction p. viii). Owen condemned laissez-faire and competition, and there were substantial differences between the circle of political economists in which Bentham had his contacts, and the society Owen advocated after 1812. At first, there were no contradictions between political economists and Owen's managerial practice. As time passed, Owen became more and more socialist, whereas Bentham tended to emphasize his own attacks launched on wealth disappointments and encroachments on property and his belief in freedom in labour markets (in particular, the rights for workers to move and choose their employers).

Actually, Bentham believed that wages would find their true levels in a free market system with state control to maintain common agreed standards. Although the poor man "knows what is his interest…, and is as well disposed and able to pursue it as they are" (Bentham, 1838, p. 7, vol. iii, cited by Bahmueller, 1981, p. 147), the unemployed have both the knowledge that their continued subsistence depends upon the investment of labour, and the disposition to invest labour. As Quinn (1997) points out, one function of the National Charity Company (a plan of Bentham that poor relief be dispensed through a national network of workhouses) was to mimic the "natural" relation between subsistence and labour. Bentham proposed that each Industry House should serve as an Employment Intelligence Office, exploiting its access to national information.

As suggested before, Bentham's methodology seems to be individualistic, whereas Owen was anti-individualistic. Owen supported creating full employment by principles of cooperative ownership and prices based on the amount of labour invested in a product, arguing against individualism which he thought to be one of the causes of poverty (see Roberts, 1997; Claeys, 2005). For him, the same as happened in Keynes (1936), inclusion of all the potential workers is more important than the sum of individual happiness. Owen educational strategy "will induce each man to have charity for all men" (Owen, 1813, p. 33).[7]

On the contrary, society for Bentham is nothing but the sum of individuals. Bentham talked of the public good as a summing up of the greatest happiness of the greatest number, thus making the public good not something perceptible on its own, but based on the interests of some individuals. Schwartz (1986) compares this to the Hobbesian society; Rosen (1992, pp. 28–39) shows that Bentham's definition of freedom is more influenced by Montesquieu. His principles were that people should only be constrained from harming others, not themselves, and that the legislator does not have the knowledge and insight possessed by the individual regarding his own interests (Rosen, 2003, p. 115).

As Halévy (1972, p. 34) notes, the whole force of Bentham's criticism is concentrated on the established institutions as a source of corruption and oppression. Actually, the education strategy of the Panopticon could be contradictory with pure individualism as institutions go beyond individual interests and knowledge in a way that the whole makes the parts better (Schlossberger, 2008). Institutions have to be designed so as to make individual interest coincide with a common non-individual interest (Trincado, 2005b).

3.3. Conclusion

So, we may conclude that Bentham's and Owen's mutual antipathies were more grounded on philosophical differences than we may have thought at first sight. Both were haughty personalities who needed recognition but who were not open to recognizing others' achievements and, in their private conversations, both had a mocking tone for each other. Bentham only seems to be taking advantage of Owen so as to obtain from New Lanark the greatest monetary profit, not considering Owen's social improvements in the factory as something relevant in a utilitarian point of view. His concerns about New Lanark were not about Owen's religious view – which he shared – but about the solidity of the business.

Finally, when Owen saw himself forced to resign as managing director of New Lanark, Bentham did not speak on behalf of Owen so as to avoid his resignation.

All these frictions have something to do with their differences in philosophies of life. According to Owen, the whole is more than the sum of the parts, and factories are corporate machines producing vice or virtue – moral institutions. Bentham will go to the utilitarian solution through a crude individualism and reductionism in psychology. Bentham's and Owen's theories differed in the nature of personal identity, something that we will explain further, and also in the rate at which social change could take place. They disagreed also about the importance of education and private property in promoting social change. These differences may nowadays make us understand the difference between two doctrines in economics and social sciences that Keynes tried to distinguish on many occasions. As we shall explain after, when talking about unemployed people, Bentham continues with the individualistic view, whereas Owen was anti-individualistic supporting the striving for full employment by principles of cooperative ownership and arguing against individualism. The same as for Keynes, who talked about income equaling aggregates of demand that may lead us to full employment, for Owen inclusion – of all the potential workers – and distribution are more important outcomes than the sum of individual happiness. As Keynes (1936, ch. 24) says:

> The authoritarian state systems of to-day seem to solve the problem of unemployment at the expense of efficiency and of freedom. It is certain that the world will not much longer tolerate the unemployment which, apart from brief intervals of excitement, is associated – and, in my opinion, inevitably associated – with present-day capitalistic individualism. But it may be possible by a right analysis of the problem to cure the disease whilst preserving efficiency and freedom.

But the great point is, as we will also see after, that Bentham's philosophy was the one that influenced the most classical economy circles and is the basis for present economics, while Owen was set aside by many of them as a radical crazy man.

Notes

1 In the only Letter we know about he sends Owen, 25 March 1815. Letter 2309, Bentham (1988, pp. 451–453).
2 The Manuscripts from Robert Owen are in The British Museum.
3 Letter 2659, 7 July 1820, from Owen (Bentham, 1994, pp. 10, 12).
4 Allen, 1847, pp. 259–264, see Cole, 1953, p. 21–23; Harvey, 1949, p. 45.
5 His parallelogram housing scheme imagined communities of up to 1,000 to live in regimented, semi-communal housing blocks overseen by superintendents at each corner (Demeter, 2007).

6 Owen proposed this scheme to a gathering of the gentlemen of the county of Lanark to substitute cooperation for competition, hoping that the government would take up his radical plan of establishing cooperative, self-supporting communities (Evans, 2004). He continued these labours to regenerate mankind in Indiana through the purchase of New Harmony.

7 This can be seen as implicit also in Bentham's idea of the progress of sympathy in the species; however, he sometimes claims charity to be absurd, as one must maximize the "good" in terms of pleasure–pain personally felt. See, for instance, *The Book of Fallacies*, part V, chapter IV in Bentham (1838–1843, p. 478) or other Bentham's writings in Stark, 1954, pp. 426–432.

Part II
Entrepreneurs

4   Entrepreneurs in theory and practice

4.1. Robert Owen as an entrepreneur

4.1.1. Periods of Owen's life (1771–1858)

In this chapter we shall cast a glance over Owen's and Bentham's experience as managers. As Harrison (1969) points out, Owen's life falls into six main periods: 1771–1799, from his boyhood in Newtown, Montgomeryshire. He had but a few years of schooling before being apprenticed to a draper in Stamford, Lincolnshire. He left home at the age of ten and after three years moved from Stamford to London, still in the drapery business. About 1788 he arrived in Manchester, a friend having secured for him a position in a draper's shop. He did not stay there long, but formed a partnership with John Jones, a machine maker, and with borrowed capital set up as a manufacturer of cotton spinning machinery. From there he moved into the cotton spinning business, and after managerial experience became a partner in the Chorlton Twist Company. He entered into the cultural life of Manchester, making friends and acquaintances in particular through the Literary and Philosophical Society. In 1799 he and his partners acquired the New Lanark Mills in Scotland from David Dale, he married Caroline Dale and in 1800 he went to live at New Lanark.

The period from 1800 to 1824 is the most splendid. He was sole manager and dominant partner of the largest cotton spinning establishment in Britain. He made New Lanark a model factory and raised a family of seven children. About 1812, however, Owen began to show signs of departure from the usual pattern of an industrialist's life. His emphasis on schemes of education and social welfare for the employees became more and more pronounced and he began to talk of extending these ideas to society at large. After the ending of the Napoleonic Wars he became increasingly absorbed in his plans for the reconstruction of society. At first he was listened to with respect, and gained support in high places. But when he went on to attack the basic institutions of society such as the family and the churches, sympathy in this quarter decreased. By 1824 he concluded that progress along this road was likely to be slow and frustrating and that a fresh start might be rewarding. In the summer of 1824 he left New Lanark and went to America to found a community.

Owen's American and communitarian phase lasted only five years (1824–1829) but it marked the end of his long association with the world of business, for he never went back to New Lanark. He sank practically the whole of his fortune in a village and estate at New Harmony, Indiana and transferred his family (though not his wife) to America. The community of New Harmony did not flourish as he had hoped and the experiment came to an end in 1827. After considering the idea of a community in Mexico, Owen returned to England, considerably poorer but not lacking his conviction and enthusiasm.

On his return he discovered that his social schemes, which were not called socialism, had attracted support among working men. The British working class movement was dominated for five years (1829–1834) by Owenite theories. A climax was reached in 1834 when Owen was for a few months at the head of a great national federation of trade unions and was the acknowledged leader of the working classes. The sudden collapse of this federation ended the fourth period of Owen's life. Then, his wife died in 1831 and all his children were in America.

Afterwards, he made over his fortune to his sons in return for a modest annuity. He lived simply and frugally in London, devoting himself to the promotion of his new view of society. The period from 1835 to 1845 was marked by the development in Britain of a sectarian organization of Owenites in which Owen played the role of patriarch. He wrote and lectured and supported another attempt at community building at Tytherly in Hampshire. The closing of this community and the ending of the chief Owenite journal, the *New Moral World*, brought to an end this phase of his career.

From 1845 to 1858 he revisited the United States and was in Paris to observe the events of the 1848 Revolution. He wrote a lot, including his autobiography; he took up spiritualism and claimed to be in communication with people who had helped him in his early days. As we shall see, this gratitude towards people from the past was quite coherent with all his life and philosophy. His final effort was an attempt to address the annual meeting of the newly formed National Association for the Promotion of Social Science in 1858 but he was unable to go on with his speech. A few days later he died in Newtown, his birthplace, which he had not seen for over seventy years.

4.1.2. The first steps of an entrepreneur

Let's then elaborate on some milestones of Owen's life. Newtown, where Owen was born, was a town in Wales of no more than 1,000 inhabitants, the center of trade of a rural region. Owen's father had a harness-making business and a hardware store. Owen was mainly self-taught as he had access to the libraries of the illustrated people of the town, and had the habit of reading a novel every day. He stood out so much that the teacher took him from the early age of seven as an assistant to teach reading, writing and arithmetic to other children. He left school when he was nine years old and began to work as an apprentice at one of the important shops of the town, working every day but living with his parents. But

Owen wanted to see the world, and when he was ten years old his parents sent him to London, where one of his brothers was established in the same trade that he had learned from his father. With those familiar recommendations he obtained apprentice's work in Stamford, a small town 160 kilometres to the north of London on the route towards Manchester and Scotland. In his autobiography, Owen (1857) always gave the commercial, technical details, such as wages and everything that would call the attention of a learned person, but that would not amaze any of his colleagues in the business at all.[1]

He had a three-year contract; the first year without pay, the second with an annual salary of eight pounds, and ten pounds for the third year. All this with housing, food and washing of his clothes in the house included. "Since then, when ten years old, nevermore *had I* needed money from my parents", Owen boasts. The businessman, James McGuffon, a renowned merchant that treated Owen as one of the family, had a library that allowed Owen to continue his readings. But he also began a managerial practical instruction. "The gentleman McGuffon carefully introduced me in the routine of the business, and taught me its details, until I got used to the order and to the exactness. The business worked according to a well designed system, with very profitable results" (p. 17). It was an important textile trade, especially of luxury clothes for woman, and many of the clients were of the highest nobility. Owen emphasizes two things that he learned from this period: the ways of those people, and the careful handling of high quality and delicate goods.

After having spent three years there, our teenager still wanted to see the world, and that meant London, London and… London. With McGuffon's recommendations he joined a great shop of fabrics in London, "Flint and Palmer", at London Bridge. He had food and housing, "and a salary of 25 pounds per year, and I, with that, considered myself rich and independent" (p. 25). Too much, although it was in London. So, Owen used his recommendations and obtained a job in an important Manchester store earning a decent salary that included the housing. He had good working conditions, the employees usually were of a good family, and Owen worked there until he was 18. But the clients were very different, many coming from a low class; and they had a cold treatment, without flattery or without bargaining over the price. In the more active season, the shop remained open from eight o'clock in the morning until eleven o'clock at night the employees had to get up early more so as to get dressed and have their hair done in mint condition. They ate something quickly taking turns, and then they continued arranging the available merchandise, now without the clients in the establishment, until two o'clock in the morning.

Then, one of the suppliers of the establishment mentioned to Owen the new machinery that the manufacturer and inventor Richard Arkwright was introducing in textile manufacture, and proposed that Owen should produce and sell those machines. Owen borrowed 100 pounds from his brother in London and embarked on his first managerial adventure. As he considered himself a better businessman than his partner, Owen established on his own account as a textile businessman, using three of the machines produced by his former company and that he received as compensation for the invested capital (pp. 31–32). Soon they had forty employees, buying the wood and the iron on credit, and the business worked well.

But he was the one who took the managerial responsibility: his partner was good at mechanical matters, but the accounting and the management of the personnel were Owen's task. Actually, he had no idea about machinery.

The naturalness with which we speak today about business, machines, workers and factories makes us forget what is a fundamental question: we are in 1790, in the years of boiling invention and developing of what today we know as Industrial Revolution, but this was not obvious to all the contemporary people (García Ruiz, 1994, p. 25). A few decades later society would be fully conscious of the immense power of multiplication of the material wealth provided by the new industry, and of the social consequences of the change in the social organization, that is to say, both of the collective misery and the possibilities of solving them.

But this was not so when an almost teenaged Owen was initiating his spectacular managerial career. The machines, the fact that the workers were gathered together in factories, the textile quality, everything was so new as the computers were for us thirty years ago, and all was pushed by its spectacular profitability and the ingenuity of mechanics and capitalists, not by the science of universities. Actually, writing in 1857, Owen still says of his first own company: "I rented a big building of new construction, or factory, as these places were beginning to be called" (p. 34). He began to make quality textiles, which nobody made at the time in England. "I earned an average of six pounds of profit each week, and I thought I was doing it well to be a novice" (p. 36).

Then an advertisement appeared in the Manchester press asking for a director for a great factory that was being installed. An important capitalist of Manchester, Peter Drinkwater, had constructed a factory to produce thin fabrics, and when the building was finished and the machinery installed, the manager, a renowned engineer, left to go to another company as a partner. Owen, 20 years old, attended the interview and asked for a salary of 300 pounds, which astonished the capitalist even more than his age. But when he convinced him that his salary was then 300 pounds, showing him the books of accounts and the functioning of his own business, he obtained the position. Suddenly, he was the manager of a company of 500 employees, which the previous manager had left the day before and without help to understand its functioning apart from the drawings and calculations of the previous manager and the capacity of work and observation of the young Owen. For six weeks he only answered yes or no to the questions on what had to be done, without giving any direct order. But after, not only was he able to know, manage and organize the business, but he produced the best quality fabric in England, which at that moment was the best textile of the world, and he made his reputation among the businessmen and professionals of the sector.

4.1.3. The key to Owen's success

So, Robert Owen is regarded as an important reformer and utopian socialist but he turned into reformer, philanthropist, and socialist only after having developed an impressive career as an industrialist of the British industrial revolution. He was a self-made man, successful businessman in textile manufacturing in

Manchester and New Lanark. His methods of management were considered exemplary, because he successfully ran a profitable business, in which caring for the condition of living of the "hands" proved to be sound human resources management. What was the key to his success? How could Owen accomplish such a performance?

His success was much about being up to date in the continuous technological innovations of the time, in the quality of the fabrics and in the provision of raw materials. But it also had much to do with the personnel management in the factory, in an age in which the factory and personnel management were new or non-existent. The workers of the factory were proving to be disciplined and simultaneously satisfied with the rules and the ways of Owen's management. Owen himself emphasizes the influence that he exercised on the workers. Writing in 1857, he attributes it to his knowledge of human nature, acquired after having left "his religious prejudices"; it did not occur to him to think that it was due to his aptitude to adequately motivate the personnel, understood as part of his natural skills and technical knowledge of management. After six months of management, "I had a complete influence on the workers, and their order and discipline was better than those of any factory in the place. They were an example of regularity and sobriety, and were gaining higher wages and were more independent than ever" (p. 42). In addition, the factory was arranged and cleaned so that it was always ready to be inspected.

Mr Drinkwater, the capitalist, scarcely set foot in the factory, but he knew well, now even better than when he dared to contract a 20-year-old person for this position, the star he had registered. He offered Owen some good conditions that might guarantee his services: 400 pounds per year for the following year, 500 for the third, and he promised that in the fourth year he would become a partner with a quarter of the capital and the profits. But when Owen had to become a partner, the matrimonial (and patrimonial) situation of the daughter of his boss stood in the way: the suitor was Samuel Oldknow, one of the most important manufacturers of the sector, and in whose plans partners such as Owen were not included. So our now renowned industrial manager set out on his own, but now not as an inexperienced one. With other two capitalist passive partners, he created the "Chorlton Twist Company", under his management, and put to work new factories, which would be waiting slightly more than two years to begin their production. Robert Owen now had contacts with capitalists and traders in Manchester and Scotland, and in no small measure, he was an established businessman.

At this moment Owen's private life and industrial career were woven together. The autobiography seems here like a Jane Austen novel, with little similarity to the future reformer who would try to abolish the institution of the family – something that evoked such a rejection between the well-off people and sanctimonious classes that they considered him to be something like the Antichrist. Owen himself says: "Now that I was established successfully as a partner in one of the most respectable companies of Manchester, I felt inclined to search for a wife" (p. 65). In the wedding of the daughter of his previous boss, and in his own wedding, Owen explains having no qualms (although today's reader may find it a questionable behaviour, unless it is taken as a passage of Austen's novels) the negotiation of the patrimonial conditions of the contract, the dowry, the possible inheritance, and the managerial bows that were created between both family companies. The wife Owen was thinking about was the daughter of David Dale, one of the most respected manufacturers of Scotland. Like Owen, he was a self-made man, the son of a shopkeeper, who after being successful as a businessman married the daughter of the important manager of the Royal Bank of Scotland.

If we had to believe Owen in his autobiography, he fell in love with Anne Caroline Dale and, since he needed the approval of his father, the best thing that occurred to him was to go into talks to buy him New Lanark. It was the summer of 1797, and Owen was 28 years old. Important friends of Owen also influenced David Dale, convincing him of Owen's virtues as a son-in-law, and on 30th September the marriage of Robert Owen and the daughter of David Dale was agreed on. Finally the "Chorlton Twist Company", of which Owen was a manager and owner of a nineth of the capital, bought the business for 60,000 pounds. In January of 1800, Owen was in charge of New Lanark, as a proprietary partner and the only manager.

Margaret Cole concludes in her Owen biography judging by the correspondence that they wrote each other, that Caroline was in love when they got married, and she loved him all her life; but that, with regard to Owen, "it is doubtful whether it was not the mills as much as the lady which attracted him" (Cole, 1969 p. 35–36). As we said before, by the tenor of his autobiography, Owen spoke about the conditions of the marriages as he referred to the conditions of the mercantile contracts, and it is possible that a successful manufacturer such as the 28-year-old Owen did not make a distinction between love and social climbing.

David Dale was an owner of the biggest textile factory in Great Britain, New Lanark, approximately 50 kilometres out from Glasgow, and found in Richard Arkwright a great partner. Arkwright had established his first factory, which used a horse as motive power, in 1772; 11 years later Arkwright had near to 5,000 employees in different factories. He searched for partners to put in some capital while he provided them with the (controversial) patents to use his machines. In 1782 Arkwright and Dale studied the jumps of the river Clyde, celebrated by poets and painters, with the idea of using its energy in the cotton industry, and created a company to develop the project. In 1784 several factories and an entire village were already constructed; then Dale bought Arkwright's part and became the only owner.

Besides being an important manufacturer, Dale was a philanthropist and religious leader. New Lanark was already an exemplary establishment with him, in spite of the awful description that Owen gives of the conditions of the workers when he arrived there. Especially impressive were the working conditions for the children. As for education, in 1796, David Dale informed the Manchester Board of Health that, out of 500 children, 80 could read, and 24 of them sufficiently well so as not to need any further education. A visitor of New Lanark wrote in

1796: "It is a truth that should be recorded in golden letters, to honor eternally the founder of New Lanark, that of the almost three thousand children who have been employed at these factories at twelve years, only fourteen have died and none have been sentenced as criminals" (Owen, Robert Dale, 1967, pp. 27–35). This reference to deaths due to accidents or malnutrition and to harsh punishments must not be taken as a joke. The children worked in the factories up to depletion, and it began to be difficult to maintain the speed that the work demanded. Physical, sometimes brutal, punishments were frequent: for being late, for speaking with other children, for some real or apparent mistake. If workers ran away from the factory they could be sent to prison, and if the manager suspected that they would run away, they were fettered. The fact that David Dale's grandson, writing almost one century later and undoubtedly with other moral and hygiene and health standards, emphasizes this as a merit exemplifies the situation in other factories. The managers of the factories were responsible for their food, clothing, housing and education, but few of them provided their workers with those necessities in humane conditions. The children, as a consequence, scarcely ever grew and were pale and showed physical malformations, and were almost always illiterate. No physical safety existed in the work, and many children died or were injured in workplace accidents.

Certainly, in that period businessmen had an immense power over the people who did not rebel against those terrible conditions. This was nourished by the lack of options for survival, by the lack of consciousness of their own dignity and also by the sympathy of political institutions.

So, New Lanark then was, before Owen came, a much more humanitarian establishment than the average, for supply, housing and education; nonetheless, it proves for a modern reader frightening just to imagine. Owen and his contemporaries described the industrial village of New Lanark as the antithesis of a village adapted for the industry: the moral depravity that they all indicate translates into alcoholism, delinquency (that includes especially thefts in the factories), absenteeism, lack of motivation and scant productivity.

But let's return to the business question. Owen becomes the manager of the biggest factory of Great Britain. He became a renowned manager who would be paid for his work 1,000 pounds per year apart from his share in the profits, and a well established and related businessman. He was transformed then into what we could today call an executive of the major company of the top sector in technology in a moment of industrial effervescence. It is true that this is not the activity for which Owen is most known; but not only do we want to emphasize this attractive facet of his biography, but also the fact that his ideas of the organization of the firm came from his experience as a businessman, in particular as a personnel manager or management controller in a moment in which that was something new. He had experience in motivating and even transforming the people to make them more productive and at the same time happier. And, therefore, much more than his political writings, his deeds were in achieving the highest peaks of the self-made man, something that we have to stress if we want to understand the most important of his contributions to the progress of humanity.

In his autobiography, written in 1857, Owen says that in New Lanark not only does he propose to develop good business management, but to do a social experiment. But until 1812 Owen has nothing to do with politics, he thinks and feels as a manufacturer and the only thing that he is worried about is how to strenghthen his position in intellectual and refined circles in spite of his Welsh accent and his scanty formal education. What is doubtless is that he did well as a businessman: the establishment increased value and yielded copious profits, as well as providing him with one of the highest wages of the time (García Ruiz, 1994, pp. 28–29).

New Lanark is the paradigm of the disruption that the Industrial Revolution meant for British society. It was a completely new village, of more than 2,000 inhabitants. Owen calls his native Newtown a market town. It had approximately 1,000 inhabitants. However, they all call New Lanark a "village": there were 2,000 workers, 500 of them being children, recruited generally from orphanages (workhouses) from Edinburgh and Glasgow – the workers were unwilling to let their children be employed at the factories. The children were suited to this work, not only because of their low cost, but also because their small size allowed them to get in and out of the machines to gather the cotton that was falling down or to check possible breakdowns. They did that all the time, while the machines were working (see Image 4.1).

Most of the workers came from remote villages in the Highlands of Scotland, and they had never seen a building of several stories, as that which sheltered the impressive device that moved the water in the basement through a great wheel, distributing to the different plants the power for the working of the looms.

Image 4.1 New Lanark's cotton factories, according to an illustration of Owen's time

The children were the real workforce of the factories. They started work at five or six years old, with a working day of up to 14 or even 16 hours, and in not many years their pallor and physical malformations were inevitable. It is not surprising that it was precisely in this area where the industrial Owen and Owen as a social reformer came together, in a feeling shared by many of the people from the well-off classes. In the first decade of the 19th century, his name meant everything except utopian socialism or critiques of religion, to the family, and to private property: it brought together the humanitarian feelings of a good part of the well-off and educated class.[2] And the evidence confirmed that in New Lanark better labouring conditions not only did not diminish, but even increased the profitability of large factories. We must remember here that Richard Arkwright, from whom we do not assume different interests than the chrematistic ones, did not allow his workers to work more than 12 hours daily, when in most of the factories the working day was of 14 hours or more (George Bentham, 1997, p. 56). Other capitalists assumed that presenteeism in the workplace is good for productivity, as they treated workers as machines (a debate not yet closed as nowadays presenteeism is still questioned and debated, see Clarke, 1994; Koopman et al., 2002; Whitehouse, 2005; Hemp, 2004; Burton et al., 2006; Middaugh, 2006; or Schultz and Edington, 2007).

4.1.4. Creating an atmosphere while seeking culture for social purposes

Owen did not have a broad cultural background. In school he learned to read, to write and the rules of arithmetic until he was 9 years old; and then he read quite a lot in his adolescence, but for Owen 2 experience in business was more important than all book knowledge. What worried him the most in this area, from his growing years, was the inferiority complex that a self-made rich man feels in the presence of educated people. But when he discovered that his direct language, with clear ideas that went directly to the aim of the argument, and with facts and information that are relevant for the topic in discussion, affected the audience of Manchester more than any other of, for instance, Coleridge's romantic rhetoric, his inferiority complex disappeared.

> Mr. Coleridge had a great fluency of words, and he could well put them together in high-sounding sentences; but my words, directly to the point, generally told well; and although the eloquence and learning were with him, the strength of the argument was generally admitted to be on my side. (Owen 1857, p. 14)

The way in which Owen mentions Coleridge in his autobiography shows that he was not a romantic at all: he shows no interest for the poetry of Coleridge and Wordsworth (unlike John Stuart Mill, see Trincado 2015). He is only worried about not being able to ascend in the social scale. He then goes on with the vanity of the Plain Man: "Many years afterwards, when he was better known and more celebrated, I presented him with a copy of my Essays on the Formation of Character and the next time I met him after he had read them, he said – 'Mr Owen, I am really ashamed of myself. I have been making use of many words in writing and speaking what is called eloquence while I find you have said much more to the purpose in plain simple language, easily to be understood, and in a short compass. I will endeavour to profit by it'" (Owen, p. 14; also in Newlyn 2002, p. 113).

In this sense, Owen seems Benthamite and shows a man not so engaged with human profound and subtle feelings, such as the ones displayed by the romantics, but with rationality and the progress of the human mind, with freedom of action in a non-subtle way. In the same vein, Leavis defines Benthamite as "to be indifferent to essential elements (essential, at any rate, from the Coleridgean point of view) in the problems one offers to be tackling. Certainly (it seems to me) Basic English exemplifies the practical spirit of Benthamism" and as Mill said it applied itself "to matters were its indifference to essential human interests that are involved is calculated to have, for those interests, disastrous consequences" (Mill 1980, p. 31).

The question is that even after Owen's promotion, when he was a rich man successful in the business area but fully devoted to the political and moral reform of society, Owen continued to be a practical man. He describes the purchase by his philanthropist partners more as a justification, in managerial terms, of his previous management: he argues that if New Lanark was costing 114,100 pounds, it must have been a well managed company since Owen and his partners bought it, in 1789, for 60,000 pounds. And the textile establishment still made profits under Owen's management no matter who were the partners.

So, Owen used rhetoric for chrematistic purposes and this business ability seemed to be a central part of his success. As Adam Smith (1983) recommended, he used the plain language lead by his "propensity to truck, barter, and exchange one thing for another" (Smith, 1976, I. ii, 1). Alfred Marshall, who shared with Owen and the utopian socialists, and with John Stuart Mill, the conviction of the moral superiority of cooperatives as a form of organization, was conscious, in 1889 that "business ability", most important in the more complex companies of the modern world, was what really hampered the generalization of cooperatives (Santos, 1994, pp. 188–191; Santos (1997), chap. 2). Curiously enough, Marshall, who had never managed a company, was fully conscious of the importance of professional management in business; whereas Robert Owen, who was one of the most renowned and best paid managers of the age, undervalued in such a way his own task in the organization of the company and in the management of human resources.

However, it is true that Owen used his rhetoric for benefiting the workforce. Used to exercising great influence on the workers, the first problem which Owen faced was that these, besides the natural resistance to changing habits, were Scotsmen on whom an English manager was imposed. On this occasion it was not six months, but six years that he needed to gain their trust. New Lanark was known worldwide as one of the first experiments for creating an acceptable working environment and living conditions for the work force without avoiding the industrial process of large-scale mechanization. Apart from the school, workers and their families were provided with better housing, with gas lighting, and hygienic conditions. Owen improved the shops, which implies, he says, an evident improvement of their health and clothing: they saved 25% of their expenses and improved the quality of the goods produced. But, as we previously said, Owen gained the trust of the workers in a more dramatic situation: in 1806 the United States interrupted his exports of cotton due to a diplomatic crisis already mentioned. The price of the raw material made the production unprofitable, and the majority of the factories stopped work and left the workers without employment until the crisis was solved, four months later. Owen stopped the production without quitting the payment of wages to the workers, 7,000 pounds in total without any counterpart apart from the maintenance of the machinery, keeping it clean and in good condition. Not even a penny of the salary was discounted from anybody. "This way of proceeding gained the confidence and the heart of the whole population" (Owen, 1857. p. 88).

Here we see something that turned out to be always essential in Owen's management: the establishment of an implicit but reliable unemployment insurance, which had a positive effect on the motivation and the labour environment of the firm; and the paternalism which means the action of a boss of whom all the workers know the face and name, whom they love and admire.

Owen was completely opposed to corporal punishments for encouraging work or education, and he believed in positive reinforcement. However, he had to invent procedures so as to control the thefts and efficiency in the factory. The first thing he did was to clarify the source of a mistake: he made a system of control that made evident at what point of the chain a tool was missing. This could mean what worker was guilty of the theft, but actually according to Owen the worker was not responsible for his action and, so, neither was he guilty. The second thing he did was the most efficient ingenuity to control the slightly diligent conduct of the workers: the "silent monitor" also mentioned above. It consisted of a piece of wood of a cubic form that could turn on an axis to show one of four visible faces, painted in four different colors: black, blue, yellow and white. There was a bucket for every employee hung on a visible place for all, and the colour revealed the behaviour of the worker on the previous day: black if it was bad, white if it was excellent, blue and yellow for regular or good behaviour. In addition, a daily record of the conduct of the workers was taken in the books of record which lasted the whole working life of the worker.[3]

Every day the overseer of every department put the silent monitor in the right position, and the boss of the factory arranged that of the overseer. If somebody did not agree, they had the right to complain to Owen, or to the person in charge of the factory if Owen was absent, before the colour was registered in the book; but these complaints were very scarce. This device improved efficiency beyond all expectations. "In this way I could see at a glance, as I went through every department of the factories, how each person had behaved during the previous day" (Owen, 1857, pp. 112, 189). The colours that prevailed went from black to

white. But what is interesting here is that Owen did not use the external punishment once it was known who was responsible for the action, but he trusted on an
intrinsic motivation or instinct of workmanship as Veblen (1899) would put it. So,
Owen argues that "the workers were observing me when I was looking at the
telegraphs [the way the people called the silent monitor] – when the colour was
black, I only looked at the employee and then the colour, but I never said any
word of reproach" (Autobiography; gathered in Morton, 1962, p. 77).

Again the question: what was the reason for this improvement in behaviour?
Was it due to better organization and control provided by the record of behaviour,
or to Owen's paternal figure, which exercised influence on the workers? Margaret
Cole (p. 58) says that "Owen treated his workers as he treated the children in the
school. The workers were not very qualified, and Owen treated the children in a
more rational way than most of his contemporaries. So this could be one of the
reasons for his success". Edmund Wilson (1940, p. 116) is even clearer, interpret-
ing Owen's look with much more meaning than that of an objective supervisor.
In his book *To the Finland Station* he says that if someone had the black colour,
Owen did not say anything to him, "he simply fixed his eyes, while passing
through, on the guilty worker" and this was enough to shame him. Pollard (1987)
makes an interpretation quite different from paternalism.

> His comparative advantage came neither from a great capacity of negotiation,
> nor from a few specially effective channels of commercialization, but it arose
> from his ability to gain the collaboration of his workers without paying them
> more than competitive wages, as well as the methodical layout of the factory,
> a ready policy of technical modernization and a careful selection and training
> of the assistant managers. It is probable that his success was owed to a great
> extent to his aptitude to handle the administrative technologies of the indus-
> trial system that, in that epoch, were totally foreign to the experience of the
> men who exploited this new form of social organization. When Owen came
> from Manchester to take charge of the direction of New Lanark's factories, he
> was endowed with a knowledge of administrative processes of the manage-
> ment of the firm that maybe was unique in that period. This allowed him to
> make the thinnest of the threads, with which the biggest profits were obtained
> that were the basis for his philanthropic projects. (Pollard, 1987, pp. 329–330)

These two possible interpretations of the success of every Owen measure in the
administration of personnel – the paternalistic one or that of the connoisseur of
the technologies of administration of the personnel (both explanations are not
necessarily contradictory) are going to be more important in the second stage of
his life, when he established communities using New Lanark's humanitarian
methods. Then, the same situation is repeated time and time again. And things
were initially right, but when Owen, who believed in the egalitarian credo,
wanted the community to continue working without him, with the managers
he had trained, it was a disaster. Not all the people are good at managing a firm

and organizing and motivating the workers; Owen was a genius in that, capitalists did not hesitate to pay well for his work.

Wilson (1940, p. 116) stresses the noble ideals of the boss: "Owen had begun his work in New Lanark with the least promising beings we may imagine. And it never occurred to him that his own character was exceptionally high, and that it was due to him, and not to the natural kindness of the children of those wretched parents, that New Lanark was a model community. He did not understand that New Lanark was a mechanism he had created and that he had to personally control and make work". However, these virtues as an industrial leader can very well be faults for team work and, so, it is only appropriate for a Taylorism factory, not for an innovative one. William Lovett, one of the leaders of cahartism who worked afterwards with Owen at the cooperative movement, affirms that Owen was fundamentally despotic and it was turning out to be practically impossible to collaborate with him on a democratic basis.[4] Turned into a social reformer, philanthropist and stubborn "man of only one idea", as called by the intellectual that first approached him with shame and admiration, it seems that he had forgotten that the capacity for business is a complex skill, more important when the economy is more complex.

In 1826, the colonists of New Harmony demanded that Robert Owen himself should personally direct the community, at least during the first year, as stipulated in the initial conditions. Owen had made attempts to form new communities in the United States, England and Ireland, and lost in them all his fortune. But Owen returned, and things seemed to improve, at least initially. In this way, on 22 March, an editorial of the New Harmony Gazette affirmed: "While we have been discussing some abstract ideas, we have neglected practical solutions. Our energies have been exhausted in useless efforts… But with the tireless attention of Mr Owen, order and system have been introduced in all the sectors of the business. In our streets there are no idle people chatting; everybody is occupied seriously in the trade he has chosen. Our public meetings, instead of being the scene of oratorical disputes, are now business meetings" (R. D. Owen, 1824, pp. 285–289). It seems to be clear that the colonists of New Harmony understood well the difference between being under the technical direction of a renowned and charismatic manager, or under the political direction of a democratic professionally incompetent committee.

4.1.5. Owen's reputation as an entrepreneur

Owen showed with his business practice prior to his political career that a new way of organization could be productive and that promoting the welfare of the work force was not only compatible with the profits of capitalism but due to them. And Owen's actual merit was his practice as a manager, not his theory. Today the theory of high wages and good conditions is accepted as a sound business principle, and Owen's views could have made him a pioneer in the promotion of investment in human capital. Owen did not state this clearly: that would have revolutionized management theory as this was not at all accepted in Owen's time (Cooke, 1979, p. 146).

Owen was a leader and he considered himself to be a leader with technical, commercial and managerial skills. But he considered that it is not risk, but the taking into account of workers' feelings and incentives that is important for the success of an entrepreneur. And those incentives are not always rewards and punishments, but an unintended consequence of sympathizing with them and being concerned for their welfare. This, Friedrich Engels explains very well (Engels, 1880, p. 7):

> At this juncture, there came forward as a reformer a manufacturer 29-years-old – a man of almost sublime, childlike simplicity of character, and at the same time one of the few born leaders of men. Robert Owen had adopted the teaching of the materialistic philosophers: that man's character is the product, on the one hand, of heredity; on the other, of the environment of the individual during his lifetime, and especially during his period of development. In the industrial revolution most of his class saw only chaos and confusion, and the opportunity of fishing in these troubled waters and making large fortunes quickly. He saw in it the opportunity of putting into practice his favorite theory, and so of bringing order out of chaos. He had already tried it with success, as superintendent of more than 500 men in a Manchester factory. From 1800 to 1829, he directed the great cotton mill at New Lanark, in Scotland, as managing partner, along the same lines, but with greater freedom of action and with a success that made him a European reputation.[5]
>
> In spite of all this, Owen was not content. The existence which he secured for his workers was, in his eyes, still far from being worthy of human beings. "The people were slaves at my mercy" (as noted by Engels 1880). The relatively favourable conditions in which he had placed them were still far from allowing a rational development of the character and of the intellect in all directions, much less of the free exercise of all their faculties.
>
> "And yet, the working part of this population of 2,500 persons was daily producing as much real wealth for society as, less than half a century before, it would have required the working part of a population of 600,000 to create. I asked myself, what became of the difference between the wealth consumed by 2,500 persons and that which would have been consumed by 600,000?[6]"
>
> The answer was clear. The wealth had been used to pay the proprietors of the establishment 5% on the capital they had laid out, in addition to over £300,000 clear profit. And that which held for New Lanark held to a still greater extent for all the factories in England.
>
> "If this new wealth had not been created by machinery, imperfectly as it has been applied, the wars of Europe, in opposition to Napoleon, and to support the aristocratic principles of society, could not have been maintained. And yet this new power was the creation of the working-classes (Note, l. c., p.22.)"

To them, therefore, the fruits of this new power belonged. The newly-created gigantic productive forces, hitherto used only to enrich individuals and to enslave the masses, offered to Owen the foundations for a reconstruction of society; they were destined, as the common property of all, to be worked for the common good of all.

Owen's communism was based upon this purely business foundation, the outcome, so to speak, of commercial calculation. His advance in the direction of Communism was the turning-point in Owen's life. As long as he was simply a philanthropist, he was rewarded with nothing but wealth, applause, honor, and glory. He was the most popular man in Europe. Not only men of his own class, but statesmen and princes listened to him approvingly. But when he came out with his Communist theories, that was quite another thing. Three great obstacles seemed to him especially to block the path to social reform:

private property,
religion,
the present form of marriage.

He knew what confronted him if he attacked these – outlawry, excommunication from official society, the loss of his whole social position. But nothing of this prevented him from attacking them without fear of consequences, and what he had foreseen happened. Banished from official society, with a conspiracy of silence against him in the press, ruined by his unsuccessful Communist experiments in America, in which he sacrificed all his fortune, he turned directly to the working-class and continued working in their midst for 30 years. Every social movement, every real advance in England on behalf of the workers links itself to the name of Robert Owen. He forced through in 1819, after five years' fighting, the first law limiting the hours of work of women and children in factories. He was president of the first Congress at which all the Trade Unions of England united in a single great trade association. He introduced as transition measures to the complete communistic organization of society, on the one hand, cooperative societies for retail trade and production. These have since that time, at least, given practical proof that the merchant and the manufacturer are socially quite unnecessary. On the other hand, he introduced labour bazaars for the exchange of the products of labour through the medium of labour-notes, whose unit was a single hour of work; institutions necessarily doomed to failure, but completely anticipating Proudhon's bank of exchange of a much later period, and differing entirely from this in that it did not claim to be the panacea for all social ills, but only a first step towards a much more radical revolution of society" (Engels, 1880).

Engels had it clear that the increase in productivity was going to pay the interest capital and the profits of the capitalists; but he does not come to understand

Owen as a businessman, prior to 1824 or even 1814. Because what Robert Owen wanted to demonstrate was that, improving the conditions of work and the education of the working class, more profitable companies would be achieved. Paradoxically, Engels and Marx longed for the revolution because they were speaking as utopian philosophers. Marx was not acquainted with the productive possibilities of capitalism (although Engels was); whereas Owen had discovered that technological innovations could increase human possibilities, but that those possibilities were not sufficiently understood by capitalist managers themselves as they did not look to the full picture of the long run but to a mean spirited and narrow-minded short term.

Actually, that was what happened in 1814 when, as a consequence of the disagreements between the partners and inheritors of other partners of New Lanark's, the whole firm of New Lanark was put up for auction. It was a clash between two rival groups inside a company, an inside fight for control. It looks nothing special. But this will mark a turning point between the two Owens: first, the successful manufacturer, of faultless reputation, respected by the manufacturers, the clients and the suppliers; later, the political agitator who connects with the masses of the working class, the tireless writer who spreads his writings, the initiator of communities, unions and cooperatives. Then, he wanted to start a new world without taking into consideration the past achievements. That was not so agreed upon by the business world, based on trust and reputation. In the final analysis, Owen was toying with a delicate equilibrium between innovation - wish to change - and recognition - fairness of treatment.

As already mentioned, when Owen says in his autobiography, written at the end of his life, that he was tired of his partners who "were only trained to buy cheap and sell dear", he is claiming that their only objective was capital gain, the price differential in the current long selling market operations, not profitability. So, those partners were not interested in the opportunity cost of investing in one activity instead of the other in terms of expected yields in the long run.

After, the partners that he assembled to get rid of the previous inconvenient ones were not businessmen. Owen was the only manager and the main shareholder – he bought the establishment for 114,100 pounds. The six partners that he looked for and that he finally found were, as we have seen, very distinguished people, most of them philanthropists, who had never had commercial contact either with the business or with Owen himself and that in principle took human development, not only accumulation, into account. John Walker of Arnos Grove, the richest of them, had inherited a fortune that made the price of New Lanark insignificant. Jeremy Bentham was also rich through inheritance. Actually, research by François Crouzet on the social origins of the entrepreneurs of Industrial Revolution concludes that "the main group are middle classes, there is no self made man" (Casado, 1998, p. 48) something that Piketty (2014) has more recently tried to demonstrate. This looks true for our investors, but Owen was in this also an exception.

In the New Lanark establishment, a recommendation was set that when the capital advanced by the partners had been returned and the education of all is sufficiently high, the management of the establishment will be entrusted to a Committee. Until then, the Committee was to be formed by 12 people chosen in an Annual General Meeting: eight will be chosen from among those members who have advanced 100 pounds or more, and four for the remaining partners (García Ruíz, 1994, p. 165). As they were not thinking in terms of a business deal, but as philanthropists, all the investors accepted Owen's conditions: he would be the only director of the business, without interferences; they will get 5 per cent of interest for the contributed capital, and the benefits (that were constantly yielding) would be devoted to the education of the children and the improvement of the living conditions of the workers. These are quite different requirements from those of the normal investors in a profitable company. Visitors, many of them illustrious men – for instance, in December 1816, Nicholas, Gran Duke and future Tsar – admired the school.

But they also imposed that education would be in accordance with the Christian religion, atheism would not be promoted, and the books that form a part of the library of the school would have to be supervised and passed by all the partners. It was from these conditions that the disagreements were going to come: Owen stumbled upon the conventional view of education of his partners that were against the play principle in education and condemned Owen's insistence on the fact that the "religious prejudice" was the origin of all evil. As the partners of Owen strongly rejected his methods, finally, the formal religious education and the old methods interfered. But this is a story that we will go into later.

For Owen, this dispute in 1813 was undoubtedly an important change in his life and in his activity as a manufacturer. "Robert Owen was very disappointed and gave up trying to change the law and decided to appeal directly to public opinion" (On 1819 Act, Santos 2000). Till then he had not even written a letter. Later he continuously wrote pamphlets, he devoted himself to political reform and to preaching for the generalization of a society that public opinion thought related to some successfully created model in New Lanark. However, the change is more profound than public opinion may think: the second Owen looked for a communist society; New Lanark wasn't it. It was not until 1895's Cotton Mills and Factories Bill that we come to a generalization of New Lanark, without being communist.

However, it was not only that his assaults on religion and the family made him bad company for the educated people; now he did not have the money of a well-off manufacturer nor the reputation of good manager, but the opposite was true: he had the reputation of a utopian visionary. Besides his ideas and his perseverance, a mixture of nobility and vanity, continued to have influence over the workers. He really got to their heart with his ideas, his proposals and his charisma. And he played an important role as a politician in Great Britain, in the Cooperative Movement and in the Grand National Consolidated Trade Union, the great union of ephemeral existence that he created.

Needless to repeat that the bibliography and reputation of Robert Owen as a social reformer is very important. However, his relevance as a pioneer of the professional management of the firm is, in general, much less regarded. His contemporaries considered Owen a man of managerial success in the leading sector of the industrial revolution. His relations and contacts were not intellectual people or politicians, but business people, and his success arrived between his 20th and 28th years, when Owen was organizing, in Manchester, a company of 500 employees, a large size for 1791 (Chaloner, 1954). And later, he was main partner and the only manager of the New Lanark's textile establishment in Scotland, with almost 2,000 employees.

Casado (1998, pp. 15–36) says that "between 1850 and 1870 the cases of large size companies and of high numbers of workers were scarce"; he mentions some siderurgy, mining industry or textile companies, and continues: "Equally, the companies that in this age had initiated a process of vertical and horizontal integration were very small. The case of the great textile factory directed by Robert Owen in New Lanark (Scotland), which reached 1,600 workers in 1817, or that of the mining – metallurgy complex of Cockeril in Belgium, are extraordinary" (p. 43). He is, then, cited as the entrepreneur leader in the sector and, precisely, of the wool textile sector in Manchester, England. According to Casado, textile firms in Manchester were smaller and more craftsman-oriented than the ones in the United States. Owen was not then a manager of the modern firm in the Chandler sense, with some complex mechanism of personnel management, but he was modern from many other points of view (García Ruiz,1994, pp. 30, 161, 164–171 places Owen in the "Modern firm in Great Britain"). It was not only one of the major textile companies of his age, but a model company from the managerial point of view. And it was precisely the success of new personnel management methods, opposed to what was considered "productive" in his age that convinced Owen that the living conditions of the workers must be improved. In particular, he claimed that the good work environment leads to a productivity increase.

The curious thing is that the first violent agitation of the workforce in 1811 and 1812 was not against the severe foremen or haughty aristocrats, but against the machines and the technological innovations, a symbol now of the Industrial Revolution.[7] The Luddite fury was centered in the textile machines. In 1733, John Kay's "flying shuttle" boosted greatly the performance of the weaver. The inventor was first expelled from Colchester after being chased from city to city, and finally he had to shelter in France. In 1758, Lawrence Earnshaw constructed a machine to spin cotton, and he broke it once he had made it "not to remove the poor from their means of living" (Sauvy, 1986, p. 45). In 1768, a mechanical spinner without any instruction, James Hargreaves invented the jenny, which replaced several wheels. The workers besieged the inventor in his own house and destroyed his machines. Hargreaves would die in misery. Towards the turn of the century, armed gangs emerged that could only be put down by the army. The death sentence was decreed in 1812 for machine destroyers and 15 luddites were executed in the city of York in 1813.

However, what drew Owen's attention was not the negative impact of machinery on workers, but how such a formidable increase in productivity was compatible with machinery leaving the workers still living in miserable conditions. His words in *A New View of Society* were:

> Many of you have long experienced in your manufacturing operations the advantages of substantial, well-contrived, and well-executed machinery… If, then, due care as to the state of your inanimate machines can produce such beneficial results, what may not be expected if you devote equal attention to your vital machines, which are far more wonderfully constructed?.. Will you not afford some of your attention to consider whether a portion of your time and capital would not be more advantageously applied to improve your living machines? (Owen, 1813, p. 8–9)

Owen was in the middle of a minefield and as a practical man he did not have any doubt that the machines were increasing the productivity and the well-being of the population. Ekelund and Hébert say: "Born in obscurity to Welsh parents, Robert Owen (1771–1858) worked his way up the ladder of success in the textile industry… Owen was especially alert to the changes in economic and social life brought about by the introduction of machinery. The mechanical marvels of Arkwright (spinning frame), Crompton (spinning mule) and Hargreaves (spinning jenny) transformed the textile business in England and helped make Owen a wealthy man, but their impact on the working class was not so apparently beneficial" (Ekelund and Hebert, 2013, p. 268)

At the end of his life he believed in spiritualism and he waited for the magnanimous souls that he had known to visit him.[8] But, for the first stages of his life, we need to have in mind the administrator of human resources in a period and a sector where technological innovations and the most important social changes were taking place. This first Owen was, not only a predecessor of the ideas being applied in the twentieth century by the followers of F. W. Taylor and Elton Mayo, but also a genius of administration able to face a new situation and to solve it applying, with explanatory crudeness but with practical efficiency, the same ideas that we discuss still today when we look at the firm to understand the perfect system of labour relations.

Actually, in the second stage of his life Owen continued to be a practical, non-intellectual, man. Socialism is undoubtedly an intellectual matter, and Owen was not an intellectual. Engels himself, as we have seen, was surprised that, unlike other utopians, Owen always included in his plans of an ideal company all the necessary calculations on costs, profits, maintenance, etc. They are the typical calculations of a businessman that he uses a lot in his autobiography. Fabian socialists, who were British, non-Marxists and non-radical, discovered the public Owen, the Owen after 1812 and they made him a great figure in socialism (Podmore, 1906). But Owen did not come to socialism by reading books or experiencing personally working class misery, but observing them from his vantage point of the manager and being convinced that the better working conditions were a win–win: productivity improves along with happiness of all the people involved. And he put his ideas into action and convinced the philanthropists and businessmen to invest in New Lanark.

After resigning in New Lanark, things were not so good for Owen. As we saw, Owen left his position as New Lanark manager in 1825. In 1824 he went to The United States, and he returned to England soon after the New Harmony inauguration, in May 1825. He returned to America in January 1826, and re-founded New Harmony based on absolute equality. By the spring of 1827, New Harmony had failed. In 1828 Owen sold his share in New Lanark. In 1829 he returned to England (Morton, 1962, p. 30).

However, New Lanark continued to be an important manufacturing centre for a long time.[9]

4.1.6. *Owen's proposal as a businessman*

As Gatrell affirms (in Owen, 1970, p. 47) in New Lanark Owen had refuted the traditional image of the workers, and he tried to do the same in the whole of England. It was this change of emphasis which – almost incidentally – made him the spokesman of the working people.

In the Address prefixed to the *Third Essay of the New View of Society* written in 1813, Owen says

> By those details you will find that from the commencement of my management I viewed the population, with the mechanism and every other part of the establishment, as a system composed of many parts, and which it was my duty and interest so to combine, as that every hand, as well as every spring, lever, and wheel, should effectually co-operate to produce the greatest pecuniary gain to the proprietors.

And he follows giving recommendations to entrepreneurs as money-makers:

> If, then, due care as to the state of your inanimate machines can produce such beneficial results, what may not be expected if you devote equal attention to your vital machines, which are far more wonderfully constructed?... From experience which cannot deceive me, I venture to assure you, that your time and money so applied, if directed by a true knowledge of the subject, would return you, not five, ten, or fifteen per cent for your capital so expended, but often fifty, and in many cases a hundred per cent. (Owen, 1813, p. 94)

In his testimony before the Parliament in 1815, Owen discussed if children at the age of five or six years must be employed in factories for 13, 14 or 16 hours, daily as that was typical of the age; or at 10 years old, the age established in New Lanark. However, he proposed 12 years old to be the perfect age and he said what he would have done if the factories were a 100 per cent of his property. Being the main proprietor and sole acting partner of New Lanark, in a town with 2,300 inhabitants out of which 1,700 worked in the factory, he was dealing with a monopsony within a Company town, and the Company could have established the wage of the workers without any competition. He could have hired children, but he did not hire children under 10 years old because it would have been preju- dicial for them and not beneficial to the proprietors.

> I have found other and very important advantages, in a pecuniary view, from this arrangement and these plans. In consequence of the individuals observing that real attention is given to their improvements, they are willing to work at much lower wages than at others at no great distance, which are esteemed to be upon the best plans in the country, with all the newest improvements.... (Robert Owen, Evidence of Robert Owen on Conditions at New Lanark, 1815)

The people knew it was true. The profits of New Lanark reached, between 1809 and 1813, 160,000 pounds. And in only two years from 1820–1821, it yielded a profit of 15,000 pounds. As Marx says in political terms, and Coase in economic terms, the capitalist does not know the theory of what he does inside the firm, but he knows how to do it (Santos, 1997, pp. 156–169). The capitalist exerting the power must understand that authority and esteem must be deserved. Leibenstein (1966, in Putterman, 1994, pp. 209–214) says that empirical studies show that psychological factors are very important for workers' motivation: small units are more productive than big ones; groups composed of friends are more productive than the ones composed of people not acquainted with one another; supervised groups are more productive than the ones not supervised; the groups that receive more information about the importance of their work are more productive, etc., etc.

Robert Owen cut down working hours, improved labour conditions, increased wages, established calculations of the profitability of workers and made theories about how they must be distributed scientifically. In this trial and error process, many other entrepreneurs went through the easy way of imposing authority through punishments and monetary rewards. Owen applied the participative model of the firm (Salas 1993, p. 138) as an efficient entrepreneurial organization, not in socialism or cooperative terms, but based on "industrial paternalism". David Dale – and Owen – was "like a father for his children" (Gatrell in Owen, 1970, p. 41). The communities he ran after New Lanark with the same organiza- tional design failed when they lacked his management. "But the emergence of personnel management and of the new ways of organizing labour will be the fruit of philanthropic thought of the utopian socialism" (Casado, 1998, p. 64).

4.2. How Jeremy Bentham became familiar with entrepreneurship

4.2.1. The contribution of Bentham (1748–1832) to philosophy: his method

But now we will go into the managerial experience of Jeremy Bentham. As Rothbard (1995) says, Bentham devoted most of his life to scribbling chaotically on endless and prolix manuscripts elaborating on his projected reforms and law codes. He wrote manuscripts in his loneliness in an increasingly dark language. In his syntax he made an excessive use of subordinated clauses, and his vocabulary of neologisms became dark, of a violent and exaggerated type. He had a language of his own, some words of which were very well received: internationally, to codify, codification, to maximize, maximization, to minimize, minimization, omnicompetent. However, most of the manuscripts remained unpublished until long after his death.

His philosophy had many influences, especially those of classic Greeks such as Arístipo de Cirene, or the English philosophers such as Bacon, Hobbes, Hume, Hélvetius and, some argue, the Bishop of Cumberland, with his book *Ligibus naturae disquisitio philosophica,* of 1672 (Bentham 1985). But, as John Stuart Mill says "We must not look for subtlety, or the power of recondite analysis, among his intellectual characteristics. In the former quality, few great thinkers have ever been so deficient" (Mill, 1980 p. 44). This lack of subtlety made James Mill complete and correct his work. Also Halévy argues that Bentham showed a certain disdain for metaphysical subtlety. For instance, he brushed aside Berkeley's arguments by assuming the existence of the material world "without scruple, notwithstanding it has been the subject of so much controversy. I assume it boldly for this reason: because in point of practice, no bad consequences can possibly arise from supposing it to be true and the world's consequences can not but arise from supposing it to be false" (UCL, p. 69). Like Epicurus, Bentham accepted the philosophical doctrine of time and space as not infinitely divisible, consisting of minimums of time, transforming movement into a series of frisks, as Aristotle would put it. Bentham was based on Hume"s philosophy of perception, and considered that, when observing external things, we can only extract a mental fiction, a subjective idea constructed by impressions. Knowledge itself is based on an imagination process, and passion consists of mental movements of attraction and repulsion. In Chrestomatia, bodies are constituted by masses of dispersed matter, by big atoms encrusted in a vacuum. Bentham thought of atoms as physical points, something that David Hume had shown to be impossible (Hume, 1964 a, p. 351). As Hume considered vacuum philosophically inconceivable, making it impossible for him to demonstrate the non-existence of vacuum, Bentham could not assume Hume's conclusions, and he said that "Hume's Treatise is a book… from which, however, in proportion to the bulk of it, no great quantity of useful instruction seemed derivable" (Bentham, 1983b, p. 275).

In moral terms, Bentham's theory was not engaged either to profound and subtle human feelings, but on his practical and calculative spirit. However, John Stuart Mill acknowledges that "A place… must be assigned to Bentham among the masters of wisdom, the great teachers and permanent intellectual ornaments of the human race. He is among those who have enriched mankind with imperishable gifts" (Mill, 1980, p. 47) as "he was not a great philosopher, but he was a great reformer in philosophy. He brought into philosophy something which it greatly needed, and for want of which it was at a standstill…. It was not his opinions, in short, but his method, that constituted the novelty and the value of what he did."

Bentham's method was not only inductive, but exact. He inclines towards induction to remove randomness from science and the scholasticism method that posits that reality exists (Stark, 1952a, p. 98). He thought, as John Stuart Mill says

> that error lurks in generalities; that the human mind is not capable of embracing a complex whole, until it has surveyed and catalogued the parts of which that whole is made up; that abstractions are not realities per se, but an abridged mode of expressing facts and that the only practical mode of dealing with them is to trace them back to the facts (Whether of experience or of consciousness) of which they are the expression. (Mill 1980, p.49–50)

He thought that the sphere of ethics was not less capable of mathematical treatment than physics, although, like Marshall, he was inclined to consider mathematics only a suitable expression (Stark, 1952a, p. 118, p. 119).

> Bentham's method may be briefly described as the method of detail; of treating wholes by separating them into their parts, abstractions by resolving them into Things, – classes and generalities by distinguishing them in the individuals of which they are made up; and breaking down every question into pieces before attempting to solve it...Hence his interminable classifications. (Mill, 1980, p. 48)

In his Manual he argues that "for the genesis of the matter of wealth... reference may for the present be made to Adam Smith, who has not left much to do, except in the way of method and precision" (Stark, 1952a, p. 49). Although Bentham praised practically no other author, he habitually referred to Adam Smith as "the father of political economy," a "great master," and a "writer of consummate genius". But, then, he justifies the need of his Manual on the basis that "At any rate, this treatise, whether better upon the whole than Dr. Smith's or not so good, is in point of method very different" (Stark, 1952a, p. 225).

In *Institute of Political Economy,* which Bentham elaborated between 1800 and 1804, the method used is geometric and he introduced, both in legislation and in moral and economic theory, a binomial method of complementary groups, which he wanted to make exhaustive and all-inclusive for science. Bentham wanted to fill the space in an orderly way and, although he did not depict graphs, he described them with great detail and he even discerned the concept of marginal utility and equimarginality (Trincado, 2004b). In short, he introduced a microeconomic method, not only in economics, but also in other social sciences.

Bentham admits that his aim is the art of economic legislation; that of Adam Smith of economic science. He raised nine other points in which his method differs from that of Smith, especially that "His object was science: my object is art... by me science is considered only as a means to an end" (Stark, 1952a, p. 224). For Bentham, the starting point of scientific reasoning must be the potential "utility" of the objects to investigate. For Smith, the economic dissertation does not necessarily look for utility, but for the description of a reality. As Bentham defined economics as a branch of the science of legislation, for him an economic treatise would be a species of code that tried to increase wealth thanks to the regulation of the State. West (1976) says that Smith was addressing the builders of constitutions but this is not completely true. With his criticism on legislators, Smith was showing a search for objectivity. Smith was really addressing the general public to criticize the mercantile system and to build a trust in freedom.

Bentham's method was a rational plan for classification of pleasures. He thinks about the science of the legislator as one of classification more than of calculation. Bentham admits that pleasures are heterogeneous and of different classes but to compare pleasures in an extensive quantity he says that the objects of pleasure must be homogeneous. In *Introduction* (Bentham, 1789) the pleasures are one of 14 categories, with 7 subordinated categories, and having simple pains 12 categories. There are pleasures or pains felt by other people, extra-regarding, and the others are self-regarding. Bentham certifies the predominance of selfishness, provided that all the pleasures enumerated by him are self regarding.

In *Table of the Springs of Action* (Bentham, 1983b) he speaks about three subordinate types of simple pleasures: of taste, of sexual pleasure and of the pleasure of novelty. In 1827 he distinguishes four immediate sources of pleasure or objects of general desire: money, power, natural reputation and factious reputation, the examination of which allows us to forget the immediate innumerable motives for doing something. However, every motive is based on the search for pleasure or aversion to pain, therefore, there is no bad motive. The intention of punishment is to teach the actions that must be considered fair or unjust in terms of pleasure pain through the fear of a penalty. So, law is exemplary punishment or an assumption of relapse of the criminal by which society defends itself from future crimes. In Introductory View he enumerates five interests that may make a civil servant leave his work. They are love: of constant comfort, of occasional revenge, of money, of power and of reputation. His classification of motives in a dichotomous way made that coupling sound as keys that, when pressed, may sing a melody.

But, how may this be applied to economics? As Mill himself says "We have arrived, then at a sort of estimate of what a philosophy like Bentham's can do. It can teach the means of organizing and regulating the merely business part of the social arrangements" (Mill, 1980, p. 73). According to Bentham, the fact that the entrepreneur directs capital in an advantageous way depends, not on the money invested, but on: 1. The choice of trade 2. The choice of directing it. The direction of capital, according to Bentham, depends on the degree of interest that the person who chooses puts in the election and the degree of knowledge and good judgement in trade. The option that a man possesses the highest powers of knowledge and judgment depends to a great extent on the degree of interest that he puts into possessing them. A person is much more interested in what affects him directly (Stark, 1952a, p. 228 from *Manual of Political Economy*). So, that makes the difference between actions *sponte acta*, agenda and non agenda posed in *Manual* and in *Institute*. According to Bentham, there is not a right relation between these three classes of actions. The distribution will differ to a very considerable degree, according to the different circumstances of the several political communities. The general rule to intervene is the desirability of any expense of the government in a subsidy comparing its possible utility with the mischief of the most harmful tax in force due to the fact that this tax could have been abolished if this incentive is not granted. The greater the degree of opulence, the greater the list of *sponte acta* – the less, therefore, that of agenda. In England, abundance of useful things was produced by individuals, which in other countries was fostered either by government, or not at all.

> Whoever takes upon him to add to national wealth by coercive, and thence vexatious measures, stands engaged to make out two propositions: – 1. That more wealth will be produced by the coercion than would have been produced without it; 2. That the comfort flowing from the extra wealth thus produced, is more than equivalent to whatever vexation may be found attached to the measure by which it was produced. (Stark, 1952a, p. 229)

In order that the state achieves an increase of wealth, for example, it must create an inclination and incentives, transferring wealth from one branch to other. But everything that stimulates A discourages B, unless the quantity of capital was unlimited or the public agent had information about the private or other interest in the branch of trade. The real problem of government, then, is asymmetric information. The individual has more information than the government, but if the government had more information, it must intervene as they could spread useful knowledge all around (Stark, 1952c, p. 359 extracted from *Institute of Political Economy*). The agency problem, however, is very difficult to solve.

> The individual acts for himself: the agent of government acts for others... The principal of the private agent is a person whom he knows, a person whom he sees, a person who is watching over him, or ready at any time so to do: a person to whom he is obliged, a person for whom he naturally enter- tains an affection, who commonly has entertained an affection for, and certainly has a good opinion of him. The principal of the government agent is an ideal being, whom nobody knows, and for whom nobody cares.[10]

For Bentham, the process of discovering information is very important. This process is so subjective and uncertain that it is not easy to transfer so as to make utility objective. Government does not know what people want and its interven- tion may obstruct their objectives:

> It is not often that one man is a better judge for another, than that other is for himself, even in cases where the adviser will take the trouble to make himself master of as many of the materials for judging, as are within the reach of the person to be advised. But the legislator is not, can not be, in the possession

of any one of these materials. – What private, can be equal to such public folly? (Stark, 1952a, p. 140, from *Defence of Usury*)

As we are seeing, although Ricardian economics was the basis of the classical school of economics, Bentham preempted with this Austrian economics. He introduced the idea of decreasing marginal utility and equimarginality; and he distinguished between goods of lower and higher order. Bentham had written quite original economic works, such as *Defence of Usury*, 1787 or *Manual of Political Economy* in 1793 and, as Schumpeter (1954a [1914]), Taylor (1955) or Trincado (2004b) state, there is a specific Bentham view of economics presented throughout his writings.[11] However, his economics does not qualify Bentham to ensure the possibility of spontaneous order, the same as Austrians nowadays think that the processes of discovery in the market is a dynamic imbalance. Institutions, for him, play a crucial role in the discovery, transmission and use of information: "Opportunity of collecting the particular information, necessary time for reflecting on it, interest in forming a right judgment, in all these particulars he falls infinitely short of the persons themselves whom he would wish to see thus employed" (Stark, 1952a, p. 202) from *Defence of Usury*).

For this reason, Bentham gives special value to the figure of the entrepreneur. Information of their modes of behaviour is crucial, we may gain a lot of experience by knowing their methods, creating a path for business history:

> The career of art, the great road which receives the footsteps of projectors, may be considered as a vast, and perhaps unbounded, plain, bestrewed with gulphs, such as Curtius was swallowed up in... If the want of perfect information of former miscarriages renders the reality of human life less happy than this picture, still the similitude must be acknowledged: and we see at once the only plain and effectual method for bringing that similitude still nearer and nearer to perfection; I mean, the framing of the history of the projects of time past, and (what may be executed in much greater perfection were but a finger held up by the hand of government) the making provision for recording, and collecting and publishing as they are brought forth, the race of those with which the womb of futurity is still pregnant. (Stark, 1952a, p. 202 from *Defence of Usury*)

4.2.2. Bentham becomes familiar with entrepreneurship

Actually, Bentham wrote in the late eighteenth century quite original economic works on entrepreneurship, such as *Defence of Usury,* 1787 or *Manual of Political Economy* in 1793. Bentham's idea of the projector-innovator, on the lines of the French tradition, will be an argument for defence of the free market, as in a centrally planned economy there will not be a projector to nurture technological innovation for its own interest.

> I mean projectors: under which invidious name I understand you to comprehend, in particular all such persons as, in the pursuit of wealth, strike out into

any new channel, and more especially into any channel of invention…; whether it consists of the production of any new article adapted to man's use, or in ameliorating the quality, or diminishing the expense, of any of those which are already known to us… whatever is now establishment, was not, at one time, innovation? (Bentham, 1818, p. 12)

Jeremy had a direct practical source to learn about entrepreneurship. It was through his brother Samuel Bentham (1757–1831), and also through Marc Isambard Brunel (1769–1849) and Henry Maudslay (1771–1831) who started mass production using interchangeable parts, at Portsmouth Block Mills, in 1802. These entrepreneurs were even paid in an entrepreneurial way, by measuring the amount of money the Navy saved with their method.

Samuel Bentham was the only surviving brother of Bentham from five other siblings (Pease, 2002). Samuel was the youngest of those seven children – and Jeremy was the eldest – and they were the only two who survived. Their father Jeremiah was a well-connected lawyer whose patron was the future Whig Prime Minister, the Earl of Shelburne. The brothers shared their inventiveness but they were opposites: Jeremy, a philosopher and jurist, was shy and scholarly. Samuel, an engineer by profession, was entrepreneurial and sociable.

Samuel was a noted mechanical engineer and naval architect credited with numerous innovations, particularly related to naval architecture, including weapons. Samuel, initially hired as a shipbuilder, constructed industrial machinery and experimented with steel production. He went to Russia in 1779 and he gradually developed contacts with the Court and by 1783 had entered the service of Catherine with the rank of lieutenant-colonel, and "accompanied Prince Potemkin to Drichev in White Russia, to assist him in his grandiose schemes for the development of the southern steppes" (Bentham 1968b, T. L. Sprigge, Introduction, Correspondence, I, p. XXXIX.). Jeremy wanted his brother to propose on his behalf his legal ideas to the Empress. The Benthams wrote to each other constantly about Samuel's escapades in Russia (see Montefiore 2001).

Eventually, Samuel began to work for the Russian Prince Grigori Potemkin, the favourite of Catherine the Great. Potemkin was already the master of an industrial empire, best-known for its factories that made Russia's most beautiful mirrors. It was while considering the difficulties of supervising the large workforce that Samuel devised the principle of central inspection, and designed the Panopticon building which would embody that principle and was later popularized by his brother Jeremy. Although Samuel came to have complete responsibility for Potemkin's factories and workshops, his main task was to build ships for Potemkin. And, for that, Samuel Bentham's budget was limitless. Sutherland, Potemkin's banker, simply arranged the credit in London. Samuel immediately saw opportunities for himself and his brother Jeremy to trade in goods between England and Russia and to benefit from the position of middlemen in Potemkin's recruiting campaign.

Father and brother, Jeremiah and Jeremy Bentham, began to work to this end in Britain. Old Jeremiah called on Lord Howe and invited the Under-Secretary of State Fraser, and two recently-returned Russian veterans to his house to discuss it. Jeremy bombarded Samuel with interminable details on a parade of candidates for posts to be created in the trading ships varying from chief of botanical garden, to milkmaid. Jeremy Bentham longed to join Samuel in Belorussia. He began to write directly to the Prince himself suggesting quixotic ideas and telling him about gardeners and chemists. In one letter Jeremy apologetically signed himself 'Here for the fourth time, Your Eternal Correspondent.' But Potemkin hated long letters and only wanted results. Samuel feared his career was being ruined by Jeremy so he told his brother off.

Meanwhile, on 28 July, 1785, Jeremy Bentham set out from Brighton. He reached Krichev in February 1786. But the people recommended by Bentham for the ships proved a disaster. There were rebellions against the Benthams led by general Benson, and some of the recruits even stole from Samuel to pay off their debts. Soon many of the recruits began to perish, a misfortune that Samuel said had more to do with their intemperate lifestyle than with the terrible climate they had to endure.

Actually, the project of the Panopticon was Sam's solution to supervising these people at Krichev: a factory constructed so that the manager could see all his workers from one central observation point. Jeremy the legal reformer could immediately see its use in prisons.

Jeremy and Samuel were also pursuing another great ambition thanks to their relation with the political power of Potemkin: to become landowners in the Crimea. "We are going to be great farmers", announced Jeremy. "I dare say he would give us a good portion of land to both of us if we wish it…". But the Benthams never became Crimean magnates, though they did get a share in one of Korsakov's estates. Yet the Benthams achieved an immense amount in Krichev. Jeremy Bentham was eagerly hoping to meet Prince Potemkin whom he called the "Prince of Princes" but he never met him. By 1787, after more than a year in Belorussia he was on his way home to England.

Jeremy Bentham also dreamt of reforming Russian law under Catherine the Great but during this stay in Russia he also became interested in economics, adopting Adam Smith's newly stated laissez faire theory. This, he carried further than Smith himself writing *Defence of Usury*, which he sent back to England for publication. It was a letter to Smith, but by his publication he was, obviously, trying to be famous on his return thanks to Adam Smith's fame.

After his tour in Russia and China, Samuel returned to England in 1791 and, for the next few years, was involved with his brother Jeremy in trying to promote the Panopticon scheme and he designed machinery for use in it. In March 1796, Samuel was appointed Inspector General of Naval Works, a post which involved a lot of travel. He produced many suggestions for improvements, which included the introduction of steam power to the dockyards and the mechanisation of many production processes. However, his superiors at the Navy Board were resistant to change and many of his suggestions were not implemented. Samuel Bentham is credited with helping to revolutionise the production of the wooden pulley blocks used in ships' rigging, devising woodworking machinery to improve production efficiency (Brindle, 2006; Burke, 1978).

In 1805 Samuel returned to Russia, this time on government business, and remained there for two years with his family, chartering an entire ship to take his establishment, his servants and his companions (Christie, 1993). He planned to construct an amphibious vessel and an articulated barge for Catherine the Great (Morris 1997, p. 262). Samuel's mission for the British Government in Russia was blocked by constant obstacles and he returned home in 1807 without having achieved any of his official objectives. During this time he supervised the construction of a Panopticon School of Arts on the banks of the Okhta River in St. Petersburg, the design which he had first conceived while in Krichev in 1786. The building was destroyed by fire. Bentham also designed a full cast-iron nine-arch bridge for the Butterly company for Vauxhall Bridge in London, which would have been the first iron-built bridge over the Thames. In 1814, he and his family relocated to the south of France, where they lived until 1826.

The family of Samuel travelled a great deal in France before settling in 1820 at the Château de Restinclières, in the region of Languedoc-Roussillon. Their new house was large, with extensive grounds, and Samuel planned to cultivate the land for profit, with his son George managing most of the operation. Samuel also imported agricultural machinery as yet unknown in France, and installed a complex system of irrigation on his land. They were reasonably prosperous, but eventually returned to England in 1826. One factor in their decision was a threatened lawsuit from neighbouring farmers, who claimed that Samuel's irrigation system was diverting the local water supply (see G. Bentham, 1997 and Gabbay and Woods, 2008).

In August 1826, George travelled to London with his sisters, with the hope of securing his uncle's support. When it became clear that he would not get financial support from Jeremy, George decided to enroll in Lincoln's Inn and trained as a lawyer, something that infuriated Jeremy (G. Bentham 1997, p. 246-7). George says: "[M]y uncle has imagined that he makes my fortune in giving me his logical papers to make a book of; That if I succeed in putting it into intelligible French, Bossanges [the publisher] may give me something – but as for a fortune, if I get any from my uncle, it must be in a more direct way than through the medium of his manuscripts" (G. Bentham, 1997, p. 31).

4.2.3. *Jeremy Bentham's own experience as an entrepreneur*

But, as we have already commented, Jeremy Bentham also invented some devices. His real estate investments were also numerous. But those inventions and investments led him to important financial losses. As his friend George Wilson scolded: "But your history, since I have known you, has been to be always running from a good scheme to a better. In the meantime, life passes away and nothing is completed" (George Wilson to Bentham, 26 Februrary 1787, Correspondence, III, p. 526). Actually, New Lanark was for Bentham his only profitable investment. Bentham's own projects could be described as failures or as not appropriate for the time and place.

Bentham spent hundreds of pounds devising those plans and undertakings. Fortunately, an inheritance received in 1796 provided him with financial stability and, so, he devised such projects as his Panopticon, his Chrestomathic school, some heat treatments and sealing devices for meats, vegetables and fruits; he built in his own back garden a huge frigidarium, he also tried to interest the Treasury in currency schemes and speaking tubes, he suggested a scheme of a train of carts drawn at speed between London and Edinburgh, and he suggested to the Americans that they should build a canal through Panama. He also told the Bank of England how to create an unforgeable banknote. His mind teemed with many other projects - an essay on paper currency, another on the sinking fund, improvements in House of Commons procedure. One of his more bizarre ideas was to rename the country and call it "Brithibernia". This was just one manifestation of his eccentricity, along with having a cat named The Reverend Dr John Langhorn and a walking stick called Dapple, and that he requested in his will that his body were preserved. C. W. Everett (1931) and Bahmueller (1981) noted that Bentham went far beyond merely drawing up plans. He also tried to put them into practice.

The main objective of all Bentham's investments and projects was the representing for him of the greatest happiness of the greatest number. For instance, in September 1800, Bentham proposed the authorities should freeze large quantities of vegetables so that fresh peas would be available at Christmas and tried to invent a "frigidarium" or ice-house for the preservation of fish, fruits, and vegetables (Works, x, 346; in Stephen 1900). Cohen (1997) says that Jeremy Bentham's frigidarium manuscripts form a little known excursion by Bentham into the science of food preservation. These manuscripts are mentioned by Bentham in a letter to his brother Samuel and in two letters to Peter Mark Roget (1779–1869), a physician who in October 1800 spent six weeks with Jeremy Bentham discussing Bentham's scheme for the utilization of the sewage of big metropolises and this frigidarium (these were related projects). Most of the frigidarium manuscripts are rough outlines and sketches of ideas composed between 1794–1809, a period of war and food shortages throughout the continent and Britain. The panic from the grain shortage and the subsequent riots in 1795 and 1800, coupled with the widespread perception that conditions of the lower classes had markedly deteriorated, and the market distortions caused by the war in Europe, made Bentham realize the vast potential benefits of a method of storing food for long periods of time. The dangers of scarcity in most minds were connected with violent Revolution, something to which Bentham was quite unsympathetic. The frigidarium would save the nation from starvation and keep inflation in check. The price of food would remain constant, since there would now be a more constant supply. Bentham's loss of interest for the project in the 1810s probably has to do with the turning of the tide of the war in Europe in Britain's favour, which was accompanied by fewer food shortages, and new developments in food preservation and cooling that would revolutionize the food industry. These changes would make superfluous the well intended frigidarium.

At the same time that he was working on the frigidarium, Bentham was writing his papers on the Panopticon and the National Charity Company. The Panopticon is the best known project from Bentham. As defined by its inventor to Brissot, the Panopticon – a model prison where all prisoners would be observable by (unseen) guards at all times – was a "mill for grinding rogues honest, and idle men industrious" (Bentham, 1838–1843, vol. x, pp. 226, quoted in Mitchell (1918, p. 194)). The Panopticon is based on the "geometry of thought", a structure organized by an internalized visuality and the simulation of optical space for a surveillance mechanism. Actually, also New Lanark was an early model biosphere: a geodesic between environmentalism and economic output, similarly describing a relation between structuralised "landscape" and the aesthetics of utopian visual repose.

Bentham establishes multiple rules in the penitentiary house, but in the rule of economy, he raises two management options: based on contract or based on trust. He chooses the management by contract. This consists of a man who treats with the government who is in charge of guarding and supporting the prisoners for an amount per head and applying the work and industry of these for his personal profit. From whom can we expect more for zeal and vigilance at the head of this establishment?, asks Bentham. From the one whose earnings depend on good conduct instead of having fixed emoluments, be it badly or well administered, as is the case with a civil servant, subject to misappropriation or negligence. So, the Panopticon would be administered by a businessman with a life contract, under the reservations of good conduct. We need to remember that Bentham lived in the last stage of prisons being privately owned and he thought that it should be an institution that was profit driven (Bentham, 1979).

In 1785, Bentham briefly joined his brother Samuel in Russia, where he hoped to interest the Czarina Catherine the Great in the Panopticon. The loss of most of Bentham's letters to Samuel for these years, leave us to infer what they said. But by 1784, Jeremy's plan to join his brother in Russia was taking shape (Tusseau, 2014). He stayed in Russia for two years. Bentham had hoped to present Catherine the Great with an immense code of law, and went to Russia in 1785, in part with this endeavour in mind. But, as J. H. Burns has written: "Catherine never saw either the Code or its author. Bentham remained secluded in western Russia, translating his work into French; and when the empress visited the district he stayed – stubbornly diffident – in his cottage" (Burns, 1966, p. 95). He returned to England in 1788 and shortly after came the French Revolution. For some 20 years Bentham pursued the idea fruitlessly and at great expense.

In March 1792 he made a proposal to the government offering to undertake the charge of a thousand convicts upon the Panopticon system. After delays suspicious in the eyes of Bentham, an act of parliament was obtained in 1794 to adopt his schemes. Bentham had already been making preparations. He says (14 September 1794) that he had already spent £6,000, and is spending at the rate of £2,000 a year, while his income was under £600 a year. He obtained, however, £2,000 from the government. It was not until 1799 that he at last acquired for £12,000 an estate at Millbank, which seemed to be suitable. Meanwhile the finance committee, appointed in 1797, heard evidence from Bentham's friend, Patrick Colquhoun, upon the Panopticon, and a report recommending it was proposed by R. Pole Carew, a friend of Samuel Bentham. Although this report was suppressed, the scheme apparently received an impetus. The Millbank estate was bought as a consequence of these proceedings, and a sum of only £1,000 was wanted to buy out the tenant of one piece of land. Bentham was constantly in attendance at a public office, expecting a final warrant for the money. It never came, and Bentham believed that the delay was due to the malice of George III. Bentham seems to have struggled vainly for a time. He appealed to Pitt's friend, Wilberforce; he appealed to his step-brother Abbot; he wrote to members of parliament, but all was in vain (Works 9, 144). The actual end did not come till 1811. A committee then reported against the scheme. The committee recommended a different plan; and the result was the foundation of Millbank penitentiary, opened in 1816 (Griffiths, 1884). Bentham ultimately received £23,000 by way of compensation in 1813.

In January 1802 he writes to Dumont (Works 10: 381) proposing to send him a trifling specimen of the Panopticon, a set of hollow fire-irons invented by his brother, which may attract the attention of Buonaparte and Talleyrand. He proceeds to expound the merits of Samuel's invention for making wheels by machinery. Dumont replies that fire-irons are 'superfluities' and that the Panopticon itself was coldly received (Stephen, 1900).

Another plan from Bentham was devised in 1815 for a "Chrestomathic school", which was to give a sound education of proper utilitarian tendencies to the upper and middle classes. This system of schooling was to be free of religious instruction and physical punishment, as was the case with Owen's scheme.[12] Brougham, Mackintosh, Ricardo, William Allen, and Place were all interested in this undertaking. Bentham offered a site at Queen's Square Place, and though the scheme never came to birth, he wrote a series of papers during his first year at Ford Abbey upon the theory of education, published in 1816 as Chrestomathia (Bentham 1983c). William Thompson wrote in 1819 to Jeremy Bentham on the subject of establishing a Chrestomathic school in Cork. Bentham replied on 7 April, and subsequently wrote inviting him to his house at Queen's Square, London. Bentham finding the church in his way, had little difficulty in discovering that the whole ecclesiastical system was part of the general complex of abuse against which he was warring. Actually, he observed passively how Owen made the same mistake.

Bentham also recommended the discretional issue of a governmental banknote that should render an interest rate or annuity, the Annuity Notes (from which we have four boxes of material in 1400 sheets). In an unpublished "Proposal for the Circulation of a [New] Species of Paper Currency" (1796), Bentham proposes that the government should monopolize all issues of paper notes in the kingdom. It could then issue the notes, preferably non-interest bearing ad libitum, and save itself the interest. In his later writings on the subject, Bentham searched for some limits to paper issue, if unsuccessfully. In his unfinished "Circulating Annuities" (1800) he continues calling for the elimination of bank paper for the benefit of a government monopoly of paper issue (in the fragmentary "Paper Mischief Exposed," 1801). Finally, in his "The True Alarm" (1801) Bentham continues the full-employment motif that will be basic for the twentieth century; but all those proposals were not much taken into account in the monetary debates of the nineteenth century.

At the end of his life, when he failed to establish those projects, Bentham's reaction was to devise a fantastic world based on his Panopticon, the world of the *Ptenotrophium*, an immense factory of battery chickens, to construct the *Sotimion* or establishment for the preservation of female delicacy and reputation or the *Nothotrophium* or "Asylum for the innocent offspring of clandestine love", in which, in spite of their innocence, contractors would use the work of the children for good effect... (Everett, 1996, pp. 72–73).

Bentham's real estate investments were also important. In 1807 he took a house at Barrow Green, near Oxted, in Surrey; but in 1814, probably as a consequence of his compensation for the Panopticon, took a larger place, Ford Abbey, near Chard in Somersetshire. It was a superb residence, with chapel, cloisters, and corridors, a hall 80 feet long by 30 feet high, and a great dining parlor. The place, for which he paid £315 a year, was very nice. He liked it so much that he would have taken it for life, but for the loss of £8,000 or £10,000 in a Devonshire marble-quarry (Works 10, p. 479, p. 573), in 1818 he gave it up, and thereinafter rarely left Queen's Square Place.

4.2.4. Bentham versus Smith on entrepreneurship

In his *Defence of Usury*, Bentham (1818) reproaches Adam Smith for having underestimated the role of the "men of talent" that, thanks to their invention and imagination, are responsible for the progress and wealth of the nations, provided that they find new channels of trade and open new ways towards the future. According to Bentham, Smith presented a businessman who faces risk as something routine. But Bentham is criticizing Smith's theory and defending theoretically the projector with some "vested interests". In so doing, he was defending the way of life of his brother Samuel, who was a successful engineer and projector, and something of an adventurer, but he also was justifying his own way of living, as a narcissistic constructor of chimeras. With his failures and bankruptcies, Bentham would have actually been a marvellous example of projector in Adam Smith's theory. This difference of Bentham with Smith is quite relevant, and needs further explanation.

There has been criticism of Smith's figure of the entrepreneur, as he neglected his importance in capitalism, but actually Smith proposed his theory very consciously. He was trying to criticize the Cantillon figure of the entrepreneur, champion of adventurers and speculators (Spengler, 1975). Hébert and Link (1988, pp. 50–54) gather Bentham's work on the businessman and emphasize that he had more links with the intellectual French tradition of Cantillon and Say than most other of his contemporaries.[13] It is to be noted that this tradition is based on supply more than on demand (Hébert and Link, 2006).

Bentham says that the businessman introduces improvements, and here, Bentham uses italics for the word improvement due to the fact that he distinguishes between improvement (a new method of combining resources for productive purposes) and invention (scientific progress). Projectors create utility, Bentham (1952, p. 170) argued, by effecting improvements, whether such improvements consist of the production of any new article adapted to man's use, or in ameliorating the quality, or reducing the expense, of any of those which are already known to us.[14] The function of the entrepreneur, then, is to capture the utility of the final good beforehand, having foreseen the pleasures of the public in an uncertainty context.

Bentham speaks to us about the productivity increased by new arrangements of the means of production, especially in manufactures. Innovation is the force that drives development because "what is now an institution, once was an innovation" (Stark, 1952b, p. 355).Though the business may fail, society as a whole remains intact because others will try not to make the same mistakes and the innovations introduced in the productive process or machinery will expand across the economic system. This is risk management and diversification of risk applied to business practices, a theory brought into question by the recent financial crisis, at least by those who argue for more regulation in cases of imperfect competition.[15]

Bentham says that the designer introduces an improvement, his expense enters unknown paths or the production of a new good adapted to the human use or the improvement of his quality. He calls designers to all who, in the culture of these arts that have been useful, direct their efforts to any of these departments in which their usefulness seems to be more unquestionable. His function, therefore, is as we have said to catch the utility of the final good, providing the pleasures of the public in contexts of uncertainty. All these fit Samuel Bentham's managerial activity, and even the Panopticon, an administrative innovation that Bentham considered could create economic incentives (Hébert and Link, 2006, p. 591).

Bentham also complains that Smith relates prodigals with speculators. The second do not follow routine models of behaviour, they stand out from the masses, so they are a very restricted elite that needs couragement and genius. Bentham shows himself here as "aristocratic" or "entrepreneurial", in a Schumpeterian individualistic sense, conception: projectors depart from routine patterns of behaviour; break away from the common herd; and in the process discover new markets, find new sources of supply, improve existing products, or lower costs of production For instance, the Panopticon is an administrative innovation that Bentham considered could create economic incentives (Hébert and Link, 2006, p. 591). So, Bentham is near the figure of the businessman described by Kirzner, in which the role of surprise and discovery is typical of the managerial creative function.[16]

He mentions two cases in which courage, not genius is necessary for an entrepreneur: the opening of a new market and the search for a new source of supply. When we add another two determinants of innovation – the production of a new good and the introduction of a new method of production – we have four of the five new combinations that Schumpeter mentions in *Theory of Economic Development*. It is surprising that Schumpeter, apart from a brief reference (in Schumpeter, 1949, p. 64) does not mention Bentham when talking about the central role of the managerial function.[17] Nevertheless, he considered that Bentham was the one who most clearly perceived the importance and nature of the managerial function, though his opinions about the topic slipped by economists.[18] Actually, an intermediate view of innovation is the one raised by the evolutionary theories of economic change, with transformations of the organization which are cumulative and based on "natural selection". Firms are motivated by profit but they are not maximizers – though they have abilities and rules of decision.[19]

On the other hand, according to Schumpeter (1954b, p. 555), Smith did not have a theory of the entrepreneur. The capitalist risks the means of production but the entrepreneur is a capitalist that supervises his business to ensure his profits. Knight (1921[1947]) says that Smith admits that the profit contains an element that is not the interest of capital. According to Hollander (1973, p. 170) Smith formulated the concept of profit as a compensation for the uncertainty of the revenue drawn from the use of capital when you run a firm.

But the entrepreneur figure is presented in the *Wealth of Nations* at least in three ways: the entrepreneur as an adventurer, those that have so much faith in their success and put their capital at risk by investing in the most difficult companies. They do this, not to anticipate the utility of the consumer, but to persuade others and convince them to be of their opinion by the use of language (Smith, 1994, p. 167). The second type of entrepreneur is the speculator (the projector), towards whom in Smith's time there already was a hostile attitude. Smith treats them with irony or scorn; they entertain the public with their "stories" of the immense profits that they can obtain, and embark on expensive and uncertain projects that also lead to bankruptcy for most of those who involve themselves in the project. But Smith's hostility to these speculators is not due to the fact that they plan projects, something characteristic of the capitalist class.[20] The problem with speculators is that they are a haughty and imprudent people, that is to say, that they do not take into account the unpredictability of time. These plans of whose opportunity they have convinced many people make public stop trusting the mercantile traffic, something bad in the long run. For that reason, Smith defended the establishment of a legal maximum to the interest rate without which only the prodigals and speculators might take loans. The frauds or losses of the businessman not only concern the parties but subdues the investor to a moral risk under the bias of asymmetric information.

Finally, Smith speaks about the prudent man who saves and invests to obtain the ordinary profit in lines of production more or less known. He has the quality of abstinence and he is the man of slow but sure progress, who contents himself with small accumulations. He makes his projects with enough current information and taking into account the relation between expected profit and an acceptable risk, provided that he knows that only if he saves or does sound business will he be able to increase the quantity of his capital in a constant way.[21]

Bentham wanted Smith to check his opinion about the function of the prudent man in his system. Nevertheless, Smith did not change his theory. As Pesciarelli (1989) says, Smith considered the "ideal man" the current and frugal man whereas Bentham – and Schumpeter – enthrone the exceptional and adventurous individual. The vision of Smith contrasts with that of Schumpeter, who says that "Talent in economic life rides to success on its debts" (Schumpeter, 1934, p 70).[22] According to the Smithian theory, Bentham's idea of managerial activity introduces Messianism, which could be similar to that introduced by mercantilism with the state. Whenever the market or the individuals cannot face the process of growth, it is necessary to have a Messiah with semi-divine characteristics. Owen was also against this idea, and he thought that a normal person could handle a firm. And he was the entrepreneur. He did not consider entrepreneurship as something to do with risk, but with prudence and the taking into account of the worker's feelings and incentives. The same as Smith, he assumes equality between men, on the basis that we do not have inborn ideas and that the Lockian tabula rasa is underlying: we cannot assume that the adventurers have more knowledge of the future than others. If Bentham shows an aristocratic attitude, Smith shows a certain preference for the middle and low conditions of society, and especially for the middle, the saving class according to Smith.[23] People from the middle classes, who have not been born rich but who have a small quantity of capital, save and invest it.[24] As Santos (1997) says, we can relate this explanation to Milton Friedman's theory of consumption, based on the concept of "permanent revenue". This relates to demand and consumption attitudes, even in the business context, instead of supply and technology, as was the case of Bentham, who assumes the entrepreneurial function.

According to Smith, the adventurers and speculators are a "type" of people who, due to their habits, have some differential features with regard to the majority of men, who trust in the future though they have a concern for it. The adventurer and speculator differ in that they are specialized in taking risks. Their character would even be used to it and they will have lost the spring of prudence. But these are concerning the psychology of the common people, influenced by imitation and ostentation in managerial customs and prodigality. These risky attitudes, in fact, lead to an increase in the interest rate. This idea, Smith takes from Hume and in a certain way it runs counter to the universality of the trend to work and saving typical of Smith's theory.[25] On the contrary, for Bentham risk is a foreseen "pleasure" and for him the pleasures are more intense the more uncertain they are (Dube, 1991, p. 97).

Besides, for Smith the managerial risk that only looks for innovations and technological changes can only give profits temporarily, and in brief other companies will assume the innovation and will cut down the profit margin with competition, it being impossible to force to any channel a major quota that naturally would flow towards it spontaneously (Smith, 1994, p. 173). Obviously, however Smith was not conscious of the Industrial Revolution that began about 1776, the year of publication of the *Wealth of Nations*. The pin factory of which Smith speaks had 10 or 12 employees, and there was no need to administer the personnel apart from the attentive supervision of a capitalist or a trustworthy man.

The nub of controversy between Smith and Bentham is also on the theory of value, as according to Bentham the projector satisfies a desire previous to the sale, although it may be unconscious.[26] As Schumpeter (1934, Chapter II "The Fundamental Phenomenon of Economic Developement", II, p. 65) says:

> ... we must always start from the satisfaction of wants, since they are the end of all production, and the given economic situation at any time must be understood from this aspect. Yet innovations in the economic system do not as a rule take place in such a way that first new wants arise spontaneously in consumers and then the productive apparatus swings round through their pressure. We do not deny the presence of this nexus. It is, however, the producer who as a rule initiates economic change, and consumers are educated by him if necessary; they are, as it were, taught to want new things, or things which differ in some respect or other from those which they have been in the habit of using. Therefore, while it is permissible and even necessary to consider consumers' wants as an independent and indeed the fundamental force in a theory of the circular flow, we must take a different attitude as soon as we analyse change.

In the twentieth century, the discussion involves the role of government and publicity: Galbraith (1958) considers that advertising induces "false" needs; Hayek (1961) that most wants are socially induced.

4.3. Conclusion: different philosophies of life

Owen's idea of management is somewhat different from the utilitarian idea, and in particular Bentham's concept of the entrepreneur. Actually, they both had a different philosophy of life. Owen considered progress and development to be the objective of happiness, the present being the time and space where we live. In contrast, Bentham considered the accomplishment of some expectation of the future the path to happiness which is lived in a succession of time. As we shall see, in economics, this implies a very important difference between development economics that relies on objectivity and some concept of freedom that makes the future indeterminate, versus microeconomic analysis that relies on subjective and deterministic hypotheses (see Trincado, 2008a).

Was Owen the prudent man of Adam Smith? At least it is what Owen thought of himself. He thought that, what makes capital increase is neither major inventiveness nor the "exceptional man", but "the skill and judgment with which normally the work is done".[27] Owen considered that it is not risk, but the taking into account of the worker's feelings and incentives that is important for success. And those incentives are not always rewards and punishments, but an unintended consequence of sympathizing with them and having concern for their welfare. This, Friedrich Engels explains very well (Engels, 1880, 7).

Bentham's idea of the projector-innovator seemed to be embodied in the practice of Owen 1 as an entrepreneur. But for Bentham, the role of technological change in economic growth is very important. Owen was against the justification of technological innovation morally and economically (Carlisle and Manning, 1996).

In Bentham, this could be an argument for the defence of a free market, as the projector in a centrally planned economy will not nurture technological innovation for his own interest. Technological innovation is not for Bentham an exogenous variable, but a continual disequilibrium of the market, as Austrians would put it (Trincado, 2004).

Actually, Bentham, trying to justify the market, was a pioneer of the "black box" picture of the firm, typical of neoclassical economics; Owen dealt with power inside the firm, then opening the black box. This silent work of pioneering in Owen's case was too ahead of his time. Even Foucault has had little or no impact outside the specialist niche of accounting history (Hoskin and Macve, 1986; Miller and O'Leary, 1987). Owen was disclosing what was happening inside institutions, the cornerstone of our understanding of the deployment of power/knowledge of the early nineteenth century. In non-democratic governments, power needed not to be questioned; when democracy is extended worldwide, the organizing principles of power began to be unwrapped (see Rosenberg, 1982 and Demsetz, 1997).

But Bentham stepped forward and constructed a theory based on the hope of progress of some fictional society. So, as we shall see, he conceives of society as a great puzzle in which the pieces' movement makes the shapes fit and paints beauty predetermined by the very same constructor of the game – let us say, the state. For Bentham, the conception of time is similar to the so-called "Judaeo-Christian conception", focused on the future and on a perfect world created by imagination. Man pursues a utopian fiction of his own mind's creation. The present is never satisfactory when we compare it with that future world, but man is proud of being better than past generations were. Time is linear, and the theory is based on the idea of perfectibility. That is to say, new generations do not slide into "the best of all possible worlds", rather they are susceptible to continual improvement, until the moment when the perfect world arrives. According to Bentham's absolutism, to arrive to that perfect world it is necessary to manipulate individual present pleasure as a way of achieving a greater future pleasure. Then, he created a new religion, that of social utility. His utilitarian heaven on earth can only have one canon: the greater happiness of the greater number, a famous phrase pronounced by Francis Hutcheson (Spiegel, 1999, p. 274).

Mill has Bentham's position on time and progressiveness clear, comparing him with Coleridge: "in the main, Bentham was a Progressive philosopher, Coleridge a Conservative one. The influence of the former has made itself felt chiefly on minds of the Progressive class; of the latter, on those of the Conservative: and the two systems of concentric circles with the shock given by them is spreading over the ocean of mind, they have only just begun to meet and intersect" (Mill, 1980, p. 40). However, it is interesting to note that utilitarian ethics, basic in the descriptive level, is absent from the theories in use on human moral development in which the Kantian path represented by Jean Piaget and Lawrence Kohlberg has been more fruitful (Tasset, 1994).

On the other hand, Owen's perception of time is not so based on anticipation of the future. It is based on present otherness, which is neither objective nor measurable. This has much to do with gratitude, which implies the break with the homo economicus definition of human action (Trincado, 2014a). This term "economic man" was used by Bentham for the first time in the early nineteenth century when he describes action in maximization terms (Stark, 1954, *The Psychology of Economic Man*, p. 435).[28] But, according to Owen's plan, man seeks the affection of people in the present and creates a relationship with current things at the present time. Then, men do not make judgements as a maximization of their subjectively defined ends, but they reciprocate with reality (in modern ethics, the concept of "homo reciprocans" has been forged to make a contrast with individual utilitarianism homo economicus, see Godelier, 1999). Besides, there is an emphasis made on intrinsic versus extrinsic motivation (see Frey, 1992, Caruso, 2012), whereas Bentham considers motivation to be extrinsic and when we motivate one industry other industry seems to be less motivated. As commented in Trincado (2014a), this research project, related to economics, was begun by Adam Smith who linked sensibility to self-command. As Adam Smith says, the propriety of our feelings and sensations seems to be exactly in propor-tion to the force and vivacity with which we enter into and conceive the feelings and sensations of others. The individual that feels more the joys and grief of others is better endowed to obtain the fullest control of his own joys and grief (Smith, 1976, p. 152).

Indeed, Owen's conception has much to do with Adam Smith's theory. As Fleischacker (2015) says, Smith thought that the state could foster the productive-ness of their economies only by the rule of law, but he did not favour as hands-off an approach as some of his self-proclaimed followers do today – he believed that states could and should redistribute wealth to some degree, and defend the poor and disadvantaged against those who wield power over them in the private sector (see also Fleischacker 2004, p. 57). Smith believed in the importance of local knowledge to economic decision-making, and consequently thought that business should be left to prudent people, who understand the particular situations in which they work far better than any government official (see Hayek, 1978 and C. Smith, 2013). But, by the same token, governance should be kept out of the hands of businesspeople, since they are likely to use it to promote their particular interests, and not be concerned for the well-being of the citizenry as a whole: Smith's oppo-sition to the East India Company is based on this principle (see Muthu, 2008).

But Owen's own activity is not that coherent with his political theory after-wards. As a utopian socialist, he defended the cooperative as an instrument of moral and political reform, based on the perfectibility of human beings by means of education and the improvement of their environment. The cooperative organi-zation, in which the workers are the owners of the firm, is supposed to give the greatest incentive to work. Efficiency, then will take us to abundance, which in turn will facilitate moral reform. However, in his activity as a businessman, the main proposal was to focus on human relations within the factory, as afterwards will be proposed by Taylor, Fayol or Elton Mayo.

The same, when Owen deals with industrial justice, he, like Adam Smith, is not talking about a utilitarian justice based on a code invented by the legislator to punish the pain maker so as to achieve the greatest happiness of the greatest number. For him, the origin of justice is previous to law, found in a natural feeling of a spectator of injustice, that is to say, in indignation. Law only respects this feeling, it does not create it.[29] And in this period, as we have seen, industrialisation had led to workers having longer working days and being packed into factories. Nowadays many studies demonstrate, with hindsight, that wages were increasing and that those who seemed to be "exploited industrial workers" were, in many cases, former country folk who had escaped from the isolation of the village in the Highlands and whose only possibility for bettering their condition seemed to be working in the new industrial towns. But, of course, it is clear that this form of developed capitalism was guilty of more and more excesses in its labour practices. And empathy led to criticism of this historical evolution of capitalism. Curiously enough, criticism came both from conservatism and from socialism. Before 1812, Owen was clear that in the industrial world the change could be held by the good and empathic entrepreneur and that "the good boss" paternalism that the conservative Carlyle defended was enough for bettering people's condition. After 1812, when he began to look, not only inside the firm, but also outside the firm, he began to realize that capitalists and unions were interested in maintaining the capitalist system, and they were only concerned about organised workers and not the non-organised (the people excluded from direct productive process, etc.).

Besides, Owen's ideas are also more in the line of Adam Smith in his considering that the normal person could run a firm and assuming the equality between men. However, it is to be noted that for Smith, natural is opposed to historic or conventional (Griswold, 1999, pp. 349–354). For Owen 2 (the communist Owen) natural is opposed to individual and, as we will see, for Owen the present is collective. "Facts prove, however – First – that character is universally formed for, and not by the individual. Second – that any habits and sentiments may be given to mankind. Third – that the affections are not under the control of the individual" (Owen, 1816). Adam Smith's theory is based on methodological individualism, considering economics to be a science close to the moral philosophy from which it was derived. But Owen's theory is one of the turning points from methodological individualism to collectivism, a change that finally affected the semantics of the paths to freedom. Actually, a different concept of freedom underlies Owen's and Smith's theory, in Owen's case being similar to some historical materialists (see Trincado, 2004a). Freedom then is not the contingency of individual freedom and for Owen, as for instance for Rosa Luxemburg, "The unconscious comes before the conscious" (Luxemburg, 1904, p. 102). In this context, the search for real freedom is related to the idea of "the whole", an objective ego which is not reactive, opposing reality but it acts freely in a communicative unity or totality. The ego itself is developed in time. However, unlike historical materialism, for Owen it is not history, but institutions and human interaction that creates personal identity and can release it. The temporal character of human experience is emphasized in this case, taking into account both memory and oblivion (Ricoeur, 1983; Vovelle, 1985; Trincado, 2013).

Notes

1 It is noteworthy that Owen's political writings are repetitive and unattractive, but his autobiography is one of many autobiographies of successful businessmen, and is written in a simple language and full of information. It is the only attractive and agreeable book by Owen.
2 "The factory represented the puritanical conscience the perfect image of hell", says García Ruiz, 1994, p. 29, quoting Mantoux.
3 Cole (1969, p. 57) says that Samuel Oldknow, a manufacturer known by Owen and mentioned a lot in his autobiography, had already established, 20 years before, an individual record in his own factory, which Owen could have seen. What was original to Owen was the bucket so that the record of the conduct was visible to all.
4 Morton, 1962, pp. 177–178, from an extract of William Lovett, *Life and Struggles* [1876], pp. 44–45. Also in Wilson, 1940, p. 117.
5 However, Owen sailed for America in the autumn of 1824. In that year Walker took control of New Lanark. "Owen sold the controlling interest in the mill in 1825 to Charles and Henry Walker, sons of one of his partners" (see Quarter (2000) p. 11).
6 From Owen 1849, The Revolution in Mind and Practice, p.21, a memorial addressed by Owen to all the "red Republicans, Communists and Socialists of Europe," and sent to the provisional government of France, 1848, and also "to Queen Victoria and her responsible advisers."
7 http://spartacus.schoolnet.co.uk/Prluddites.htm.
8 Morton 1962, p. 172. Also he became a follower of Phrenology, fashionable pseudoscience at the time. Wilson (1972) makes fun of these beliefs of Owen, considering them to be senile; but we have to bear in mind that they were very common in England then.
9 However, in 1968 the old wheels had been replaced with turbines that produced electricity for the factory. The combination of changes in technology and on the markets expelled the establishment out of the business. In 1968 production stopped, and only 50 people were living there. Now it is an important tourist centre.
10 Stark (1952b, pp. 146–147) from *Plan for the Augmentation of Revenue.*
11 This economics may be labelled as preclassical on occasion and, generally speaking, too advanced for his time and more linked to subsequent marginalism or the public choice theory, precursor of Keynes or Hayek (Trincado 2004, 2005a). Besides, Schumpeter (1954) says that already in his first economic writings we find that Bentham's purely economic thought is independent of his philosophy (quoted in Sigot, 1996, p. 195).
12 Owen, however, argued that the best way of eradicating the evils that beset society at the time was not the system of punishments and rewards advocated by Bentham (1748–1832), but by rational education and universal enlightenment (Marshall, 1984, pp. 310–11).
13 See Santos Redondo (1997: 35).The French tradition has been anaylzed by Menudo and O'Kean (2006).
14 See Stark (1952 a: 170) from Defence of Usury and Hébert and Link (2006, 302).
15 See Hellwig (2009), Allen and Carletti (2006), Allen and Gale (2006).
16 See Kirzner, 1998, pp. 275–276 in Annexe; and Huerta de Soto, 2000, p. 189.
17 Heberton, 1949, pp. 337–338.
18 Schumpeter, 1966, pp. 255–272, 1949, pp. 337–338.
19 See Nelson and Winter, 1982.
20 Smith (1994, p. 342). Tuttle (1927) thinks that for Smith to organize and to manage work is the determining element of the function with which profit is associated.
21 Prudence is very important for Smith in economics (Fleischacker 2004), in ethics (Griswold, 1999, pp. 202–209) and in the political body (Evensky, 2005) precisely because without prudence there would not be self-control (on the self-control in Smith, see Wild, 2004). However, let's not forget that prudence, as it is something usual, is not

the most admirable virtue according to Smith. The most admirable virtue is self-control directed justice.

22 Schumpeter is quoting German economist Eugen Schmalenbach "Auf Schulden reitet das Genie zum Erfolg".

23 Smith (1997, p. 132) and Smith (1997, pp. 140–141)

24 Turgot (1769–1770, p. 100).

25 Smith (1994, p. 604); Smith (1994, p. 149).

26 Stark (1954, p. 425), Hayek (1961), Schumpeter (1934), see Trincado (2009).

27 Smith (1994, p. 27). As Khan (1954) says, Smith gives importance to capital and it is not industry but parsimony or abstinence that is the reason for accumulation. But once capital is being accumulated, money makes money almost in an immediate way. Based on this, Smith created a theory of the stadiums and development begins in small-scale agriculture.

28 Afterwards, the critiques by John Stuart Mill (1836) stressed the idea. See Persky 1995, Zabieglik 2002 and Santos 2000.

29 Smithian justice is dealt with in Haakonssen, 1981; Griswold, 1999; Vivenza, 2001; or Trincado, 2000.

Part III
Social reformers
Utopians and utilitarians

5 Owen and Bentham as social reformers

5.1. Two utopians in the nineteenth century

Marxists popularized the epithet utopian as a derogatory label for Owenite socialism (chiefly for Marx and Engels (1848) *Communist Manifesto* and Engels (1880) *Socialism, Utopian and Scientific*). But utopianism has historically been the basis of the idea of progress. Without it, philosophers would have found it difficult to criticize society or show new paths of change.

The utopian idea, which is rooted back into the Republic of Plato, emerged in the Renaissance with Christian humanism. This went beyond the Greek cyclical idea of time or the consideration of original sin as the beginning of all human evil. Renaissance utopians tried to struggle against the Machiavellian idea of politics that considered it useless to rebel against laws of politics. *Utopia*, the famous book by Thomas More (1517) is "no place", an eloquent image of a perfect society on a faraway island that enabled More to compare the venal current institutions in Europe with those of utopia. More, instead of explaining dogmatically how society must be transformed, he daydreamed of an institutional utopia, a society in which men, instead of the mean ambition of looking for their own salvation, made a reality the idea of the whole as something more than the mere addition of the parts. Then, in utopia, the same as in the perfect world finally defended by Owen, distributive justice was achieved by dissolving private property and creating a community of goods in which there is no domain and houses are changed randomly every 10 years. Tommaso Campanella (1901 [1602]) in "The City of the Sun" also proposes a utopia based on the *raison d'etat*. He placed it in Taprobana Island, which was a community of goods. Francis Bacon (1989 [1627]) also imagined *The New Atlantis* as an imaginary technocratic counter-utopia.

The longed for utopias did not become exhausted in the Renaissance. The eighteenth and nineteenth centuries are full of utopian ambitions. Especially, at the end of the eighteenth century there is an emergence of utopias based on the new philosophy of utilitarianism that many saw as a rehabilitation of the idea of man in search of a happy life. There, the concept of institution reappears as an element of change that creates a "socially desirable" structure of incentives. Following the educationist theory, William Godwin (1756–1836) raised a new utopia (Godwin, 1793). The legislator is a pedagogue who uses punishment to achieve the objective of man loving what is just. Though the motive is always pleasant, the selfish motives must be eliminated through pedagogy that, unlike education that is restricted to infancy, is the construction of institutions that influence lifelong instruction adapting men to rational intelligence and allowing their intellectual emancipation. According to Godwin, the current institutions are against perfection and happiness and they are instruments of power. Godwin especially criticizes the institutions of property and marriage, which must be replaced with a system of free and flexible unions. The only objection that he poses is "the population principle". But Godwin minimizes it saying that centuries could pass until the globe was full and when this moment comes, men, whose thought would have established the empire on the body, would stop multiplying, as they are released from need. The utopian end of this form of government is, in fact, the suppression of the state.

This is the case with Bentham's theory. Based on the "scientific psychology" of James Mill (2001 [1829]) who defines pleasures as a collection of simple predictable and reproducible elements, Bentham considered that the state can make an artificial identification of interests and reform social institutions to arrive to a perfect world through pedagogy. The utilitarianism of Jeremy Bentham reduced the social world to two principles: the association of ideas; and the idea of the greatest happiness understood as the search of pleasure and avoidance of pain. The men agree in the end, but the connections of the associations differ between them.

Also, the Marquis of Condorcet (1795) imagines a Utopia. Thanks to the development of contraceptive methods and technical advances, the principle of population would surrender society to a rational control. Condorcet underlines the accumulative and progressive character of social and institutional change and he thinks that progress is unavoidable less for moral reasons that from a historical vision of accumulation of knowledge and possibility of communication. According to him, institutions are not the spontaneous expression of the needs or ideal of a society, but obstacles to the free game of reason, a machine deliberately constructed to oppress the masses and keep them linked. The consequences of the French Revolution made him reflect on the ability of that reason alone to produce social perfection. The problem was that social development is more unequal than that of knowledge. The delay of social development is due to the fact that history, up to his age, had been the history of individuals, not of the masses; and the wellbeing of society had been sacrificed to that of a few persons. In this way, he anticipates two topics of the nineteenth century: the idea of natural laws of historical development; and the collectivist vision of history as a study of the masses.

Owen's theory was within this collectivist vision of society. In the nineteenth century, the major costs of social changes produced by the French Revolution, the Declaration of Independence of the USA of 1776 and the introduction of industrialism, were supported by the working class. For that reason, the post-revolutionary utopias included the previous mirrored images, but denounced as oppressive the economic structure of the Industrial Revolution and insisted that the declaration of the rights of man does not solve the matter. In this way, the so-called utopian socialists – Saint-Simon and Fourier, about whom we will talk later, and Owen himself – constitute a critique of the way in which the industrial revolution was taking place. They considered capitalism irrational and unjust and repudiated laissez faire but they were optimistic with regard to the perfectibility of man and social order. They tried to replace competition with a system of coop-eration and democratic control of the economy and to reorganize society radically on the basis of science. Like the utopians of the renaissance, the utopian socialists tried to free politics – and economics – from necessity.

Owen's utopia implied the extension of communal property, fitting in Tomas More's utopia: where there is private property and measures in money, it is diffi-cult to achieve a fair and well governed state. Besides, in Utopia craftsmen would be able to devote only six hours to work, because they would not have to tolerate unproductive and useless work. Those are destined to promote luxury, inevitable when everything measures up in money. The lack of effective demand in capital-ism is part of the story here.

As we are showing, both Bentham's and Owen's theories were utopianism. But in Neusüss' (1968) terminology, Owen's utopia is a "horizontal" one, whereas Bentham's is "vertical". In the vertical case, utopia will constitute the crowning of a linear development of history evolving to the supreme good. Freedom in Bentham comes through market devices and through the aesthetics of prices instead of the ethics of time. In the horizontal case utopia will act perpendicularly across the historical process, renewing at every instant the contrast between reality and the ideal, fragmenting the accomplishment of utopian intention. The first utopian ideal is teleological; the second one, ethical, and it is not compulsory to think that utopia will definitely be achieved. In Bentham's case, he is talking about an "aesthetic man" in Kierkegaard's (1965) terminology, devoted to pleasure seeking, who avoids pain and tedium, flies always towards new satisfactions, going for the passion of the moment and flee-ing from his own responsibility with the past. This is a condition of permanent dissatisfaction, of travelling without option of hope and rest. Bentham's man then is this fugitive man, who values things capriciously. But in Owen's heaven, the main character is the "ethic man" who follows subsequent principles of prop-erty in his behaviour.

5.2. Owen as a social reformer

As Harrison (1969) says, from Elizabethan times in England the responsibility for looking after its own poor was laid upon each parish, under the direction of the Justices of the Peace. With the spread of enclosures after 1760 and the rise in food prices during the French Wars, the number of poor increased and the poor rates jumped accordingly, provoking protest. In many districts the practice of granting outdoor relief to the unemployed had grown and in 1795 the relief became semi regularized as the Speenhamland system. They ensured that each family had a minimum income calculated according to the price of bread and number of dependents, but the effect was to subsidize low wages out of poor rates.

Owen's name was linked with successful, paternalistic schemes for bettering the lot of the poor. He improved working and living conditions at New Lanark, then made an educational reform and after he restricted child labour in factories. Then, he turned into a social reformer. The distress which followed the peace of 1815 turned his attention to problems of the unemployed. In the fourth essay of *New View of Society* he suggested a reform of the Poor Laws which he thought encouraged idleness and crime, and a programme of public works to provide employment where necessary on road and canal construction. By the summer of 1816 public concern caused the *Association for the Relief of the Manufacturing and Labouring Poor,* headed by the Duke of York and the Archbishop of Canterbury, to convene a public meeting in London, at which Owen was invited to speak. The Report to the Committee of the previously mentioned *Association for the Relief of the Manufacturing and Labouring Poor* was referred in March 1817 to the Select Committee of the House of Commons on the Poor Laws of Sturges-Bourne. The Report diagnosed the cause of unemployment as a combination of the effects of peace and the spread of machinery. There was wartime demand that introduced machinery, thus, both the decreased demand and the increased productive power led to depreciation in the value of human labour which was the cause of the distress. The remedy proposed was the creation of self-supporting communities of about 1,200 persons, with accommodation arranged in a parallelogram of buildings, and provision for all the educational and social needs of the inhabitants. The plan found little favour with the Select Committee, which only sought economic purposes. But in September 1817 Owen was using millennial language and equating his plan with the emancipation of mankind: the villages of Unity and Mutual Cooperation were not to include all classes, and he gave greater details in the Report to the County of Lanark submitted in May 1820. However, many contemporaries still thought of Owen's plan as an improved system of pauper management. And it probably was.

Besides, Owen was the inspirer of secularism and other social reform movements of the 1860s and 1870s with which many old Owenites were associated (see Holyoake, 1896 and Harrison, 1969). After 1812, when Owen began to look, not only inside the firm, but also outside the firm, going from methodological individualism to collectivism, he began to use a different semantics of the paths to freedom (Harvey, 1949). True principles set forth in Owen's Report to the County of Lanark in 1821 were very clear and simple:

> True and False Principles: every society which now exists, as well as every society history records, has been formed and governed on a belief in the notions, assumed as first principles:
>
> First – that it is in the power of every individual to form his own character. Hence the various systems called by the name of religion, codes of law and punishments. Hence also the angry passions entertained by individuals and nations towards each other.

Second – that the affections are at the command of the individual. Hence insincerity and degradation of character. Hence the miseries of domestic life, and more than one-half of the crimes of mankind.

Third – that it is necessary that a large portion of mankind should exist in ignorance and poverty, in order to secure the remaining part of such a degree of happiness as they now enjoy. Hence a system of counteraction in the pursuits of man, a general opposition among individuals to the interests of each other, and the necessary effects of such a system – ignorance, poverty, and vice.

Facts prove, however –

First – that character is universally formed for, and not by the individual.

Second – that any habits and sentiments may be given to mankind.

Third – that affections are not under the control of the individual.

Fourth – that every individual may be trained to produce far more than he can consume, while there is a sufficiency of soil left for him to cultivate.

Fifth – that nature has provided means by which populations may be at all times maintained in the proper state to give the greatest happiness to every individual, without one check of vice or misery.

Sixth – that any community may be arranged, on a due combination of the foregoing principles, in such a manner, as not only to withdraw vice, poverty, and, in a great degree, misery, from the world, but also to place in every individual under such circumstances in which he shall enjoy more permanent happiness than can be given to any individual under the principles which have hitherto regulated society.

Seventh – that all the assumed fundamental principles on which society has hitherto been founded are erroneous, and may be demonstrated to be contrary to fact. And –

Eighth – that the change which would follow the abandonment of these erroneous maxims which bring misery to the world, and the adoption of principles of truth, unfolding a system which shall remove and for ever exclude that misery, may be effected without the slightest injury to any human being. (in Morton, 1962, pp. 58–59)

As Rocker (2004) says, ten years later in 1831, when Owen had presented his plans for the reconstruction of society before a meeting of delegates of the Builders' Union in Manchester, his plans amounted to a kind of guild socialism and called for the establishment of producers' co-operatives under the control of the trade unions. The proposals were adopted, and shortly after this the Builders' Union was involved in a long series of severe conflicts, with unhappy outcomes. However, Owen did not let himself be discouraged by this, but carried on his activities with renewed zeal. In 1833 Owen exhaustively explained his plan for social reconstruction by the workers themselves in a conference of trade unions and co-operative organizations in London. From the reports of the delegates one can see what an influence these ideas had already gained and what a creative spirit then animated the advanced circles of the English working class. The Poor

Man's Guardian summed up its report of the conference in these words: "But far different from the paltry objects of all former combinations is that now aimed at by the congress of delegates. Their reports show that an entire change in society–a change amounting to a complete subversion of the existing order of the world–is contemplated by the working classes. They aspire to be at the top instead of the bottom of society–or rather that there should be no bottom or top at all." Owen began to think that capitalism was not a good means to acknowledge the real value of effort or worth and, so, he dreamt of a complete subversion that opened doors for the poor people. He considered inclusion, not utility, the main objective of politics and power.

The immediate result of this conference was the founding of the GNC, the Grand National Consolidated Trade Union of Great Britain and Ireland at the beginning of 1834, gathering the scattered organisations into one great federation. Innumerable strikes and lock-outs were staged, and the number of workers organized in trade unions rapidly peaked at 800,000. The GNC set itself the goal of overthrowing the capitalist economy as a whole and replacing it with the co-operative labour of all producers, which should no longer have in view profits for all individuals, but the satisfaction of the needs of all. The organizers wanted to put together the industrial and agricultural workers and group them according to their special branches of production. The exchange of products of the co-operative plants was to be made through so-called labour bazaars and the use of special exchange-money or labour tickets. By the steady spread of these institutions they hoped to achieve a complete reorganization of society that avoided competition and fluctuations of trade and commerce so that the working man might be supplied at little above wholesale prices. These organizations were destined to take over the functions of the present entrepreneurs; with common ownership of all social wealth there would no longer be any need for political institutions (see Oliver, 1964; Hollis, 1973; Cook, 2005; Claeys, 2002).

5.3. Bentham as a social reformer

5.3.1. Introduction

But, to see the difference of this proposal of social reform with that of Bentham, we need to go back to the roots of Bentham's thought. It is not clear if Bentham took the sentence of the greatest happiness of the greatest number from Helvétius, Beccaria or Priestley. Although he says that he took it from Priestley, probably it was from a translation of Hutcheson or Beccaria as Priestley wrote about it after in 1768. Paley also developed the utilitarian ideas, this time with a theological base, in vogue in England, as well as Brown, who critiqued, like Bentham, the idea of a moral sense. His book was published as a University of Cambridge textbook, with that of Locke. However, we know that Bentham took his method of comparing utilities from two basic authors for him: Helvétius and Beccaria.[1] Social reform and economics is, in Bentham, based on his theory of ethics. He read Helvétius in 1769, who defended an artificial identification of interests and a moral determinism, as men are the product of education who can reform them indefinitely (Hélvetius, 1759). Education makes individuals identify their own interest with the general interest. We may learn a pedagogic art to inspire passions whose principles are as certain as those of geometry (Hélvetius, 1810). Beccaria tried to apply this theory in Italy to penal law. *Dei delitti e delle pene* was published in 1764 (Beccaria, 1996). However, apart from those, we may find in Bentham influences from Mackintosh, Paine, Godwin and Condorcet. They all appealed to the self interest of governors to seek the common good and they criticized natural law.

Bentham wanted to apply the principle of utility to morality and legislation so that reason ruled over instinct and feeling. The change in old hedonistic morality is the insistence on the need of a calculation of the consequences of our actions, a moral arithmetic that provides us with the necessary information to decide on our conduct and to know if we have satisfied the principle of utility (Bentham, 1996).

Bentham's view may have the flavour of harmony of interests and of spontaneous order and sensationalism. However, Bentham's political proposals show an opposite view to spontaneous order. He proposed political constitutions for all liberal countries that made them be ruled by the principle of utility. So, he was thinking about a rationalist contractualism that imposes an external rule of behaviour. Bentham appears to be a model of what Michael Oakeshott had described as "Rationalism on Politics".[2] Although he recognized that the controlling person could not be controlled, he made up constitutions so that the interest of the ruler would be the same as that of the public. Bentham wanted to put his ideas into practice and in 1811 he submitted his code to the President of the USA, James Madison, and after to Russian and Polish rulers (Bentham, 1998). In 1820 he did the same with Spain and Portugal. Although Bentham proposes a constitution to be enforced in all nations professing liberal opinions, he was aware of the fact that constitutions were based on the presumptuousness of people that think that they are wiser than posterity and that dead men may chain people alive.[3] But he continued proposing a type of contractualism – that some scholars have considered similar to that of Hayek[4] – and he defended despotism as a way of making the people free.[5] He devised a glass prison in politics that would reverberate to public choice theory (Buchanan, 1977).

The philosophy of Benthamites, then, is not interpersonal in nature, and he actually did not accept different ways of thinking to his own. Mill says "Bentham would have regarded Coleridge with a peculiar measure of the good-humoured contempt with which he was accustomed to regard all modes of philosophizing different from his own. Coleridge would probably have made Bentham one of the exceptions to the enlarged and liberal appreciation which (to the credit of his mode of philosophizing) he extended to most thinkers of any eminence, from whom he differed" (Mill, 1980, p. 101).

Bentham's theory does not allow for the existence of otherness. He was a pure individualist who considered that man is able to classify his pleasures on his own, without external imposition – on some occasions he does it unconsciously, as he is the only one who knows his preferences.[6] But, while using the famous statement of Hutcheson, he noticed that nothing prevented his theory from sanctioning the greater number, let's say half plus one, being happy by crushing the smaller number, let's say the half minus one. So, in the end, he broke with the utilitarian principle to be left, in 1831, with the maxim "the greater happiness", that is to say, the social maximisation of happiness. As the last unit of pleasure decreases as we add new units (the finding of the decreasing marginal utility, discerned by Bentham and other contemporaries[7]), a social criterion can be that of the equalization of wealth, and afterwards we must leave man to choose his own utilities freely.

To achieve this social criterion, Bentham made two assumptions. First, each person is to count for one and only for one in making the assessment. Second, there is no pleasure, no matter how heinous it might seem to a given person, which ought to be condemned without a hearing. Any pleasure, taken in itself, is a good for the individual who experiences it. If it is to be condemned as criminal or immoral, it must be shown that it is detrimental to the happiness of others who are affected. This implies that pleasure is something objective and measurable.

Bentham did not believe in genuine self-sacrifice. "All men who are actuated by regard for any thing but self, are fools; those whose only regard is confined to self, are wise. I am of the number of the wise" (Stark 1952, p. 426). Benthamian theory is based not only on methodological individualism, but also on normative individualism. It advises us to be selfish because, if we are not, we risk being left with no objects of pleasure while others, with more eagerness, take advantage of our ingenuousness. Predominance of self-regard over other impulses is, for Bentham, almost an axiom. He underlines the philosophical concept of the necessary reference to self. Whatever man "demands for himself" can be considered pleasure. Whatever he avoids, is considered pain.[8]

In this sense, Bentham was less paternalistic than other progressive utilitarians, like John Stuart Mill who, despite the fact that he criticized Benthamism, decided to weigh up the sum of pleasures, making a hierarchy of those that he considered of greater value or superior and those that he thought vulgar or of less emotional content. Until man has had the opportunity to experience a pleasure, he does not have the freedom to choose it.[9]

So, Bentham moves away from the focus on character evaluation of Hume and towards act-evaluation (Schneewind, 1990). Character – that is, a person's true character – is known, if known at all, only by that person and it isn't a practical focus for legislation. Even, habit of character is considered by Bentham as something faulty. Men must assess pleasures, not be led by instinct or habit. Fighting also against habit, Bentham tried to create a language of his own to free words from the "poisoned" connotations which they could have acquired in time. Bentham gave a special importance to language in the interpretation of reality and, even, in the creation of it. Ogden (1932, p. xxvi) argued the importance and originality of Bentham's contributions toward understanding the linguistic basis of philosophy.[10]

In the same way, Bentham criticizes conservatism authors for having overvalued habit. According to Hume (1964c) the very same perception of reality depends on habit, and the possibility of transgressing these habit rules causes great anxiety that leads him to defend the preservation of rules. In Hume institutions must be valued for their survival: this is "institutional Darwinism", in which we become strongly devoted to past social constructions, forged by habit, because we sense in them an implicit knowledge that feeble human reason is not always capable of distinguishing. Bentham criticized this conservatism, which was typical of the English jurist Blackstone. Blackstone (1855 [1765]) defended in his *Commentaries* the common law's tradition on which the law of nations was based. Bentham creates a new term, international law that seeks for the future a universal and perpetual peace (see Janis, 2010).

In the same vein, Bentham wanted to change the language of morality. According to Bentham, utilitarianism explains altruistic as well as "selfish" actions, so the difference between altruism and selfishness is not reality-based.

> That which in the language of sentimentalism is a sacrifice of private to public interest, [is] but a sacrifice of a self-supposed private interest in one shape to a self-supposed private interest in another shape: for example, of an interest corresponding to the love of power, to an interest corresponding to love of reputation: – of that reputation, of which power is the expected fruit.[11]

This criticism of self sacrifice is also criticism of established religion. However he was convinced that the people would look with hostility at his suggestions for greater sexual and religious freedom, so, using a utilitarian calculation, he suppressed those suggestions, in the main until 1818. In this, Owen was much more honest and authentic than him. For Bentham, there was little to be gained and much to be lost in trying to show, for example, that homosexuality was not only wrongly punished but that it was a positive good, or that incest ought not to be a crime. "The herd of the people must for a long time perhaps forever be sway'd chiefly by authority: but of those who by their authority are in a way to lead them there are enough whose circumstances admit of their being sway'd by reason" (UC 27, 9. 135). It would be the task of the legislator, then, to convince the people of the utility of reform (Steintrager, 1977). Although he held that any sovereign who was truly interested in reform could overcome popular prejudice, he warned against running too hard against popular feelings, even if rooted in prejudice and false morality.

5.3.2. Bentham's social theory updated

As we have said, Jeremy Bentham, as opposed to Owen, was a theorist of the rules and anticipated many ideas of the present theory of public choice. He contemplates the legislative process as a continuous "rent seeking" that emphasizes the role of the pressure groups (with some sinister interests in Bentham's terminology): trying to catch the greatest number of votes possible, taxes, subsidies, regulations are used with a consequent increasing of the wellbeing of the most influential groups implying losses for society. The problem is that the privileges obtained by the special interest groups become permanent.

Bentham, then, was worried about the difficulty of cutting public expenditure once created, provided that it implies inflicting a pain in the affected agents. His ideas are based once more on the principle of prevention of disappointment. A loss of a non-compensated reform implies that, to the pain suffered by the implied part, we must add the alarm in other individuals who may be harmed by a similar reform, implying a precedent for future actions. The compensation will reduce the opposition to reform and will make its establishment easier.

Bentham deals extensively with the voting rules. At first, he denies democracy, considering it to be synonymous with anarchy, and unnecessary for his principle of utility, which might be imposed by a benevolent despot; but, hereinafter, he thought that the fact that the leaders did not accept his plans for reform was due to their selfishness. Then, on the basis of Priestley's claim of identification of interests of the government with the governed, he defended that governors must have the dread of being dismissed from their post if they do not consult the interests of the people.[12] The people must be included in the government to arrive to his "ideal republic". [13] The acceptance of democracy was then, due to the fact that most of the monarchs had rejected his advice on reform (Schofield, 1998).

So, in a first analysis, Bentham's utilitarianism defended the enforcement of laws by a benevolent Monarch. But Mary Mack (1962) argued that Bentham was fully committed to democratic reform by 1789 and that his failure to push ahead with concrete reform proposals was a retreat forced upon him by the turn of events. By 1791 he began to be disillusioned by the increasingly radical turn the Revolution was taking in France. The French were taking the notions of equal rights quite seriously. For almost two decades he not only wrote nothing on behalf of parliamentary reform but he wrote almost nothing about politics proper (Burns, 1966, p. 59).It was in 1809 and due to some advice from James Mill, that Bentham fully accepted representative democracy showing as an example the American Government (Steintrager, 1977, p. 78). First, he did not believe in universal suffrage as, immersed in his intellectualism, he thought that passions of uneducated people will reign. But afterwards Cartwright suggested to Bentham and Mill the convenience of universal and secret suffrage. However, radicals did not believe, as Godwin did, in the possibility of a progress in intelligence that will lead to the abolition of government. They only aspired to artificial harmonization of individual interests.

The first published work where Bentham presents the radical doctrine of universal suffrage and representative government would be *A Plan of Parliamentary Reform* of 1817 that he developed further in the *Radical Reform Bill* (Bentham, 1819).[14] There he defends elections with secret and universal suffrage, based on the rule of the majority. But he does not defend egalitarianism in voting as the consequence could be the subversion of established order and it is "to desire that folly should have the same influence as wisdom, and that merit should exist without motive and without reward" (Bentham, 1840a, p. 359). He urges the centralization of responsibility in the all-competent legislators, proposing the One Chamber, and the centralization of responsibility in judges, claiming that the popular jury dilutes responsibility.

For Buchanan (1999 [1962], 1977), ideology is no more a significant element to explain the behaviour of the political and bureaucratic entities. The politicians, motivated by their own interest, seek to maximize their probability of reelection and power; the bureaucrats their prestige, income and budget; and the voters, vote according to their economic interest. The same, Bentham considers the ideology from the utilitarian point of view: he does not hope that the individual will sacrifice his private interest for the public interest. For him, this is the language of "sentimentalism": the state must force him to seek the image of the social good. When a person is said to sacrifice his interest for the public – for example when a man accepts a smaller salary for having accepted a public position – Bentham says that he is replacing a private interest (wealth) with another one (power or reputation). But the same as utilitarianism considers the citizen self centred, the governor is also self centred, and we must try to lead him, through controls and sanctions, to act for the social good. So, the labour of statistical and registral advertising is fundamental in bureaucracy. Bentham is very exhaustive in the details that will lead to maximizing the aptitude of the civil servants and to minimizing their expenses (Bentham, 1993).

Bentham considers the division and the independence of power a fiction. For him, it is impossible to prevent the reciprocal influences: the judge is for him a subordinate of the legislator. He is interested in the notion of political society as a sociological reality, which leads him to the consideration of the state as a purely technical and neutral concept. The highest power is absolute, unless it is limited by a specific convention, and to say that an act of the supreme power is void, illegal or that it constitutes power in excess is an abuse of language, except if there is a specific convention.

Bentham's theory also sounds like the traditional perspective of the economic analysis of the law. As the current economic analysis, it introduces the methodology of the *homo oeconomicus* in law. Nevertheless, it adds his critical stance, which tries to adopt a system of pressures calculated to suppress crime from the source and to mechanically transform the criminals into honest men. Also he develops an elaborate theory of the elites, adding here the critical element that, to reduce power, a procedural and constitutional rule must be developed to keep it in the correct terms, with the rewards and punishments, the right remunerations and punishments. There is a clash between two interest groups: the leaders, the lesser number, and the subjects, the greatest number. Bentham wanted to establish securities against ill-government of this lesser number based on the Tribunal of Public Opinion, a judicature that should prevent the existence of sinister interests (Bentham, 1983a). In addition, he introduces other reservations: he proposes the ineligibility of elected members of the legislature for the following two and three years, and he introduces a penal council for the members of the legislature who are suspected of criminal delinquency. Bentham (1993) is very exhaustive in the details that will lead to maximizing the aptitude of the civil servants and to minimize their expenses. The statistical advertising and record of actions is basic to control public servants. To maximize the intellectual and active aptitude of the civil servants he appeals to the public examination, to pecuniary competition in which the candidates compete for a position at the least wage possible, and to the principle of administration of responsibility. In order to maximize the moral aptitude in a way that the civil servants search for the greatest happiness of the greatest number, we need once more to frighten them with punishments and incentive them with rewards.

All in all, Bentham transforms Hume´s previous descriptive utilitarianism into a critical doctrine.

5.3.3. Law as an artificial entity

According to Bentham, men have no natural rights that exist prior to civil society: all rights are drawn from law.

> Of natural right who has any idea? I, for my part, have none: a natural right is a round square – an incorporeal body. What a legal right is I know (…) Right is with me the child of law: from different operations of the law there result different sorts of rights. A natural right is a son that never had a father (…) When a man is bent upon having things his own way and gives no reasons for it, he says: I have a right to have them so. (Stark, 1952a, pp. 334–335: *Supply without Burden*)

Rights, duty, immunity, privilege, property, security, freedom, are not objects of offense, but fictitious entities that the law creates and that are at their disposal. They are moral not for being virtuous but because they are desired for their social consequences in terms of pleasure or pain on the individuals.

Bentham (1821, 1948) wants to apply the principle of utility to morality and legislation in order that reason will reign over instinct and feeling. With regard to pleasure, law must learn how to leave it the same, protected against disturbance. For as to giving them by the power of the legislator to anybody beyond a very inconsiderable amount, it is neither needful, nor possible. This fact is due more to lack of information, than to a true impossibility.[15] As the state does not have information about the utility felt by every man, he must only try to relieve or anticipate pain produced by human agency or by another type of agent – such as natural calamities – in magnitude and number of the individuals who suffer it. And the reason to avoid the pain produced by one man on others is that the pleasure that a person can derive from the contemplation of the pain suffered by another one is not as great as the pain suffered by the patient. So, for Bentham the pain of the victim is valued in the same way as the pleasure of the offender and we may only think of an act as unfair by assuming that the victim suffers more than the offender enjoys. If this pleasure of the offender is produced after another offence, this is to be called revenge.[16] Human dignity is, so, reduced to the principle of pleasure. Then, Bentham is against Aristotelian natural law, which considered that law is not a restriction on liberty and dignity and that justice is a principle beyond that of utility.

Bentham stays faithful to this idea to the point that when he talks about sexual violence he considers that the enjoyment of the offender is equal, or even greater, than the suffering of the offended part, in which case there is no first order evil. Nevertheless, finally he considers rape punishable for the possible social alarm that it can create in third parties, which he calls second order evil. Certainly, Bentham (1997) distinguishes two types of evils: the crime produces a first order evil inflicting a suffering on the victim. But there is a second order evil creating an alarm and danger in society. The punishment produces an evil of first order by inflicting suffering to the delinquent. But there is a second order effect. It avoids the danger of the crime, but at the same time it creates another evil: by threatening the person who wants to commit the act defined as crime, it creates an alarm and danger.

Bentham identified the theory of natural rights of man with anarchism. The assertion made by Article 1 of the French Declaration that all "men are born and remain free and equal in rights" was for him an "extravagant proposition" as every law is a violation of the rights of man. Without a state law, says Bentham, society would not exist and the state is the only one that can inflict pain so as to avoid the disappearance of society. But the good state must seek the greatest happiness of the greatest number, although from the subordinate ends – security, subsistence, abundance and equality – security is the most important one.

The first critique of the legislation that Bentham would make was his clash with William Blackstone, previously mentioned, whose lessons he attended as an youth, already in 1763 (Everett, 1996, p. 17). Bentham then rejected the Common Law: the idea that custom is "immemorial" gives an emotional load to unwritten laws by the simple fact of having existed, independently of the criterion of utility (Bentham, 1977). In this way, he considers the fear of innovation to be sophistry that needs to be eradicated and he substitutes the idea of law as historical process by the idea of law as a mental process.[17] Bentham thinks that Blackstone's principal fault was that he did not distinguish between the explanatory and the critical jurisprudence, so that he seemed to approve what he studied.

As there is no underlying "natural justice" that could lead a man to feel the reasons for being liable to be punished, learning by heart of the law is necessary. For comfort and protection of the citizens, all the laws should be gathered in a code that forms a Pannomion, and they need to be written completely ex-novo, based on a social welfare function that the legislator is able to know (Schwartz, 1988, p. 59). For that reason, the Pannomion follows a binomial classification of the crimes so that they are easier to be memorized. The uniformity of provision is one of the first excellences of law. Bentham criticizes the body of the laws of those times that were not very accessible to the capacity of memory.[18] The universal code of the utilitarian morality would speak a familiar language to everyone: every person might consult it as he needed.[19] Nevertheless, Bentham perceives even the possibility of a "natural law" of the memory. The laws that are opposite to feelings and to reason have a natural inability to become known by the people as they refuse to keep them in mind. [20]

Bentham was a positivist between the jurisprudence of concepts and that of interests, which supposes a way of "iusnaturalism". So, actually, Bentham ends up by defending a utilitarian iusnaturalism: the way of judging law is the measure in which it contributes to the general happiness and this fruit of the imagination can justify any action, as there is no superior principle different from utility (Trincado, 2003a). Public interest is the sum of interests of the members of a community. Nevertheless, from that it does not follow that the aggregate of anything that the individuals consider to be their interest in a particular moment is the public interest. The interest of members of a society at any time is a normative and empirical concept, which can be discovered by consulting the individuals. The government can make a man resign his freedom to achieve that of the greatest number, so that we can come to what has been called a "totalitarian democracy", something John Stuart Mill (1980) denounced (see Schwartz, 1986). This was something that Bentham was aware of, and for that reason he renounced his sentence the greatest happiness of the greatest number to keep only the principle of "the greatest happiness".

So, the concept of the greatest happiness ("social") is different from that of greatest happiness of the greatest number ("the sum of individuals") and, therefore, it looks as if society is different from the sum of the parts, something that Bentham denied on other occasions. Even the idea of the "greatest number" has been criticized by utilitarians: Later utilitarians thought that the greatest number had to be the average of the individuals. Edgeworth (1881, p. 117–118) dismissed what Hutcheson called "the greatest happiness for the greatest numbers" as meaningless, like "greatest illumination with the greatest number of lamps".

As Schwartz (1988, p. 67) says, a peculiarity of the philosophy of law of Bentham that throws light on his philosophical foundation is the subordinated place given to civil law in the Pannomion. For Bentham, civil law is the branch of law that grants rights and the penal law is the one that suppresses transgressions; but Bentham wants to have in every part of the civil code a reference to be made to the corresponding section of the penal code. The idea of constraint and intimidation, therefore, is fundamental, and there is no right whose fulfillment should not rest in a repression for having broken the law.

As we have said, law is always for Bentham an exemplary punishment. The ideal of a punishment is that it inspires in possible criminals a feeling of alarm without inflicting the punishment that, not for nothing, is a pain. Without the external effect of a punishment, given by its advertising, punishment loses its sense. In order to make punishment exemplary, Bentham says, it must turn into a theatre, "provided that the real punishment is what does the whole evil and an apparent punishment what does all the good" (Bentham, 1981c, p. 358). We must make the most of the former so as to increase the latter. So, for instance, Bentham considered well-taken acts those of torture and infanticide. He did not approve of torture committed in the Europe of his age, but he proposed to put some requisites to use torture in a way that vital information for the public was obtained (Dinwiddy, 1995).

5.3.4. The social contract and the constitutions

From Hume on, the idea of an implicit unsigned contract that forces us to obey the coercive mandates, not matter what they are, was criticized (Riley, 2006).

This social contract idea, typical of the Age of Enlightenment, addressed the questions of the origin of society and the legitimacy of the authority of the state over the individual. It was discussed by Grotius (1625), Hobbes (2012 [1651]), Pufendorf (1927 [1673]), Locke (1996 [1689]), Rousseau (1762a) and Kant (1996 [1797]) and was invoked in the United States' *Declaration of Independence*. However, the idea was eclipsed in the nineteenthth century in favour of utilitarianism. Many considered that this idea was the basis for despotism. The defenders of the idea of the social contract find it difficult to criticize prevalent institutions as the original contract binds the citizens to existing institutions and power with a view to the superior good of safety. For instance, Hume, as against contemporary contractualist authors, such as Hobbes, left the door open for revolt. Hume gave great importance to the concept of legal convention. He quotes the classical example of two men who operate the oars of a boat who do it by agreement or convention, though no reciprocal promise has been made between them. Experience confirms them in the convenience of keeping rowing (Tasset, 1999, pp. 203–205). So, the distinction between an asocial human condition and the social one that is in the origin of the legal convention is, in sum, a distinction, not of a chronological, but of a psychological order (Fassò, 1982, p. 217).

Contractualism is based on a Kantian rationalism that, as Brandt (1994, pp. 294–295) says, does not offer us a fixed parameter of impartiality. Certainly, the categorical imperative denotes absolute, unconditional requirement that must be obeyed in all the circumstances. It implies acting according to that maxim whereby you can, at the same time, will that it should become a universal law (Kant, 1977, p. 414). This is compatible with utilitarianism, as moral judgements based on the utility granted to those involved are simply extended to include others in decisions. However, the requirement of generality can be satisfied by a carefully articulated principle, in such a way that allows the conduct of some people to be of a type that the author of the principle would not really wish with regard to the whole world. As Abbott (1909) says, it is enough to establish the suitable restrictions in order that the Kantian imperative "always" could justify its own action.

Actually, Bentham warns about the dangers of the chimera of a social contract. He thought that the utility principle would be a better explanation of the social link than that of contract. "In fact, part of his [of Bentham] criticism of Lockean constitutional theory was that its notions of a state of nature, a social contract and natural rights were dangerous fictions which might encourage reckless and revolutionary disobedience to the Municipal laws" (Steintrager, 1977, p. 16). Bentham tried to break with the moral subjectivity; however, it has been argued that utility is not a static criterion of the law. The value of an action based on utility is not intrinsic to the action, but extrinsic and due to an imaginary expectation of pleasure obtained by it (Manning, 1968, p. 39). It consists of fleeting sensations or desires. Actually, Wolff (1993, pp. 87–90) says that with Bentham's argumentation we could also reject the theory of a Benthamian political obligation based on the general utility.

For these and some other reasons, John Stuart Mill and others thought that hedonism was not to be a good basis for the guarantee of human rights and Bentham himself admitted that he was not a theorist of human rights, but of social change. His "humanism" is perverted into the spirit of a system, the result of social engineering and a crude behaviourism. It is the social utilitarian plan which develops, not the man (Trincado, 2003b, pp. 205–207).

However, when we look at Bentham's influence on different countries and his attempts to implement a "liberal" intervention, we see that he did not manage to make any change in society, as Bentham tried to impose it externally on the political theatre. Bentham was a strong defender of institutional, legal and economic reform. Not only did he work in the construction of constitutions on paper: he projected from London an influence on the most notable politicians of his age of all the countries; and he intervened in the drafting of many constitutional texts, such as those of New York State, South Carolina and Louisiana. A Panopticon was done in Russia and the Emperor Alexandre asked for Bentham's cooperation in the production of a code. He exercised special influence in Spain and Portugal, and in the Spanish-American countries, where he supported the revolutions and offered his codes for the arrangement of its inhabitants: Bolivia, Argentina, Chile, Guatemala, Colombia, Venezuela.[21] He gave the same prescriptions for all, as there is no need to adapt the codes to time and place since mankind is one and we all are equally governed by pain and pleasure (see Bentham, 1998).

But the only way to enforce these utilitarian codes could be through the punishment of the state or of the public opinion tribunal, which acts as the watchman of the Panopticon.

This is the case with Bentham's attempts to establish codes in Spain and Portugal.[22] The particular story of these two important countries for Bentham is as follows. Étienne Dumont tried to spread Bentham's work in Europe translating some of his works into Russian, German, Spanish, Swedish, Italian, Portuguese and English. Dumont's reviews, which were adaptations of Bentham's unpublished works, were known in the whole of Europe, as the *Traité de législation civile et pénale,* that appeared in Paris in 1802 and became a bestseller. Especially, in Spain and Portugal, Bentham was read through these Dumont editions.

The Constitution of Cadiz, the Spanish Constitution of 1812, one of the most liberal of its time, set up Benthamian ideas. The constitution established the principle of universal male suffrage, national sovereignty, division of powers, free trade, land reform and freedom of press. An example is his initial declaration in Article 13: "The object of Governments is the welfare of nations; as is the happiness of the individuals who compose them, that of all political societies". This constitution was established by Spain's first national sovereign assembly in refuge in Cádiz during the Peninsular War against Napoleon. But it never entered fully into effect as much of Spain was ruled by the French, while the rest of the country was in the hands of interim *junta* governments focused on resistance to the Bonapartes rather than on the immediate establishment of a constitutional regime.

Between 1821 and 1823 Bentham wrote *Rid Yourself of Ultramaria* (Bentham, 1995), in which he discussed the harmful effects of a colonial empire on the

Constitution of Cadiz. Bentham had already talked about the independence of colonies in the period of the French Revolution, in which he asked for the independence of the French colonies.[23] In *Rid Yourself of Ultramaria*, he insisted upon the convenience of the emancipation of the Spanish colonies, especially because the ministers do not worry about the unfavourable consequences of their policies abroad as they will lose visibility for Public Opinion Tribunal.[24] Though Spanish liberalism already had benefited from some liberal British influences,[25] Bentham tried to show the dangers that were hovering over the liberal regime due to the deficiencies of the Constitution of 1812.[26] Nevertheless, he was not able to finish it due to the violent frustration of the Liberal Triennium (1820–23).[27]

In addition, in 1821 Bentham published in London the work defending free trade Observations on the restrictive and prohibitory commercial system: especially with reference to the Decree of the Spanish Cortes of July, 1820 (Schwartz and Rodríguez Braun, 1992). Joaquín de Mora, liberal journalist from Cadiz who would be a propagator of Bentham's work in Spanish America in the following decade, translated Three Tracts Relative to Spanish and Portuguese Affairs. Bentham also wrote a series of letters to Toreno, three of which were translated and published in Madrid in 1822 as Cartas de Jeremías Bentham, al señor conde de Toreno sobre el Proyecto de Código Penal.

In Portugal, Bentham's name was also used as an argument of authority. Catherine Fuller (2000) reports how Bentham tried to intervene in Portugal.[28] The liberal graduates of Coimbra's university prevailed in the new Parliament of Lisbon in 1821. Bentham was a partisan of Portugal adopting the Spanish Constitution. Little wonder that the above mentioned article 13 and the article 4 read: "The nation is obliged, by wise and just laws, to protect the liberty, property and all other legitimate rights, of every individual which composes it". So, they proclaimed as only legitimate end of government the greatest happiness of the greatest number based on the sum of the felicity of individuals and on the continuity and enforcement of individual property rights, the conservative and liberal response to the French Revolution that Bentham defended.

In the constituent debates in Portugal, many references about Bentham and others of the classic school economists appear. Although in Portugal also actual contact with political economy began with the translation of the *Wealth of Nations* into Portuguese (Lisbon (1811–1812) or Lisbon (1804)) and the influence of intellectual expatriates after the liberal revolution of 1820 (see Mata, 2001), the *Diário das Cortes* shows that few Members of Parliament took political economy principles seriously and in fact the leaders of the Revolution of 1820 did not look favourably upon them (Cardoso, 2001b, p. 158). In addition, though the intention of the Constituent was the writing of a constitutional code or "Soberano Congresso ", for it they had to discuss economic, social and political interests of difficult commitment. For example, they spoke about reinforcing the conditions of the Brazilian colonial agreement, interrupted by the opening of the ports in 1808, which implied a protectionist strategy that tried to satisfy economic interests of the manufacturers and farmers. Economic liberalism was set aside, but the rhetoric of political liberalism was used (Cardoso, 1997, pp. 138–139).

In a letter of November, 1821 to Joâo Baptista Felgueiras, Secretary of the Portuguese Parliament, Bentham offered to write the penal, civil and constitutional codes for Portugal. Bentham received a receipt of the letter of acceptance of the Portuguese Parliament in April, 1822 (apparently the letter of acceptance did not come into his hands, but learning about his acceptance, he wrote asking for confirmation and a copy of the letter). Bentham began to write a constitutional code based on the idea of the greatest happiness of the greatest number, on the basis of which the civil and penal codes should be created. Between April and August 1822, Bentham prepared four essays, published in *First Principles preparatory to the Constitutional Code,* where he defended universal suffrage, annual legislatures, equal constituencies, the secret vote and fixed salary for the members of parliament and denied the need of a second chamber, different from the Commons.

It was a graduate from Coimbra's University and one of the writers of the Constitution, Jose Joaquím Ferreira de Moura, who proposed to the Parliament that Bentham's books should be translated into the Portuguese language. In 1822 the Parliament published the translation of Dumont *Théorie des peines et des recompenses* with two volumes, as they were then writing a penal code.[29]

At the same time, Bentham heard that Manuel Fernandes Tomás, one of the principal liberals of the Portuguese Parliament, had said that if Brazil wanted to separate from Portugal it would be better not to try to avoid it by using force. But that was what Bentham had defended in *Rid Yourselves of Ultramaria!* So, he decided to send to his brother, Jose Fernandes Tomas, Secretary of the Portuguese Embassy in London, a letter in April 1822 with a copy of the essays opposing the Spanish control over their colonies. Between April and June 1822, Bentham sent to Tomás and to San Martin another set of essays against subordination at so great a distance, if *we are thinking about a constitution with a minimal sparkle of freedom in her.* After Tomás's death in November 1822, Bentham lost hope that the work would be published in Portugal. Bentham, in correspondence with Carvalho, advised him to emancipate Brazil. The Parliament rejected these offers to grant any degree of self-government to Brazil and this led to the Revolt in 1822, something that Bentham had already foreseen (Bentham, 1995, p. 156). In fact, Manuel Fernandes Tomás in *Relatório sobre o Estado e a Admnistraçao do Reino* in February, 1821, when he was trying to achieve the regeneration led by groups with diversified economic and political interests, already showed his concern for the transformation that was taking place on a slow and gradual path, and he weighted the risks of adopting extreme positions and overcoming the differences or making consensus easier (Cardoso, 1997, p. 147). Carvalho, in a letter of July 1822, shows Bentham his concern for the arrests and the fear that the realists would frustrate the liberal regime.[30]

Joâo Rodrigues de Brito asked the inhabitants of El Salvador to replace their religious books with the treatise of political economy, in benefit of national prosperity. But, although more importance was to be given in Portugal to the new doctrines of the utilitarians or political economists, their influence continued to be marginal and the authors had many doubts on their applicability and utility for

Portugal. The politically confused environment did not facilitate the diffusion of these theories (Cardoso, 2001a, p. 59).

As Rosen and Burns report in the introduction of the *Constitutional Code,* in 1822 Bentham published a leaflet of introduction in Spanish, *Propuesta de codificación para cualquier nación que profese opiniones liberales* that he published in English in 1930 in London as *Constitutional code; for the use of All Nations and All Governments professing Liberal Opinions.* He harboured hopes that the Iberian liberals would also entrust to him the writing of one of their codes (Bentham, 1983a). But, in spite of the fact that the political *Constituçâo politica da monarchia portugueza* was promulgated on 4 October 4 1822, the liberal Portuguese regime succumbed in 1822, and the Spanish in 1823 (the following Portuguese economic thought is in Mata (1988) and (2001)). In the course of time, the moderate legislative measures lead to the slow dismemberment of the structures of the *Ancien Regime.* In the parliamentary works of the Constituent Courts there was a political worry about regulating by law everything that before was regulated by tradition and fixing procedures and rules relative to the definition of individual rights and duties of the citizen (Cardoso, 1997, pp. 139–140). That would have implied a total reorganization of the social institutions.

In Bentham's portrait by Henry William Pickersgill, from the National Portrait Gallery, and one that forms a part of the College Art Collections of University College London, the importance of Portugal for Bentham is made evident: on the table, close to Locke's *Essay* and his *Introduction to the Principles of morality and the legislation,* there is a copy of the *Diarios das Cortes,* which included those of the meetings of the Portuguese Parliament from the period 1821–1823 and the resolution of the Parliament of 26 November 1821 in which Bentham's proposal to write the penal, civil and constitutional codes was accepted.

Bentham's influence spread later to Spanish-American countries, where, as we have said, he supported the revolutions and offered his codes for the arrangement of their inhabitants: Bolivia, Argentina, Chile, Guatemala, Colombia, Venezuela (see Schwartz and Rodríguez Braun, 1986).

The theory of regulation predicts that political power creates laws or codes in the same way that producers create goods; i.e., regulation is understood as a commodity, with a supply and a demand, in this case the supplier being the power and the consumer the citizens who seek income and privileges from this power. Indeed, Ekelund and Tollison (1981) tried to apply this theory of rent seeking to mercantilism, where the consumers (businessmen or merchants) are expecting to obtain some profit from a monopolistic privilege of the suppliers (monarchs, members of parliament or state legislators), that in turn receive money or votes in exchange for the granting of privilege. The peculiarity of the mercantilist period is that an absolute monarch was the supplier of privileges and the costs of supply and demand of regulations were lower as compared to a system with division of power.

When the supply of regulation became more costly because the political system changed and they needed to ask for permission from Parliament, mercantilism disappeared (see Perdices and Reeder, 1998, or Perdices, 2003, p. 45).

But, what will happen if we apply this methodology of rent-seeking to the code supply of Bentham? The supply of regulation might be considered infinite: Bentham was ready to write some regulation or code (the Pannomion) at any price, so that the supply is inelastic. In places were there was a group of liberal people very willing to establish such a liberal constitution, such as Spain and Portugal, and some places in South America, Bentham found a demand. Nevertheless, what Bentham was looking for was the heteronomous imposition of an idea of General Will or the self-imposition of a rule of conduct, a way of self-command based on reason. But the reality was that political systems, and even the mentalities, did not allow it to be firmly established. Institutions in Spain and Portugal, for example, were not prepared to allow the imposition of such a rationalist utilitarian and administrative system that needs an institutionally deep transformation and the extension of a bureaucracy and administration. This would have probably increased even more the transaction costs and turned the Iberian Peninsula into a bureaucratic and still authoritarian states, in the style of Russian tsarism (see Trincado, 2005b).

However, Bentham did influence British society, which followed the utilitarian message for some hundred and fifty years. But this statement might turn out to be too exaggerated if we consider his influence abroad, since his ideas were only used as an arsenal of useful weapons for local contests (something that, in any case, his philosophy of self interest predicted).

Actually, Bentham did not manage to elaborate this total code for any of the countries in which he proposed to do it. It is even to be doubted if his influence was real. What is undoubtable is that Bentham was a critical voice to be heard that, as Mill says, broke the spell on many thoughts

> Who before Bentham (whatever controversies might exist on points of detail) dared to speak disrespectfully, in express terms, of the British constitution, or the English Law? He did so; and his arguments and his example together encouraged others. We do not mean that his writings caused the Reform Bill or that the Appropriation Clause owes him as its parent: the changes which have been made, and the greater changes which will be made, in our institutions, are not the work of philosophers, but of the interests and instincts of large portions of society recently grown into strength. But Bentham gave voice to those interests and instincts: until he spoke out, those who found our institutions unsuited to them did not dare to say so, did not dare consciously to think so; they had never heard of the excellence of those institutions questioned by cultivated men, by men of acknowledged intellect; and it is not in the nature of uninstructed minds to resist the united authority of the instructed. Bentham broke the spell. (Mill 1980, p. 41)

5.3.5. *The horror vacui*

Steintrager says that for Bentham "There could be a substantial reduction in the level of unhappiness simply by reducing the common law to statutes, and by vigorously and systematically promulgating those statutes... In a map of the law executed upon such a plan there are no terrae incognitae, no blank spaces... This can only be done by way of bipartition, dividing each superior branch into two, and but two, immediate subordinate ones" (Steintrager, 1977, p. 22). Certainly, as a defender of codification, Bentham will be lead to a horror vacui of the law. He wanted to legislate every area of crime so that there was none without punishment, something which goes against the above mentioned principle of memorization and simplification. As every law creates a counter-law to evade it, when it comes up to a so-called motorized legislation, there is an anxiety and neurosis of wanting to avoid any avoidable pain through legislation. The legislator is the supplier of pleasures and pains in society, he creates the moral order and the balance of interests and the society is the result of his artifices (Bentham, 1989, pp. 123–149). Therefore, the sensation of need of a legislator and the terror of its disappearance are very pressing. Bentham himself had some neurotic features; for example, an eccentricity of his was that he never began a new page without beginning a new paragraph.

But legislation is for Bentham also regulation. Bentham gives special importance to organization in all the branches he touches, and we might even call all his philosophy "administrative". He raises a procedural code in *An Introductory View of the Rationale of Evidence* in 1812 and in *Rationale of Judicial Evidence* of 1827, which Dumont extends in *A Treatise on Judicial Evidence*. First of all, Bentham denied religious formalities. From his childhood, he suffered from the perjury he committed in Oxford, when he had to swear under oath that he respected some bylaws and customs that he ignored and he accepted the 39 articles of the Anglican Church in which he did not believe. He took revenge for the perjury imposed on him with a blasphemous and violent campaign on the formality of the judicial oath in a chapter of *Introductory view of the Theory of Evidence* that he published in 1817 with the title *Swear not at all*; and in a chapter of *Rationale of Judicial Evidence*.

Bentham thought that the administrative law might turn into an exact and mathematical science. The administrative law also has two ends: the direct and the collateral one. The direct end is to execute justice as exactly as possible, spending all the necessary time and money. The collateral ends demonstrate that the loss of time, money and vexations are evils that must be avoided, so that justice is done with the minor expense and the minor delays and possible vexations. Between the direct and the collateral end, there is a contradiction whose solution is reducible, according to Bentham, to a calculation of pleasures and pains. In this sense, he connects his theory of the procedure with the moral arithmetic, concluding that the procedure is the sum of means to endow legal punishment with a certainty element.

The procedure laws are work of the judges but the judges, as a class, do not have equal interests to the citizens and favour the judicial corporation. The general procedure of the members of the judicial corporation, "Judge and Co", as Bentham calls it, to make justice more lucrative and easier consisted of increasing the number of judicial formalities that make the procedure unclear, long and costly. This meaningfully complicated system is the "technical system" as opposed to the "natural system". There is a method older than the technical rules, that of the domestic court, and in the way the father behaves with the children and the serfs we will find the original characteristics of justice that we are now not able to see. A good judge, Bentham says, is a good head of household that works on a large scale.

In fact, Bentham condemns the system of multiplicity of judges and wanted the judge to sit down alone in front of the defendant and to be totally responsible. He despised the institution of the juror, the pride of liberalism, and thought that the advertising of the debates would make sufficiently responsible the one judge who might eliminate the system of appeals, which only serves to delay the case in time. This "one judge" of Bentham is an "illustrated despot" who is inspired in a free ideal public opinion of philosophers.

All Bentham's intentions of simplifying administrative laws were to be criticized by the liberal followers of Montesquieu, who thought that the simplest institutions are more adequate for despotic states and the complex ones for the free states. According to Montesquieu (1748), the judicial formalities and the complex constitutions with several balanced organs would guarantee individual freedom against the executive and judiciary power.

However, due to Dumont's protests, Bentham introduced a quasi-juror's concept, with fewer attributions, which would be a consultative organ that would ensure a representation of public opinion in the court, besides forcing the people to enter into the debates, which, according to Bentham, would be an open school of morality. That is to say, when the English men were proud of the local self-government that made them the prototype of free people in Europe, Bentham was pleading for a system of administrative centralizations, inspired by the French system. With the simplification of the parliamentary routine he sought to make the execution of the governmental measures less costly. The liberals, with the multiplication of the judicial organization, wanted to prolong the deliberations that precede the act.

Bentham says that if law consists of the respect for certain traditional, unintelligible formalities for the man of laws who does not know the history of the judicial corporation, the adoption of the technical or formalist system makes the science of law more difficult and necessitates the intervention of an agent acting between the judge and the defender, entrusted to the interpretation of the mystery of the law, that is to say, the attorney. As the judge finds it in his interest that the lawsuit lasts as long as possible and is as costly as possible, the attorney will prefer avoiding the presence of his clients in the debates, so that all is arranged within the servants of the law, that is to say, individuals affiliated to the same corporation. Justice becomes a business in which the interests of dealers are different from those of the judged parties. So, in 1791 *Draught of Judicial Establishment,* Bentham defends pro se legal representation, i.e., advocating on one's behalf before a court, and that anyone could be an attorney of the other. In *Rationale of Judicial Evidence* he repeats that *A man may be a judge in his own case* and the economic formula *Every man is the best judge of his own interests.*

Besides, Bentham rejects the plurality of jurisdictions – civilian, criminal – that according to some liberals, such as Adam Smith (1978), could bring in a healthy principle of emulation. According to Bentham, to foster competition, we need the rival courts to have equal competition and procedure. So, competition will benefit justice only if the area divides into lesser areas. Then, all judges must be able to judge everything and, in the division of jurisdictions, it is better the geographical than the logical principle. In Bentham's opinion, the logical principle is confusing, based on some legal fictions only understandable by attorneys and judges. It is preferred by the professionals, precisely, because it is less clear.

Another characteristic of the natural procedure that Bentham defends is that no evidence must be excluded – in England the judge could take evidence out of the trial if he considered it to be irrelevant – and that all the actors of the judicial drama were free to ask all the questions they wanted when they wanted, that is to say, that they had freedom of asking orally in all directions and without rules. It is true, Bentham argues, that so much freedom can finish in anarchy. So, looking for the collateral end of justice of avoiding losses of time, money and vexations of the parties, he proposes that the judge must assess how much time he will devote to examining the evidence according to the importance of the case. These considerations must be left, therefore, to the discretion of the judge, like a father who judges the fights arising from his children or servants. This contradicted liberal prejudice. But utilitarianism is not liberalism, as we have said, and because of it freedom is not something good as such.

Also Bentham speaks about the way of financing justice. English judges were paid via rates of the parties, which made the judge interested in the greatest cost for the parties. In order that the judges are interested in being honest, they must be paid a wage. In addition, an equitable method of dividing the expenses is to free the litigators and make non-litigators pay for them because the object of utilitarian justice is not to repair the committed crimes, but to anticipate future crimes. Those who go before the law already pay with vexations inflicted on them and the objective is the future good of creating an alarm for other possible future criminals, and, so, non-disputants are the real beneficiaries of the safety that is enjoyed.

5.3.6. Space and visibility: personalize to exercise power

The concern for space was constantly present in the texts of the French Revolution. Not for nothing, in the eighteenth century the space was specified and was becoming functional and everything began to be spatial in political economy as well, in which the main focus was placed in the topic of emigration and displacements, the spread of the species. Like his contemporaries, Bentham found a problem in human being overcrowding and he gave a lot of importance to space and architecture. He even described the space of the place where the ministers should have their debates, or the preferable shape of the table – oval. Likewise, he spacializes in the science of legislation. Thus, he tries to make a division between districts, subdistricts, bi-subdistricts and, if it is necessary, tri-subdistricts. On having favoured a simple form of government as opposed to a federal structure, he thought that in every subdepartment, there had to be only a secretary and a civil servant had to administer each office. Bentham was trying to centralize responsibility –as was the case for judges – and, when it was not possible to grant it to a person, he opposed meetings and advice that might dilute it. Under the sway of the prime minister, he makes explicit the 13 ministries and subdepartments; and the functions that these ministers would carry out, but he does not indicate the extension of government nor the legislation that his experts would create. As a matter of fact, the change in circumstances will make necessary the replacement of all of them: but only the Pannomion would remain in spite of the changes.

But in this set of laws visibility would also be fundamental: the advertising and reputation of laws became basic for Bentham, who demanded a codification to create certainty and the approval of a complete code based on the idea that "it will not be a law what is not in the legal body". He proposed the dismemberment of the code into so many codes or plots as different classes of persons are affected, to make everyone know and understand his specific code.

The architecture of the Panopticon also represents the political organization that Bentham defended. There is a key phrase in the project: every comrade turns into a watchman, recalling the sentence of *The Emile* of Rousseau (1762) who said that every watchman must be a comrade. The spring of justice will be that of opinion and maximum publicity: not to punish the people, but to make them not be able to act badly as they feel absorbed in a field of total visibility in which the opinion and the sight of others prevents them from doing what is harmful. It is an immediate, collective and anonymous look, without any area of shade.

The optical procedure was Bentham's great innovation to exercise power well and easily. In his jail, it would not even be possible to make plans of escape. Not only for the circular pit that he projected in the outside of the building, but architecture allows control inside, making people visible. This architecture should make the transformation of the individual easier, since it would allow the capture of his conduct.

So, we need to "individualize", to create prominent figures of a play set in motion by power. As Foucault (1984, p. 203–204) says, he is seen, but he does not see; he is an object of information, never subject in a communication.[31] The effect is to induce in the prisoner a conscious and permanent condition of visibility that guarantees the automatic operation of power and tends to make the exercise of power useless. With the individualization of the subdued, "The multitude, compact mass … individualities that are fused, collective effect … From the point of view of the guardian it is replaced by a multiplicity enumerable and controlled, from the point of view of the arrested, by a hijacked and observed loneliness" (Foucault, 1984, pp. 203–204). Power is automated and unpersonalised through a fictitious relation, so that it is not necessary to resort to violence to force the condemnation of good conduct. This reduces the administrative cost. The one that is submitted to a field of visibility and that is conscious of it, reproduces the constraints on his own, he makes them be born spontaneously.

In fact, the Panopticon can turn into a species of laboratory, as a machine of experiences to modify behaviour and to channel conducts. Bentham says that it is based less on a person than on a certain compound distribution of bodies, of surfaces, of lights, of looks; on a whole the internal mechanisms produce the relation in which the individuals are inserted. Consequently, it matters little who exercises power. An individual, taken almost at random, can make the machine work. The Panopticon is this "wonderful machine" that, from the most different desires, creates homogeneous effects of power.[32]

5.3.7. The Public Opinion Tribunal

Bentham changed his mind throughout his life on not many occasions, but he did so especially in relation to the possibility of checking power and controlling the controller. Firstly, he rejected the idea that the division of powers constitutes a safeguard to the arbitrariness of the state. Division of powers is a fiction that, in the last analysis, makes power disperse and be less fair. However, he embarked on the promotion of written constitutions that power has to impose in different countries. According to Bentham, only if their own individual interest coincides with that of the public, will hedonistic rulers be ruled by this constitution. But as Postema (1986) says, Bentham never recognized an artificial identification of interests between the politician and the citizen as possible, and in fact all the controls that he tried to set up – "externally to the political theatre" – are a symptom that the interest of the legislator does not coincide with that of the electorate (see Schofield, 1996).

How can the interest of the legislator be made to coincide with that of the public? As we have said, after some conflicting ideas, Bentham accepts that the only way of achieving that goal is through the democratic vote. Bentham rejected the fashionable idea of the natural right to vote, so he based democracy on two core principles (Hume, 1981).

First, providing that the secret ballot is guaranteed, within a democratic system the people can reveal their preferences to the public policies. Second, the only way of controlling the utilitarian government is through a fictitious entity, the "Public Opinion Tribunal" (Bentham, 1990, pp. 27–29). The power of this hypothetical entity will be exercised through the vote and the media, and it will search for the interest of the majority of the people. Authority is then imposed by the people on the people themselves. Here arises the problem posed by Rousseau. How can a man be at the same time free and forced to adapt his will to those of others? Rousseau solved it saying that the man might vote depending on an idea of "social well-being". This proposal by Rousseau divides the individual into two selves: the private person and the citizen (Goodwin, 1988, p. 255).

Bentham presents the "fiction" of the Public Opinion Tribunal, which he imagined as incorruptible: it is not possible to corrupt everybody in society and people do not have the means of corruption that the leaders have. Nevertheless, this Tribunal acts by representation; and seeks the "public interest" which depends on the interests of the people that have managed to have voice and influence in public opinion (see Cutler, 1999).

Bentham emphasized four functions of the Public Opinion Tribunal: the statistical function, i.e. it needs to gather facts and evidence so as to judge any act or public institution; the censorial function, i.e. it must express approval or disapproval on the basis of the gathered evidence; the executive function, i.e. public opinion is a moral reward or punishment; and suggest improvements and reforms. Finally, the political function of the media seems to be the exemplary punishment that frightens government members.

But a deeper function of the media (and of the government) is to promote social change through political education and to seek the development of the mental powers of the people, something first considered by Priestley, and predicted as necessary progress (Miller, 1993; Passmore, 1964). The media qualify the people to understand their real, probably subconscious, interests. Bentham (1983b, p. 172) draws up in his *Deontology* a law of progress of the sympathy of species. With economic growth, the individual is wrapped in an ever growing number of social circles; the more they live in public, the more influenced they are by the moral sanction, and they become more virtuous, until they reach perfection. Finally, the individuals will be so hermetically tied and linked, they will feel so constantly observed, that it will no longer be possible to draw a line between sympathetic and selfish feelings. This, and many other ideas of Bentham, have many flavours of Hayek's theory (Dube, 1990, p. 72)

As we have said, this Benthamian utopia is exemplified in the Panopticon by his "principle of universal inspection", in which the prisoners could not see the watchman thanks to a system of blinds and, thus, the fear of being observed would be constant. Janet Semple has found a note that registers Bentham's intention of playing cat and mouse with the prisoners of the Panopticon: "I will keep an unintermittent watch upon him. I will watch until I observe a transgression. I will minute it down. I will wait for another: I will note that down too. I will lie by for a whole day... the next day I produce the list to him. You thought yourself undiscovered: you abused my indulgence: see how you were mistaken" (Tumim, 1994, pp. 81–82). This Bentham utopia resembles the novel *1984*; as Rothbard (2000, pp. 82–89) rightly says, it is a version of the utilitarian Big Brother. Certainly, there should be no punishment that did not put on display its magnificence publicly and was made well-known. In this way, people will be frightened and ashamed of having abused the "general interest".

5.4. Bentham as an economist

5.4.1. Property rights

As we see, Bentham's proposals of social and political reform are interlinked with his law and economics. For Bentham, the distinction between real and fictitious entities is very important. "Power, right, prohibition, duty, obligation, burden, immunity, exemption, privilege, property, security, liberty – all these with a multitude of others that might be named are so many fictitious entities which the law upon one occasion or another is considered in common speech as creating or disposing of" (Hart, 1970, p. 251). "Because the common law was filled with such fictions, it would not be possible to end all the existing defects merely by turning the common law into adequately classified and promulgated statutory law" (Steintrager, 1977, p. 23).

Property, Bentham says, is only a creation of the law. We base our hopes on drawing a certain profit from our possessions on property relations. So, property is no more than the hope to draw a certain profit from the thing possessed as a result of the relations of it with law. If we admit that it is useful for social good that the product of work is property of the worker because it reinforces the feeling of expectation without which he would not work, the thief must be threatened by a pain of equal intensity to the pleasure of stealing. The enforcement of property rights, actually, fosters growth that reverts to the whole society. But, apart from that, Bentham thought that the government could do little to promote abundance. The individual investor is most likely to be the best judge as to what industry or occupation will increase his own wealth and so the wealth of the nation. Government might be able to gather information which would assist individual investors, patent protections should be given to encourage new inventions and it might even be defensible to provide temporary protection for a nascent industry. But the rule must be free market.

The objects of property can be real or corporal and fictitious or incorporeal, but Bentham, like Locke or Hume, considers property to be an external relation with an external object.[33] The essence of property is that the proprietor derives a benefit or pleasure from the acts that have their completion in an external thing and their beginning in a person.

In addition, Bentham introduces the principle of prevention of disappointment, which is the basis of the civil and penal branches of property rights. Without the idea of expectation, there would be no difference between a person that possesses a thing and a usurper, if both feel equal pleasure in possessing the thing and, so, property is the enforcement of vested interests. Due to the principle of non-disappointment, the rich man expects his opulence the same as the poor accepts his fate. So, in emphasizing the expectation, Bentham based his concept of property rights in the future and he opens the path to a gradualist programme of redistribution. Thus, his concept of time in the transformation of the law is futurist, gradualist, and continuist (Bentham, 1981c, p. 118).

Bentham, then identifies propriety with the human feelings of pleasure, security and expectation, but, after the French Revolution, he was terrified by the idea of a revolutionary change in distribution

> A revolution in property! It is an idea big with horror, a horror which cannot be felt in a stronger degree by any man than it is by me… it involves the idea of possessions disturbed, of expectations thwarted… of opulence reduced to beggary, of the fruits of industry made the prey of rapacity and dissipation – of the levelling of all distinctions, of the confusion of all order and the destruction of all security.[34]

So, Bentham defends the maintenance of the status quo:

> In all the instances, what ought to be the primary object of government? Steadiness. This ought to be the first object of its wishes at any rate, if not of its measures.
>   Why so? Since what is lost to one man by a change of price is just so much gained to another, both of them members of the community, the interest of each forming an equal poertion of the interest of the community. True: but such is the constitution of human nature that the enjoyment resulting from a gain is never equal to the suffering resulting from a loss.
>   Steadiness of price is a branch of that species of security which has property for its object.[35]

However, there are reasons to look for equality: the poor can use the principle of minimization of the inequality and, in addition, a mass of given wealth produces more happiness when it is distributed between a greater number of individuals. Bentham says that any inequality which is not justified by a special utility is an injustice.[36]

This does not mean that Bentham's theory relates property rights with human rights, or that he criticizes the relation of man with other men or with nature. Bentham condemns the theory of Natural Law as he thought that all the laws are artificial and passed by the state for some utility.[37] The question of whether human beings may be objects of property, Bentham answers that in principle, they must not be, or at least not in an unconditional way, but he says that, since the experience has not taught another condition to the slaves, these do not perceive their subordination as something so abominable: "the difference between freedom and slavery is not so big as for certain ardent and well-prepared men, because the habit of evil and with a great more reason the inexperience of the best diminishes the interval that separates these two conditions so opposite to the first sight" (Bentham, 1981c, p. 196). There is no reason, then, to carry out an emancipation without indemnification and he asks for the gradual abolition of the personal obligations on slavery, maximizing thus the principle of non disappointment both for the owners and for the slaves, as well as the productivity of work.

He distinguished between human trafficking, of which he disapproved (forbidden by Spanish and English people in 1817) and slavery itself, which he did not condemn clearly. He seemed to be more worried about the fate of animals than of slaves themselves (Rodríguez Braun, 1989, p. 126).[38] Then Bentham is not absolutely opposed to human property: due to their expectations, children, women, convicts, apprentices or poor people are scarcely defrauded. The one that does not expect anything is not driven to despair. In this way, for example, the poorhouses may lodge children in the condition of human property. Human rights theorists such as Nozick (1974) criticize this idea of utilitarianism as it does not specify what the state must never do, no matter what the price. If, as Bentham says, law and freedom are opposed, to maximize safety can be, on occasions, crushing on dignity. In the same vein, Bahmueller says that in the society that Bentham proposed the citizens were lacking dignity and they "were to be divested from personality and formed into a common mould, much like soldiers upon joining an army" (Bahmueller, 1981, p. 72).

5.4.2. Defence of usury

We have already talked about *Defence of Usury* (1787) with regard to the entrepreneur theory of Bentham. But Defence of Usury was really a result of a rumour that Bentham had heard according to which the secretary Pitt planned to reduce the legal interest rate of 5 % to 4 %. As Stark says, that meant that more people would be chased for the felony of usury! But, in the *Introduction to the Principles of Morals and Legislation* (1781), Bentham was unable to find a place for usury, so for him it was an imaginary offence.

> Usury, if it must be an offence, is an offence committed with consent, that is, with the consent of the party supposed to be injured, it cannot merit a place in the catalogue of offences, unless the consent were either unfairly obtained or unfreely: in the first case, it coincides with defraudment; in the other, with extortion. (Stark, 1952a, p. 23)

In addition, from the harmful effects of fixing a maximum interest rate, Bentham emphasizes the decrease in the number of possible lenders and the emergence of a black market of credit. The earnings of the banker will be limited and he will be more cautious in fixing the margins of risk involved in the projects. The loans will be granted only to the businessmen who operate in known ways of production and distribution, with low risk. So, Bentham thinks that the effect of a maximum rate of interest will be to block any innovation and to obstruct the mechanism of development itself. Therefore, it is necessary to trust market forces.

In his *Defence*, Bentham reproached Smith that he did not understand that the same hatred towards the word "usury" and moral prejudices were responsible for the law of usury. Here, Bentham was missing Smith's arguments, who was not speaking about moral justice, but considered that the market rate of interest, agreed by the people, is the "price of time" that a solvent businessman will accept (provided that, according to Smith, men are generally prudent). In any case, Bentham ended his *Defence of Usury* in May 1787 and ordered the manuscript for George Wilson, an attorney of Lincoln's Inn who gave it to press. The book appeared towards the end of 1787. In a letter to Bentham on 4 December 1789, Wilson wrote:

> Did I ever tell you what Dr. Adam Smith said to Mr. William Adam, the Council M.P., last summer in Scotland? The Doctor's expressions were that "the Defence of Usury" was the work of a very superior man, and that tho' he had given him some hard knocks, it was done in so handsome a way that he could not complain, and seemed to admit that you were right. (Rae, 1895, pp. 423–424)

Bentham referred to this alleged conversion in the second edition of his *Defences*, in 1790, but he was careful to say that he was not present at Smith's transformation. He looked for the open recognition of the change in opinion and sent a letter to Smith, that he received in the last days of his life. All that Smith did was to order a dedicated copy of *The Wealth of Nations* for Bentham, as Bentham admits in *The True Alarm* (written in 1801). And it is difficult to believe the conversion of Smith, who, actually, reinforced in the course of time the importance of the prudent man in his system.

Smith and Bentham had two different visions of economic development: in *Defence*, Bentham considers development to be characterized by constant changes determined by improvements, and, therefore, with a non-linear trend; Smith thinks that development is something slow, gradual, uniform and not capable of sudden variations. Besides, Pesciarelli argues that each had a different view of human progress. Smith's entrepreneur is a common type, one who exercises self-control in economic activity in order to receive the approbation of his fellow man. "The prudent man unconsciously promotes the interest of society because he consciously sets limits on the pursuit of his own interests. He is the visible promoter of the invisible hand; he is the fulcrum but also the limit of Smith's belief in the working of a self-adjusting mechanism" (Pesciarelli, 1989, pp. 534–535). For Bentham, economic development is activated by discontinuous changes involving improvements (in the broadest sense), and resulting in a non-linear path of progress. Smith's notion of economic progress is slow, gradual, uniform, and not subject to sudden variations. In some way, Bentham was based on some foreseeable idea, that is to say, image, of the future, whereas Adam Smith tried to base his theory on present reality and memories, not on imagination. A theory based on an image tends to explain parallel and irregular conditions, somewhat exceptional (as happened in Hume's theory, see Stewart, 1977, pp. 172–173).[39]

As we have already said, in this Owen is nearer to Smith than to Bentham, as, for him, progress needs to be checked and accompanied by human progress, not taking so much into account the monetary stimulus, but also the slow development of the human race.

Defence was immediately praised by the *Monthly Review*, May, 1788. Besides being highly appreciated in England (Thomas Reid quotes and defends the work), *Defence* was appreciated in France (Mirabeau quotes it as well and also defends his ideas) or in America, where it had great influence (his principles were adopted in the state of Mississippi in 1817, in Alabama, in Virginia and in New Hampshire). The liberals accepted his arguments, and the bill presented on 15 February 1788 in Ireland, supporting a reduction of the legal maximum the interest rate, was refused maybe based on the publication of *Defence* in Dublin the same year. *Defence* also received critiques, but the first of them appeared 30 years after the date of Bentham's attack on Smith.[40]

In any case, as Stark (1952a, p. 33) says, the specialized literature admits that *Defence of Usury* owes its success more to stylistic brilliance than to the depth of its thought. Bentham was becoming famous for defending the freedom of the market, beyond that of "Adam Smith himself" and, nevertheless, his argument was consciously "cheating". Actually, Bentham defended at the same time a maximum price on grain in *Defence of a Maximum* – though he did not find a publisher for this work – and there he stands up from inconsistency admitting that, really, in *Defence of Usury* he was arguing against a maximum – seeking to argue with Smith – and now, in *Defence of a Maximum*, he was in favour of a maximum – seeking to argue with Charles Long (see Hutchison, 1956 and Harrison, 1989).

In this pamphlet, which he wrote at the end of 1801, the problem that Bentham approached was that of the shortage of provisions in general and of grain for bread in particular, something that happened in 1799 and that was threatening famines and massive misery. Probably Bentham would not have decided to take part in the discussion if he had not found a valuable adversary: Charles Long, who published in 1800 a pamphlet under the title *A Temperate Discussion of the Causes which have led to the present High Price of Bread*. Here, he rejected the exigency of the people who asked for the legal imposition of a maximum price of wheat. Bentham at first did not defend this measure but, when Long presented his arguments, he thought more about the topic and came to the conclusion that a law of maximum would be a measure that was defendable. Without a maximum, the cultivators and merchants may want to retain what they have of the good with the hope of a later increase of prices and profit. And, to answer Long's objection that consumption depends on the price and a low price will stimulate consumption, Bentham mentions the Marshallian problem of the elasticity of demand, although he does not develop it fully (Stark 1952c, pp. 247–302). [41]

In many other cases Bentham tried to achieve attention from some famous men of letters. He thought of writing to Edmund Burke to interest him in particular reforms (UC 169, p. 74) and also tried, with success, to bring himself to the attention of Lord Shelburne (Norris, 1963, pp. 141–143).

But, after 14 years, Bentham returns to the argument of *Defence of Usury* and, though he does not retract it in the Preface he admits that the fixing of a maximum interest rate has a merit that had not occurred to him in 1797 and that he might have approved the measure of maximum interest rate: it makes it possible for the government to borrow on more favourable terms, especially in time of war. In the last analysis, Bentham might have defended the reduction of the interest rate with a somewhat Keynesian analysis with the argument of a benefit of trade.[42] Nevertheless, maybe to continue supporting the thesis that he initially defended, in *Institute* he affirms that cheap money policy with a forced reduction of the interest rates is a direct tax on the lenders that will not increase, but it will reduce, capital, as they will travel to countries with higher interest rates.[43]

For modern economists, the most notable fault of the *Defence of Usury* is the absence of a theory of interest. But there are some ideas in *Defence* that later Bentham develops as a theory of interest and capital. He refused to accept that money was sterile, but he was not attracted either by a theory of physical productivity. His theory approaches more to a monetary theory of the interest rate, in which the expectation becomes pivotal. This is proved by his definition of lending as an exchange of present money for future money,[44] or that of saver as one that has decided to sacrifice the present for the future.[45] In letter III, he reports that the desire of a man to save, and his degree of saving, is a response to

> which of two pains may be of greater force and value to him, the present pain of restraining his present desires, or the future contingent pain he may be exposed to suffer from the want to which the expense of gratifying these desires may hereafter have reduced him. (Stark, 1952a, p. 133 from *Defence of Usury*: Letter III)

In other essays, he expresses himself in a similar way, and the loans are seen "not for risk of lending, but for mere self-denial in not spending" (Stark, 1952b, p. 294) from *Abstractor compressed view of to Tract intituled Circulating Annuities*). Here, Bentham not only anticipates Menger, Jevons or Marshall, but also Boehm-Bawerk explanations of the interest rate. If the value of the future pleasure does not only depend on the intensity and duration, but on the certainty and propinquity, it is smaller the more uncertain and more distant it is. Therefore, a risk premium will emerge. Bentham says:

> Intense, long, certain, speedy, fruitful, pure
> Such marks in pleasures and in pains endure
> Such pleasures seek, if private be thy end.
> If it be public, wide let them extend.
> Such pains avoid, whichever be thy view
> If pains must come, let them extend to few.
> (Stark, 1954, p. 435, *The Psychology of Economic Man*)

This analysis is coherent with his final idea of *Defence of Usury* that the maintenance of usury laws only can come from a moral prejudice as: "Those who have the resolution to sacrifice the present to the future are natural objects of envy to those who have sacrificed the future to the present. The children who have eaten their cake are the natural enemies of the children who have theirs" (Stark, 1952a, p. 159 from *Defence of Usury*).

5.4.3 The theory of value: the calculus of felicity

"Adam Smith has turned into light a great mass of smoke: but there are cases also where he has turned into smoke what was light before".[46] This is the description that Bentham makes of the theory of value of Adam Smith, and in similar terms he will criticize, in the margin of Table of the Springs of Action, the idea of the tendency to exchange – why not to say that the individuals maximize their utility instead of having some strange propensity to exchange? he asks.[47]

For Bentham, the starting point of scientific reasoning must be the potential "utility" of the objects to investigate. Bentham defined economics as a branch of the science of legislation. "He frequently compared legislation with medicine.

It was, however, the art and science of healing on a grand scale, of ministering to the sickness of the body politic" (Steintrager, 1977, p. 20).

For that reason, Bentham was a friend of statistical methods (Stark, 1952b, p. 143). Statistics, more than the fundamentals, was for Bentham the justification of the plans he designed. For example, in chapter 5 of *Escheat vice Taxation* entitled "Produce", he finds it impossible to calculate the magnitudes involved in a financial plan that he had elaborated to re-live the law of Escheat. In spite of the fact that he had merely come to a few solvent numbers, he proposed with vehemence the Escheat instead of taxes to the secretary Charles Long. Obviously, he already knew, before beginning the work, what his induction had to defend.

Stark includes an anthology of Bentham's writings that he calls "the psychology of economic man". This is the concept of the *homo oeconomicus* accepted by many economists and who then would be used by the school of marginal utility as a definition of human behaviour. According to Bentham, happiness is an "idea", the expectation of the future pleasure and pain that influences the interested and expected action. In *The True Alarm*, he defines wealth on the basis of two elements: there must be a sensitive object and the object must be a matter of use and desire. In chapter 5 he discusses the notion of value: "All value is founded on utility".

But what is pleasure or utility for Bentham? Anything that the individual or the self "asks for himself" can be considered to be a pleasure. What the self rejects, is to be considered a pain. The approximation of pleasure – avoidance of pain, according to Bentham, explains the altruistic actions – we can feel pleasure when we feel that we are generous – the same as the traditionally so called "selfish" actions. Therefore, the difference between altruism-egoism disappears. The predominance of the self-preference or self-regard on other impulses is for Bentham an axiom of human nature and it is implicit in the philosophical concept of personal identity where there is a necessary reference of men to their own hedonic self. "All men that are actuated by regard for anything but self, are fools; those only whose regard is confined to self are wise. I am of the number of the wise".[48]

As previously noted, the philosophy of Benthamites, then, is not interpersonal in nature: actually Bentham does not accept different ways of thinking to his own. On the basis of this psychology, the society that Bentham presents is a fortuit and atomistic gathering of rival men.

Social life is not a natural phenomenon, but is only possible by repression of the human beast.[49] According to Bentham, and as against Smith or Hume, sympathy is not a natural feeling (Trincado, 2003b, 2008a). Our greed for the pleasant things is immense, whereas the number of good things is small. The result is a fight where antipathy, a desire to see others as bad as we are, arises.

> The preparation in the human bosom for antipathy towards other men is, under all circumstances, most unhappily, copious and active. The boundless range of human desires, and the very limited number of objects adapted to satisfy them, unavoidably leads a man to consider those with whom he is

obliged to share such objects, as inconvenient rivals who narrow his own extent of enjoyment. (Stark, 1954, p. 430)

Concluding, Bentham's individualism is both philosophical and methodological and even normative: the man must be an egoist, at the risk of being an idiot. Man, therefore, seeks to maximize a sum of expected pleasures and to minimize a sum of expected pains. But are there impulsive actions previous to this calculation, with positive – negative amounts? For Bentham, even passion calculates, although in a disordered way and, by the way, passion is not regular behaviour "As to the proposition that passion does not calculate, this, like most of these very general and oracular propositions, is not true… Passion calculates more or less in every man."[50]

As Mitchell (1918, p. 4) says, Bentham does not stand out for being utilitarian. There are many philosophers that had proposed the doctrine of utility, for instance, Richard Cumberland in 1672. What makes Bentham different is his desire to introduce the exact method in utility issues. Bentham says that we may quantify physical experiences so as to yield specific numbers on mental assessments, which are endogenous and in constant change (Lapidus and Sigot, 2000). And these assessments are actually made whenever a monetary price is mentioned. We may take money as the measure of individual pleasure or pain and Bentham makes this measure in some way a "subjective objectivity". Value of a monetary unit is high for those who do not have much money and high for those who have much money, so that value of the relative money is related to some real preferences and absolute necessities. Then, we may make interpersonal comparisons between men: if *ceteris paribus* two men of equal circumstances lose the same quantity of money in relation to their wealth, we may assume that they will lose the same quantity of happiness.[51]

In particular, Bentham makes the Smithian distinction between value in use and value in exchange, but he criticizes Adam Smith: water can have value in exchange in some cases, whereas diamonds can be useful.[52] Bentham's ideas are always near to the importance of the principle of marginal utility. In Axioms, the reader finds a clear exhibition of the idea of "sensitive minimum" of wealth in the "mass of produced pleasure".[53]

Besides, Bentham presents the idea of the decreasing marginal utility principle:[54]

> The magnitude of the pleasure produced by it does not increase in so great a ration as that in which the magnitude of the cause increases. Take, for instance, the same cause as before: namely money. Take thereupon any individual: give him a certain quantity of money, you will produce in his mind a certain quantity of pleasure. Give him again the same quantity, you will make an addition to the quantity of his pleasure. But the magnitude of the pleasure produced by the second sum will not be twice the magnitude of the pleasure produced by the first.[55]

The principle of decreasing marginal utility is not only applied to money, but to whatever gratification: high degree of exciting matter applied to the organ makes his sensitivity be somehow exhausted.

With regard to his theory of exchange, Bentham did not see clearly that, provided men have different utilities and given their resources, both traders can benefit from voluntarily giving up a portion of their happiness for their own profit.[56] But he raises the idea of "exchange by reparation" and he even talks about a law of indifference. "Relation had to the individual in question, an evil is reparable, and exactly repaired, when, after having sustained the evil and received the compensation, it would be a matter of indifference whether to receive the like evil, coupled with the like compensation, or not".[57]

In the *Treatise* (Bentham, 1981c, pp 110–116), he studies the pathology, the sensations, affections and passions and the effects on happiness of a transfer of commodities. "Be the modification of the matter of prosperity what it may, by losing it without an equivalent, a man suffers according to, and in proportion to, the value of it in his estimation – the value ascribed to it by him".[58] To judge the effect of a portion of wealth on happiness he considers three different conditions: 1. When they are in the hands of the parties; 2. When the particles of wealth are about to enter into the hands of the parties; 3. When the particles of wealth are about to go out of the hands of the parties.

> I. Case or state of things the first.– The quantities of wealth in question, considered as being in a quiescent state, actually in the hands of the two parties in question: neither entering into, nor going out of the hand of either.
>
> Ceteris Paribus: – to every particle of the matter of wealth there corresponds a particle of the matter of happiness (…)
>
> 5 Minimum of wealth, say 10 pounds per year; – greatest excess of happiness produced by excess in the quantity of wealth, as 2 to 1: – magnitude of a particle of wealth, 1 pound a year. On these data might be grounded a scale or table, exhibiting the quantities of happiness produced, by as many additions made to the quantity of wealth at the bottom of the scale, as there are pounds between 10 pounds and 10.000 pounds (…)
>
> II. Case, or state of things the second – the particles of wealth about to enter into the hands of the parties in question
>
> 1. Fortunes unequal: – by a particle of wealth, if added to the wealth of him who has least, more happiness will be produced, than if added to the wealth of him who has most (…)
>
> 3. On these data there might be grounded a scale, exhibiting the quantities of happiness produced, by so many additions made as above to the minimum of wealth, to the respective happiness of any number of persons, whose respective quantities of wealth exceed one another, by the amount of a particle in each instance.
>
> III. Case, or state of things the third, – the particles of wealth about to go out of the hands of the parties (…)
>
> 6. The larger the fortune of the individual in question, the greater the probability that, by the subtraction of a given quantity of the matter of wealth, no subtraction at all wil be made from the quantity of his happiness."[59]

Bentham, with his geometric method that shows the static consequences of pleasure of a transfer, was thinking on a scale that reminds one of graphs of utility that after were drawn by economists. Besides, he is very near to the equimarginal principle in exchange, although he does not define it clearly.

> IV. Case or state or things the fourth, – the particles of wealth about to go out of the hands of the one party into the hands of the other.
>   1. Fortunes equal: – take from the one party a portion of the matter of wealth and give it to the other,- the quantity of happiness gained to the gainer of the wealth will not be so great as the quantity of happiness lost to the loser of the wealth.
>   2. Fortunes unequal:- the poorer the loser, the richer the gainer: greater in this case is the reduction produced in the mass of happiness by the transfer, than in the last mentioned case.
>   3. Fortunes again unequal: – the richer the loser, the poorer the gainer: the effect produced on happiness by the transfer may in this case be either loss or gain.[60]

Bentham's theory is very near to Menger's doctrine, not only due to subjectivism, but because of his distinction between high and low order goods, production and consumption goods. The same as Menger (1984), he distinguishes goods by their nearness to consumption: "Between "real service and its reward" the exact common measure is the least quantity of the matter of reward that he who is able to render the service consents to take in return for it. This is the measure of all prices: this is the measure of the value of all good things that are at once valuable and tangible".[61] According to Bentham there are goods of immediate or intrinsic value, as food, and goods of a derivative or servile value, such as tools:

> Immediate utility admits not of degrees: but of unimmediate utility, as above, degrees may have a place in any number. The scale, to which these degrees belong, may be termed the scale of vicinity to use. Instruments, the station of which is on the highest degree of the scale – say the first degree – the degree nearest to immediate use – may be termed instruments of the 1st order: those, next to them, i.e. next below them, instruments of the 2d order; and so on, through any number of degrees, which in any system of connected instruments may at any time be found exemplified.[62]

Price and cost must take into account the final prices paid by the final consumer, the lower order goods, not production goods, the higher order goods. Bentham talks about this for the first time applying to the definitive and the preliminary prices (in Stark 1954, p. 113, *The True Alarm*). Goods nearer to use exclude pain or administer pleasure directly and are not subservient or instrumental to production. In the distinction between the primary and the derivative part of national revenue, and between the natural and conventional revenue, there is an echo in Bentham of the physiocratic doctrine. The difference between agriculture, manufacture and crafts, says Bentham, is the greater division of labour, the greater quantity of intermediate uses and the degree in which the instruments approach the "vicinity to use", that is to say, the greater production time.

In *Institute of Political Economy*, he displays a theory of the factors of production different from that of Ricardo. He points to three factors: inclination, knowledge and power (the will to produce wealth; the knowledge of how to produce it; and the power on external things necessary for this intention). The inclination is given in unlimited quantity, flows from the constitution of the man and does not need to be stimulated. Knowledge is a fruit of the inclination, so that the legislator does not have to stimulate it either. But power, that is to say, the control of capital and capital goods, is the bounding factor, provided that it is scanty. The problem is that it is difficult for government to take effective steps towards avoiding this shortage of a natural factor. Therefore, as a whole, for Bentham laissez-faire is the appropriate attitude.

A feature of Bentham's theory is his inclusion of people as a part of wealth, as they are a source of services. Inhabitants are a part of the productive capital of the country. Besides, labour is "only" an instrumental good, not one of lower order, and the labourer's pain of working could only be compensated for by the monetary pleasure of a wage: "Aversion – not desire, is the emotion – the only emotion – which labour, taken by itself, is qualified to produce… Insofar as labour is taken in its proper sense, love of labour is a contradiction in terms".[63]

This allows Bentham to defend a communist rationale: "If, on the ground of delinquency, in the name of punishment, it be right that any man should be rendered unhappy, it is not that his happiness has less claim to regard than another man's, but that it is necessary for the greatest happiness of the greatest number that a portion of the happiness of that one be sacrificed".[64] So, Bentham defends a tendency to equality founded on marginal decreasing utility of wealth and on a quasi mathematical method that foresees Jevon's proposals and will set the path for microeconomics.[65]

Nevertheless, utilitarianism is so inconsistent and fleeting that another principle allows Bentham to justify economic conservatism: the legislator must maintain the distribution of the property not interfering in the total mass of expectations. The principle of minimization of disappointment and uncertainty cancels out the happiness that the redistribution would produce and, Bentham says, may even cancel existence itself.[66]

The legislator is the one that provides pleasures – and existence itself. Thus, Bentham's theory is completely static. There is a clear difference between Bentham's theory and Smithian dynamics, as for Smith transactions and transfers are not measured by the "mass" of pleasure produced but growth is something different. For Bentham, state redistribution would not have more negative effects than the static of the disappointment for the derogation of property, and even, a redistribution towards the rich people might have positive effects, if the measure enriches the people who have a propensity to save.[67] Besides, the State might make pleasures objective and not interpersonal in nature. For instance, Bentham says, jewels are purchased for ostentation and emulation and "A custom of this sort when it has once got footing lays people under a kind of obligation of conforming to it, not for any satisfaction if affords them, but to avoid contempt. If they were relieved from this obligation they might spend their money more to their satisfaction in another way" and in doing so they might give a boost to domestic trade (UC 72, p. 67). So, then Bentham was willing to consider that the government might be right in placing high taxes on luxury items such as jewellery.

Bentham makes the "increase of the stock of wealth depend on the advantages of the direction given to it and of the interest put into it. The interest that a man takes in the matters of others…, for example a sovereign for his subjects, is probably not so important as the interest that each one takes in himself; much less when this other one is a perfect stranger for him" (Stark, 1952a, p. 229). In order that the State increases wealth, it must create incentives, transferring wealth from one branch to the other.

In the unpublished *Manual of Political Economy* (1795), Bentham continued the laissez faire theme of "No more trade than capital". The government, he emphasized, can only divert investment funds from the private to the public sector; it cannot raise the total level of investment. "Whatever is given to any one branch is so much taken from the rest… Every statesman who thinks by regulation to increase the sum of trade, is the child whose eye is bigger than his belly." However, he states that government paper money could increase capital if resources were not "fully employed".

In defending this famous "only economic principle" of the limitation of trade by existing capital, he cites Adam Smith as an argument of authority. In short, he will use this economic principle in the same systematic way as the greatest happiness of the greatest number principle is used in ethics and legislation. This idea that capital limits trade is accompanied by a definition of capital as "Capital is the aggregate of the produce of labour of preceding ages minus the consumption which has taken place by destruction or use" (Stark, 1954, p. 74). According to Bentham, "All wealth is the joint result or product of land and labour: of human labour operating either immediately upon land, or upon something is using more or less" (Stark, 1952a, p. 226). This physiocratic bias makes us come to the conclusion that capital can neither grow beyond nor be different from the product of the land. "Labour, operating upon land and the produce of land, is the source and only source, of wealth" (Stark, 1952b, p. 333).

5.4.4. The theory of money

In an unpublished "Proposal for the Circulation of a [New] type of Paper Currency" (1796), as Rothbard (1995, chapter 2.1) says, Bentham happily wedded his "projecting" and constructivist spirit to his newfound inflationism.

Instead of floating bonds and paying interest on them, the government, he proposed, should monopolize all issue of paper notes in the kingdom. It could then issue the notes, preferably non-interest bearing, *ad libitum*, and save itself the interest. But Bentham did not say what limit there might be to this government paper issue. The limit, he answered, would obviously be "the amount of paper currency in the country." Stark, Bentham's editor, is scornful about this: "It is like saying "the sky's the limit" when we do not know how high the sky may be" (Stark, 1952b, Introduction, II, 18–19). In his later writings on the subject, Bentham searched for some limits to paper issue, if unsuccessfully. In his unfinished "Circulating Annuities" (1800) he criticizes the Turgot-Smith-Say insights and actually declares that employment of labour is directly proportional to the quantity of money. After once again calling for the elimination of bank paper for the benefit of a government monopoly of paper issue (in the fragmentary "Paper Mischief Exposed", 1801), Bentham reached the maximum of inflationism in his *The True Alarm* (1801). In this unpublished work, Bentham not only continued the full-employment motif, but also complained about the allegedly bad effects of hoarding, of money saved that went into hoards instead of investment. In that case, prices, profits and production will fall. Nowhere does Bentham recognize that hoarding and a general fall in prices also means a fall in costs, and no necessary reduction in investment or production. Again treating his earlier views on usury, Bentham denied that he had ever believed in any self-adjusting and equilibrating tendencies of the market, or that interest rates properly adjust saving and investment. According to Rothbard (1995), Bentham worked around to the Mandeville fallacy about the beneficial effects of luxurious spending. In the mercantilist and proto-Keynesian manner, saving is evil hoarding while luxury consumption animates production. How capital can be maintained, much less increased, without saving, is not explained in this model.

Bentham places great importance on money, although in the course of time he changed the emphasis placed on inflation. He defended the monetary authority of a Central Bank to carry out an anti-cyclical policy, introducing such important concepts as "forced saving". If the capital is used at full capacity and resources for investment do not come from voluntary saving, they must come from involuntary saving. The additional capital accumulation is obtained "by force" from the fixed income collectors through the price increase (see Méndez, introduction to Thornton, 2000).

> Suppose, according to Hume's supposition, the money in each man's pocket was to be doubled instantaneously. It is not true that (as he says) the wealth [of the country] would not be increased by this.[68]

In the long run, an increase in prices will occur, which works as two taxes: one on the capital of wealthy men that have lent money at interest; the other on consumption. But Bentham sees two possible consequences even before the price increase happens. Either metal increases or it is replaced by notes and is melted and the wealth in knives, spoons will increase. But if there are unemployed resources, another possibility emerges: the unemployed will join the process of production, when the tenants of money give wage increases, or the demand for labour will increase. So, the quantity of labour and the productivity of a given quantity can increase. Recalling the theory of rational expectations, Bentham affirms that if the increase in the quantity of notes is unexpected, the price increase will not occur immediately and the increase in the quantity of money possibly will affect activity and employment positively.

> Buy gold and silver money to the same amount, the same mischief would (it is true) be produced, and in the same degree; but the magnitude of the mischief is in proportion to the suddenness of the addition, not to the absolute quantum of it; and, in the shape of cash, the influx is not susceptible to any such suddenness as in the shape of paper.[69]

As the issuing of new paper money can stimulate the economy, as we have said Bentham recommended the discretionary issue of a governmental banknote that should render an interest rate or annuity, the Annuity Notes (from which we have four boxes of material in 1,400 sheets). Bentham's could be seen as a primitive scheme of nationalization that aims to transfer lucrative transactions from private to public hands.[70] Banking "in the sense of deposit", Bentham says, is an area where the government can surpass other bankers in security. There is no argument, neither utilitarian nor legal, against a state system of paper money, as government credit is the best one. Besides, it is easy to borrow, he says. But it is not so to lend. Bentham is not thinking about more important economic functions of banking, directing the productive credit flow; he is only worried about the fiscal side of the coin that affects the agenda of the state. "Saving the subject from bad paper is most perfectly in [the government's] power. Let it but supply the market with its own paper, and a simple prohibition will keep all other paper out of the market most effectually".[71]

So, government can obtain resources issuing notes, which is a "cheaper" means of exchange, but an unfair one, as it constitutes an inflationary tax. It is a temporary exchange between government expenditure at the present moment, and future expenditures of individuals. "What is a government annuity? Future money given in return for present money."[72]

Existing government bank notes (treasury bills and army bills) had, according to Bentham, four advantages for circulability: they were nominated in high amounts and, so, not many people could use them in currency traffic; they were payable after a year; the means of payment were complicated; and they did not look very appealing.[73] Treasury bills were more appropriate paper for constituting a source of income than for general circulation. However, government money could be introduced that could yield an interest (over 2%) in enough small units for daily circulation in a way that they do not interfere with the (private) Bank of England notes, whose smallest note was 5 pounds. Bentham had no doubt that the interest free notes were better, since they circulated more easily due to their manageability. But he considered the financial sacrifice of interest payments to be a sort of bait for the people to accept the new note, which could compete with other bank notes and with treasury bills. When people thought these notes were trustworthy, they would become notes without an interest rate.

In the same vein as Coase (1994), Bentham appealed to the public bank note issuer to reduce transaction costs. In particular, he talked about the supply and demand of these Annuity Notes. With regard to supply, Bentham is especially explicit in pointing out the fact that the notes should be issued on a paper that, by its size, shape, texture and fineness, should be especially prepared for circulation. In the first chapter, he details the administrative apparatus necessary for the payment and issue of annuities. He proposed the local post offices be charged with the issue of these notes.

> Dispatch, punctuality, cheapness in the transaction of the business, sufficiency of number, and equality of distribution in regard to the stations, forming the characteristics of the Post Office establishment, as compared with all other provincially-diffused official establishments.[74]

Bentham makes a comparison between annuities and bank notes, giving special importance to the time lost in finding out if it was a good idea to place money at interest and make the calculation of the interest rates over small and fractional or short period amounts. He also pays attention to the time lost in the process of demanding and obtaining payment of the interest or of the capital and interest. "But in the case of the Annuity Note no computation at all is necessary: inspection takes the place of it".[75]

Notes would have a table showing the particular value every single day, given the increasing of the interest rate.[76] Without it, there were no hopes of making the paper circulate, because every transaction meant a complex mathematical computation. This table would balance the fact that this money had a different purchasing power every day. Besides, Bentham said that to prevent forgery, human figures could be introduced on the notes. In the hands of a master, the difficulty of forging a metallic impression is not as great as that of a human figure. To the colour figure could be added one in relief without colour with paper printing. The head of the king could be the main figure and other heads of lesser dimensions could be added, perhaps persons with an official relationship with the sovereign, not represented on other occasions. He also made specifications for the borders of the banknote and the fact that the king should wear a crown – because he was hardly ever shown with it. At the same time, barons would wear an official suit because they scarcely ever exhibited themselves in that way. A difficult ingredient to erase could be added to the ink. Stark points out that it is clear that Bentham underestimated the necessity of a very simple and non-problematic means of circulation, something that in fact would have made his proposal useless.[77]

With regard to the demand for annuity notes, Bentham distinguished clearly between what he called demand for "circulation" motives and the demand for "permanent income" motives, which is speculative (he tried to avoid a reduction in interest rates compared with other securities or other branches of commerce).[78] Also, he talked about something similar to the liquidity trap.

> By the supposition they all reject the paper bearing this new and lowest rate... It is still taken, and that to the amount of 20 millions, by the customers for temporary income in the course of, and with a view to, circulation... For whatever rate of interest is accepted on the footing of permanent income, there will always be people in abundance to whom it will be worthwhile to accept the next lowest rate with a view to circulation.[79]

Furthermore, Bentham considered this money would be insurance against economic crises springing from purely monetary reasons. The new money will be a regulator as it will be used as a means of payment and as an investment or capital, according to the situation. In fact, he says, if there are unemployed resources, employment could be increased with the issue of this additional money. As Stark says, if there are, before the influx of the additional money, unemployed resources, human or material, and the influx brings them into play, inflationary measures do increase the standard of living in the country. But if, at the beginning of the operation, all resources are fully employed, no more can possibly be produced, and the only effect of an attempt to pump fresh money into the circulation is bound to be a rise in prices.[80]

Bentham investigated the possibility that the establishment of government annuity notes might increase the circulation of money and help to pay off the national debt. The possibility existed that capital would be freed for investment purposes. He argued on behalf of a nationally controlled currency and he went a long way along the road towards modern monetary policy, as noted by Stark. He ultimately dropped his plans, in part because of the want of a favourable response from the government in part because of a growing concern that the policy would have inflationary tendencies which would work particular hardship on people with fixed incomes, especially the elderly (Stark, 1952b, pp. 7–113).

In fact, already while devising his annuity notes scheme, Bentham became worried by the inflationary consequences of the plan, something that weakened his faith in the scheme. Nevertheless, he tried to deliver it to the government a year later, because he thought that the present situation increased prices even more than his project and because, as Stark points out, Bentham "could not well imagine a sound circulation without gold sovereigns" (Stark, 1954, introduction, p. 25) and was anxious to avoid the bankruptcy alarm. Annuity notes, he would say himself in November–December 1800, would, in any case, be money controlled by government, preferable to the existing one, without control.

> In the actual state of things, the amount of paper money put into circulation was beyond anybody's control: who could know what the numerous country bankers up and down the country were doing? Who could hope to impose limits on their issues? Were they not, without perhaps suspecting it, inflating the circulation and raising the price-level day after day, week after week, and

year after year? Did there not lie here a great danger for the community which ought to be energetically tackled by the government and which could best be tackled by replacing private paper with a public currency?[81]

A pamphlet that Bentham found accidentally fixed his ideas, Iniquity of Banking by W. Anderson, with a subtitle: Bank Notes proved to be injurious to the Public, and the Real Cause of the present exorbitant price of provisions. Anderson's thesis was that notes issued by provincial banks were the principal cause of the evils of the period, the lack of goods and provisions. Bentham was impressed by Anderson's arguments that assumed clearly enough that free issue of paper money always implied a danger of general bankruptcy. It was then that Bentham began Paper Mischief (Exposed) recognizing that he had thought before that moment that a positive connection between the growth of quantity of money and of wealth existed and, so, the increasing of prices was a justified sacrifice to obtain a greater good. But he now knew that connection to be a figment of his imagination. Now, the evil of inflation was for him a greater evil. And Anderson had confirmed this idea.

Then, according to Bentham, prices had doubled since 1760 and money purchasing power had decreased by half. Bentham's objective was to prevent that evil in the future and to compensate for the damage to fixed incomes in the past. It was then that Bentham introduced the forced saving theory, which he would later develop in the Institute of Political Economy in 1804 (nearly at the same time as Thornton in 1802), or, as he calls it, the theory of "Forced Frugality", which explains the connections and mechanisms of money operation, not surpassed until Keynes' theory. In this sense, Bentham accepted the possibility of artificial incentives affecting wealth, at least in the short term since growth in quantity of money is favourable to the accumulation of capital, although consumption by certain individuals with fixed incomes who do not receive the advantages of saving is produced. Government "has" the possibility to spur saving through an artificial mechanism, money issue (an inflationary tax); however, it "ought" not to do it, because it is unfair to compel people to sacrifice future wealth for present wealth.[82]

To calculate depreciation, Bentham took the figures of Sir George Shuckburgh Evelyn from his writings on weights and measures. He liked them because the price increases agreed perfectly with the increasing of paper money circulation, so a cause and effect line could nearly be shaped. He concluded that increasing paper money should be restricted and effective money increase be kept under control or, at least, we should not give it a positive incentive. These are the main monetary policies Bentham defended and developed in *The True Alarm*, May 1801, trying to attack Walter Boyd in *A letter to the Right Honourable William Pitt, on the influence of the stoppage of issues in specie at the Bank of England: on the prices of provisions, and other commodities*. In the pamphlet, Boyd showed opinions contrary to Bentham's. He considered the Bank of England, the directors' policy and, in particular, the suspension of payments in kind, responsible for the general commodities shortage. While Boyd accused the Bank of

England, he excused provincial banks, as he thought that they restricted their issue more. His notes were payable when they were demanded, whereas the Bank of England was freed from the obligation of paying their notes in kind by a licence of February 1797. According to Boyd, the Bank of England's over issue was the cause of inflation.

Conversely, according to Bentham, the Bank of England was not guilty, and the problem was found in provincial banks' freedom. Bentham gave definitive remedies: bankers must register and make patents, their number must be controlled, securities for their solvency must be given, their issue of notes should be limited and taxed and the bullion currency making must stop. He included in the false remedies the renewing of payments in kind by the Bank of England. Here, Bentham tried to calculate once again the inflation of the period. No doubt, he was a pioneer in the elaboration of this kind of index. Bentham asked Robert Watts from Sion College, September, 1801, for information and some lists of prices of cloth arrived at Charity Schools in their respective years (1772, 1777, 1780). Watt's answer is not very illustrative but Bentham, without waiting for the gathering of a corpus of statistical data broad enough to elaborate an index, continued in June and July his theoretical argumentation. In April 1801, Bentham gave his manuscripts *Circulating Annuities* to Étienne Dumont in Geneva for him to edit and translate for their publishing in France. Dumont translated them into French, but he wrote in the margin, "I've read the manuscript ten times, without understanding it" (fol. 168) "I do not understand either the original or my translation" (fol. 356).

5.5. Differences in the proposal of social reform of Bentham and Owen

The utopian socialism proposed by Owen, and the practical schemes of social reform undertaken by him, had some theoretical coincidences with Benthamian utilitarianism. For all the phrases in which Owen refers to Bentham, its basic principle of society was the same as that of the Utilitarians. But, as we have said, differences are made evident when we go in depth into their theories. Owen differed from Bentham in his view of the rate at which social change could take place and in the importance of the part education could play in promoting such change. Development is for Owen something that happens all the time, as it is evolution taken for the better understanding of things and the connection of the past into the future. On the other hand, for Bentham progress is a search for pleasures to be felt in the future and, in some way, its enjoyment is impossible to attain. Actually, as time passed, Owen's disciples came into sharp conflict with the Utilitarians. Owen became in after years more and more socialist, whereas Bentham thought that free markets would free the workers from the excess power of the capitalists.

This has to do with some essential differences in the philosophical basis of Bentham and Owen. In particular, Bentham was an idealist who, like Hume, goes against the existence of personal identity: we are a collection of different perceptions which succeed each other with an inconceivable rapidity, and are in a perpetual flux and movement. Then, self command has not much to do with happiness, and it may only be fostered externally in order to attain some public happiness. When dealing with social reform, Bentham imagines that an external agent, such as the State, may make perceptions more beautiful and, as pleasure is somehow physically measurable, we may sum up those pleasurable feelings and attain the greatest happiness of the greatest number.

To improve society, Bentham advocated a system of punishments and rewards which Owen argued against. Bentham remained dubious of the basic goodness of men and his project is based on punishment and constraint. The control devices in the Panopticon are not only exercised through central surveillance, but through seven ways of authority that aim at reforming paupers or convicts: rules, look, classification, word, tradition, sanction and education, which means an idea of community or "communities" of individuals with conflict of interests (Brunon-Ernst, 2007, p. 19, 26). Education is part of the art of government, and consists of command on the one side and subjection on the other (see Everett, 1948).

Owen seems not to share this idea of perception and happiness and, so, his thoughts are based on an idea of personal identity. Here personal evolution is possible, where self command is a part of education and where developmental economics emerges. Owen sticks to a theory of property which is obligationist or personalist. The right of people to do what they want with the goods is an illusion. Rights are only person-to-person. Any right involves a faculty in the subject to demand something from the passive subject. Therefore, a right is an obligation and it implies a negative abstention or passive obligation imposed on the whole world, the universal passive subject, bound to respect it (Castán, 1987, p. 40). But there is no internal economic content in rights as there is no relation of the person to the thing.

Bentham is talking about microeconomics and Owen about developmental economics, something that implies a change of gestalt, as shown in Trincado (2008a). Besides, Bentham is based on the aesthetic man, a certain condition "of the moment" where oblivion is acceptable, but Owen is based on memory, capabilities and reality.

With this thesis in mind, we would like to make a comparison of current theories that could clarify the differences of the theories of Owen and Bentham. Owen's view may be related to Amartya Sen's capability approach, where freedom depends on individuals' capability of achieving the kind of lives they have reason to value (Sen, 1989). As against utilitarianism, in Sen's approach, a person's capability to live a good life is defined in terms of the set of valuable beings and doings', as signaled by Wells (2016). People can internalize the harshness of their circumstances so that they do not desire what they can never expect to achieve. Therefore, evaluation that focuses only on subjective mental metrics is insufficient without considering whether that matches with what a neutral observer would perceive as their objective circumstances.

In this sense, Owen's theory is also similar to that of William Godwin (see Open University, 2016). Godwin constructed his theory of progress on the

Enlightenment premises where characters are formed by their circumstances, vice is ignorance and truth will ultimately prevail over error. Godwin and Owen equated happiness with knowledge and defended the moral regeneration of humankind and the importance of economic reform in advance of political reform. They argued that the best way of eradicating the evils that beset society at the time was not the system of punishments and rewards advocated by Bentham, but by rational education and universal enlightenment. Both condemned political agitation, but favoured instead a voluntary redistribution of wealth, which Owen later hoped would be achieved through cooperation. Their ultimate social ideal was that of a decentralised society of small self-governing communities of the kind that Owen was to propose in his village scheme (Marshall, 1984, pp. 310–11).

Although Owen was not an intellectual, his view of progress seems to be dynamic, the same as happened with some classical economists, such as Adam Smith, for whom it was not utility or a sum of felicities that we may achieve with wealth, but growth itself, and the possibility of breaking habit and creating a wishful thinking. "The progressive state is in reality the cheerful and the hearty state to all the different orders of society. The stationary is dull; the declining, melancholy" (Smith, 1994, p. 129). Certainly, in *Wealth of Nations*, Smith abandons the idea of abundance that must "promote" the State (defended in his *Lectures on Jurisprudence* of 1762–66), to present an economic growth that the State must "allow" to be left unchecked "the natural effort of every individual to better his own condition" (Smith, 1994, pp. 438, 440, 444; Smith, 1976, p. 582). In this sense, it is "not the ease, or the pleasure, which interests us" (Smith, 1997, p. 124). China, in spite of being abundant, was in Smith's time poor according to him, as the workers were earning low wages. Really, abundance does not indicate a certain level of development, but the aptitude and ability of workforce to create value in a fluid way.

On the other hand, for Bentham, the psychological principle that promotes wealth is a desire for enjoyment of the consequences of this wealth, as a type of pleasure. Bentham could be compared with Rawls' concept of justice: the task of justice is not to assess people's achievements, but rather to ensure the fairness of the conditions of participation in a society. Justice should be neutral with regard to judging different people's conceptions of the good. Bentham's concept of freedom, like that of Montesquieu, implies that people should only be constrained from harming others, not themselves. The legislator could not have the knowledge and insight possessed by the individual regarding his own interests. Actually, Bentham arrives in some way at the *maximin* principle of Rawls: the two most important subsidiary ends of government for Bentham are security and subsistence, while abundance and equality are of inferior importance. Without security there would neither be abundance nor equality, people would make little effort to create new wealth.

According to act consequentialism such as Bentham's theory, actions should be assessed only in terms of the goodness or badness of their consequences. This excludes any consideration of the morality of the process by which consequences are brought about, for example, whether it respects principles of fairness or individual agency. Besides, many philosophers have argued that without an objectively justified list of valuable capabilities, it is difficult to assess how well a society is doing, or to criticize particular shortfalls. However, having a list of central capabilities to be incorporated into national constitutions and guaranteed to all up to a certain threshold (as in Martha Nussbaum 2011) excludes, as Gore (1997) points out, valuable goods which are "irreducibly social", such as a shared language, culture, set of moral norms, or political structure. John Alexander has proposed a capability theory based on a Republican understanding of the importance of freedom as non-domination (Alexander 2008).

Then, Bentham's methodology is individualistic – society being nothing but the sum of individuals, whereas Owen's is anti-individualistic or against the individual – for him education will induce each man to have charity for all men. However, socialism will not be for Bentham in itself and out of revolutionary measures, a problem. Some might argue that the greatest happiness of the greatest number could be achieved under a dictatorship. But in the question of property, Bentham was quite near to political economists. As time passed Bentham tended to emphasize his own attacks launched on wealth disappointments and encroachments on property and his belief in some freedom in labour markets (in particular, the rights for workers to move and choose their employers).

In Bentham there is no clear concept of economic growth. He is based on a static economy, as if industrial capacity was a pecuniary capital stored forever. "In this point of view, then, money, it would seem, is the cause, and the cause sine qua non, of labour and general wealth... The truth of the matter is, that in regard to any particular species of wealth, no addition can be made (except as excepted) but by an addition to the quantity of money employed in giving birth to that particular species of wealth" (Stark, 1952b, p. 326). He also says "At the end of each year, a community is the richer in the proportion between the wealth produced and imported, and the wealth consumed and exported in the same year" (Stark, 1952b, p. 325).

Bentham raises a static economics, without the passage of time, just in a Walrasian sense and he even criticized the economic language that, on having assumed wealth as dynamic, was confusing. "It would be desirable that, in the moral department of science, men should accustom themselves to speak of the matter of wealth, of the matter of reward, of the matter of punishment, as has become customary in physical science to speak of the matter of heat" (Stark, 1954, p. 72). There is a given quantity of wealth that cannot be increased if there is not a quantity of unemployed capacity of labour. This is a mercantilism view of economics. The idea of capital as a fixed quantity leads Bentham to defending that the State can distribute the stock of wealth.

As an example of his static vision of the economy, in *Institute* Bentham affirms that, unless capital increases, men's displacement by machines will produce unemployment. In *Manual of Political Economy*, he raises the agenda and non-agenda of the State and the *sponte acta* and discusses the possibility of creating an artificial formation of capital under governmental incentives through forced saving. Bentham is eager to minimize the role of government, and he even informs us about a possible crowding-out effect, but in the notes he pleads for many state measures to achieve wellbeing. The subtle idea is that incomes and prices are not completely flexible, as Keynes would put it. "If all incomes could be raised in the exact proportion to the rise of prices and at the same time, the rise of prices would not be attended with any positive inconvenience..." (Stark, 1952b, p. 335).

So, more than defending liberalism, Bentham defends a democratic despotism (Schwartz, 1986). But, as John Stuart Mill says, "The power of the majority is salutary so long as it is used defensively, not offensively – as its exertion is tempered by respect for the personality of the individual, and deference to the superiority of cultivated intelligence. If Bentham had employed himself in pointing out the means by which fundamentally democratic institutions might be best adapted to the preservation and strengthening of those two sentiments, he would have done something more permanently valuable, and more worthy of his great intellect" (Mill, 1980, p. 88).

Notes

1 University College, xxvii 34 "Pleasures and Pains. How Measured" in Long (1990, p. 20).
2 See Oakeshott (1962, pp. 1–36) and Manning (1968).
3 Stark (1952a, pp. 98–99).
4 See Dube (1990) on Hayek (1960).
5 See Schwartz (1986, p. 70).
6 The Psychology of Economic Man: VII. In this sense, Bentham was less paternalistic than other progressive utilitarians, like John Stuart Mill who, despite the fact that he criticized Benthamism, decided to weigh up the sum of pleasures, making a hierarchy of those that he considered of greater value or superior and those that he thought vulgar or of less emotional content. Until man has not had the opportunity to experience a pleasure, he does not have the freedom to choose it (see Mill, 1984, p. 47; and Scarpe, 1996).
7 Although some authors affirm that Aristotle had already introduced the marginal utility theory, and afterwards this theory was accepted by Davanzati, Montanari, Galiani, Condillac and Bernouilli (see Vivenza (2001, p. 143)).
8 See Stark (1954, p. 422), The Psychology of Economic Man.
9 See Mill (1984, p. 47); and Scarpe (1996).
10 Other theorists have also tried to do this, introducing new words such as "catallactics" to name the market, etc... (Hayek 1988, 110–112).
11 In Stark (1954, p. 428) The Psychology of Economic Man.
12 Bentham (1948), Introduction 1xiv.
13 See Peardon, Thomas, "Bentham's Ideal Republic" in Parekh (1974), pp. 120–145.
14 Rosen (1983), pp. 5–6.
15 Stark (1952a), pp. 103–4: The Philosophy of Economic Science: XXV
16 Stark, W., 1952a: The Philosophy of Economic Science: XXV: 107.
17 Bentham (1986), p. 43. On Bentham's enmity with Blackstone see Posner (1976).
18 Stark (1952b), p. 137: A plan for Augmentation of the Revenue.
19 Bowring, vol. iii, pp. 205–9 in Halévy (1972, p. 78).
20 Stark (1952a), p. 321: Supply without Burden.
21 Harris (1999); Schwartz and Rodríguez Braun (1986) and Williford (1980)
22 The Iberian correspondence by Bentham is published in Schwartz (1979). See also Schwartz; Rodríguez Braun (1983); Rodríguez Braun (1987); Schwartz (1975); y Schwartz (1976), (1990).

23 "Jeremy Bentham to the National Convention of France", in *Emancipate Your Colonies! Addressed to the National Convention of France, Anno 1793, shewing the uselessness and mischievousness of Distant Dependencies to a European State*, London, 1830.

24 Bentham's "anti-imperialism" and "anti-militarism" have been applauded, but there are many continuities with the traditional forms of the English critique that warned about the danger of the regular armies (Winch, 1997, p. 152).

25 There had been a reception of the WN by Jovellanos and Ortiz. See Schwarz (1990).

26 See Rodriguez Braun (1985).

27 In Bentham (1995 pp. 1–344),with "Emancipation Spanish" and "Summary of a Work entitled Emancipate Your Colonies".

28 See Fuller (2000, p. 62). V. Diario das Cortes geraes, extraordinarias e constituintes da Naçào Portugueza, 7 vols., Lisboa, 1821-2, Sesión del día 13 de Abril de 1821, i. 573. Citado en Fuller (2000), p. 59.

29 The title is "Theoria das Penas Legaes" and "Theoria dos Premios Legaes" and the general title *Traducçao das obras politicas do sabio jurisconsulto Jeremias Bentham, vertidas do inglez na lingua portugueza por mandado do soberano congresso das Cortes Geraes, Extraordinarias e constituintes da mesma naçao.*

30 Letter 2901,Carvalho to Bentham, 5 July 1822, Correspondence.

31 Escamilla (1998) says that the vision of the Panopticon of Foucault is comical and that the critique to Bentham is only possible from an anthropologically positive conception: man is good and society is what makes him corrupt, so that any repression is distorting.

32 See Bentham (1979) and the critique by Foucault (1984), pp. 205–6.

33 Bentham (1981: 118).

34 Stark (1952a, p. 318) extracted from Supply without Burden.

35 Stark (1952a, pp. 364–365) extracted from Supply without Burden.

36 Stark (1952a, p. 329) extracted from Supply without Burden.

37 Mises (2001, p. 209) criticized Natural Law theory based on Bentham. However, the Austrian School of economics is compatible with iusnaturalism. As Huerta de Soto says (Mises 2001: 1xi, introduction), there are three tendencies in the Austrian School of Economics: the utilitarian-rationalism of Mises, the evolutionism of Hayek and the iusnaturalism of Rothbard and Hoppe

38 Campos Boralevi (1984, pp. 142–175) has studied Bentham's view on slavery and handling animals.

39 Urrutia (1983, p. 148) says that this depends on non-conmensurability of the whole. Any explanation can be reconstructed as atemporal without any loss of information.

40 For instance, that of Grahame, 1817, "Defence of Usury Laws against the Arguments of Mr Bentham"; that of Robert Maugham, 1824, "Treatise on the Principles of the Usury Laws; with Disquisitions on the Arguments against them by Mr Bentham"; the anonymous essay in 1825 "Reasons against the Repeal of the Usury Laws"; Francis Neale, 1826, "Essay on Money Lending... and... Answer to the Objections of Mr Bentham"; or John Whipple, 1855, "Free Trade in Money" subtitled "Stringent Usury Laws, the best Defence of the People against Hard Times".

41 From *Defence of a Maximum* containing a particular examination of the arguments on that head in the pamphlet of 1800 attributed to a late Secretary to the Treasury to which are subjointed hints respecting the selection of radical remedies against dearth and Scarcity 1801.

42 Stark (1952a, p. 192) from [Proposed] Preface [to the Second Edition] of Defence of Usury.

43 For the liberal stance of Bentham with regard to the market of credit, see Leloup (2002, pp. 7–20).

44 Stark (1952a, p. 132) from Defence of Usury: Letter II.

45 Stark (1952a, p. 159) from Defence of Usury: Letter X.

46 Stark (1954, p. 80), *The True Alarm.*

47 Bonner (1995).
48 Stark (1954, p. 426), The Psychology of Economic Man: VII.
49 Stark (1954, p. 431).
50 Stark (1954, p.434).
51 However, Bentham says, there are goods with an invariable value, as relative needs, and goods with variable and capricious value, as relative luxuries, for which the comparison of interpersonal utility is more difficult.
52 Stark (1954, p. 19) y Stark (1952a, pp. 108–9).
53 Stark (1952a, p. 118).
54 Stark (1954, p. 438); Stark (1952a, p. 108 and pp. 113–114). See Bentham (1981, pp. 110–116).
55 Stark (1954, p. 441) fromThe Psychology of Economic Man: XXIX.
56 Schwartz (1986, pp. 74–103).
57 Stark (1954, p. 438) The Psychology of Economic Man: XXVI.
58 Stark (1952a, p. 108) The Philosophy of Economic Science: XXV.
59 Stark (1952a, pp. 113–114) The Philosophy of economic Science: XXV.
60 Stark (1952a, pp. 114–115) The Philosophy of economic Science: XXV. See Schwartz (1976).
61 Stark (1952a, p. 118) The Philosophy of Economic Science: XXVII. Stark (1954, pp. 448–9 and p. 84). See Trincado (2004).
62 Stark (1954, pp. 448–9) The Psychology of Economic Man: XXXIV. Also Stark (1954: 84) The True Alarm.
63 Stark (1954, p. 428), The Psychology of Economic Man: IX.
64 Stark (1954, p. 439).
65 Marginalists have criticized Bentham's equalitarianism, but not his philosophy. Their criticism of Bentham's equalitarianism is based on a radical subjectivism and relativism. For instances, according to Edgeworth, people are unequally able to enjoy pleasure and suffer from pain (see Murphy (1984, p. 171).
66 Stark (1952a, pp. 364–5 and pp. 111–112).
67 Stark (1952a, pp. 196–198), Defence of Usury.Proscript.
68 Stark (1952a, p. 270), Manual of Political Economy.
69 Stark (1952b, p. 208), Circulating Annuities.
70 However, Bentham was brave, as he discussed the possibility of a competitive system in the issuing of notes, although he finally rejected it (Schwartz 1982, p. 691).
71 Stark (1952b, p. 157), Proposal for the circulation of a new species of paper currency.
72 Stark (1952b, p. 38), introduction.
73 Stark (1954, p. 209), Supplement of The True Alarm.
74 Stark (1952b, p. 213), Circulating Annuities.
75 Stark (1952b, p. 386), Circulating Annuities, Observations by Sir Frederick Morton Eden, (in the form of a Letter) on the Annuity Note Plan as contained in the *first three* printed sheets with the two tables: with counter-observations by the author of the plan.
76 Stark (1952b, p. 179) Proposal for the circulation of a new species of paper currency.
77 Stark (1952b, p. 51), introduction. These proposals of Bentham in the course of time have had great success: there is the euro which, in introducing all kinds of technical advances, has become a more expensive means of exchange than the previous currencies.
78 Stark (1952b, pp. 245–253), Circulating Annuities: V. Cantillon had already distinguised between demand for transaction and for precaution motives; and in his works demand for speculation motives are also stressed.
79 Stark (1952b, p. 257) Circulating Annuities.
80 Stark (1952b, p. 56) introduction.
81 Stark (1952b, p. 63) introduction
82 Hayek (1932, pp. 123–133).

6 Education in New Lanark and in Bentham's proposal

6.1. Utilitarian education

Dickens in his famous critique of utilitarian education in his novel *Hard Times* published in 1854 opens the novel with the Superintendent Mr. Gradgrind stating at his school in Coketown, "Now, what I want is, Facts". The children are taught "Facts ... nothing but Facts. Facts alone are wanted in life". Instead of by names, they are identified by numbers. "Girl number twenty" is harshly scolded for suggesting that a carpet with flowers would be a pleasant thing to have in a home (a carpet with flowers = "fancy" rather than "Fact"). Mr. Gradgrind has three younger children: Adam Smith, Malthus and Jane. Josiah Bounderby, "a man perfectly devoid of sentiment", is revealed as Gradgrind's close friend. Bounderby is a manufacturer and mill owner who is affluent as a result of his enterprise and capital. In Dickens's interpretation, the prevalence of utilitarian values in educational institutions created young adults whose imaginations had been neglected, due to an over-emphasis on facts at the expense of more imaginative pursuits. He also wished to campaign for reform of working time and conditions. Drawing upon his own childhood experiences and thanks to his visits to the factories in Manchester as early as 1839, Dickens became appalled by the environment in which workers toiled (Dickens, 1854).

Actually John Stuart Mill had that type of rigorous education consisting of analytical, logical, mathematical, and statistical exercises. In his twenties, Mill had a nervous breakdown, believing his capacity for emotion had been enervated by his father's emphasis on analysis and mathematics in his education. Although he longed to end his life, he had a transforming experience reading the English romanticism (see Trincado, 2015).

Many critiques have been made on *Hard Times*; however we will especially emphasize the critique by George Bernard Shaw, who, writing in 1912, observed that with the publication of *Hard Times*: "Here you will find no more villains and heroes, but only oppressors and victims, oppressing and suffering in spite of themselves, driven by a huge machinery which grinds to pieces the people it should nourish and ennoble, and having for its directors the basest and most foolish of us instead of the noblest and most farsighted." Shaw decreed *Hard Times* to be a novel of passionate revolt against the whole industrial order of the modern world that failed to provide an accurate account of trade unionism of the time. But it is in *Pygmalion* that Shaw gave an alternative both to imaginative and to utilitarian education (Goldberg, 1979). The play is a sharp satire of the rigid British class system of the day and a commentary on women's independence. But, in particular he raised a point with regard to education that would be applauded thereafter. Higher expectations lead to an increase in performance because people internalize their positive labels, and those with positive labels succeed accordingly. This, obviously, implies that education has more to do with self dignity than with the accumulation of facts and more facts.

Another interesting criticism is that by Levy (1999, 2000), who notes that Charles Dickens tried to stigmatize the idea of capitalism and markets backing up the criticism by Carlyle, who talked about the Dismal Science of economics, as compared to the Gay Science of art. However, Carlyle defended slavery and Jamaican genocide. Those were paternalism based on racism as he idealized slavery of benevolent masters and child-like slaves (Carlyle, 1853; 1956 and 1971).

Actually, there is something true and false in Dickens´ criticism, at least with regard to Bentham's proposals.

James Mill and Bentham got acquainted in 1810 with philanthropists obsessed then with the idea of reforming humanity through pedagogy, a method followed by Owen, at factory level, or defended by Godwin or by Francis Place, Wakefield and Brougham. These three planned with James Mill a complete system of primary and secondary education for the city of London based on the Lancaster system. Mill communicated the idea to Bentham and he offered his garden to construct the school, and made the architectural, administrative and pedagogic plan, which resulted in Chrestomatia (Bartle, 1991).

Bentham published his ideas on the Chrestomatic School fully in 1817. There he presents the order in which the academic topics should be taught justified by the principle of diminishing utility, so that no pupil who left the establishment would lose the benefit of his years of education. The classical education was eliminated and the scientific one was justified by its utility. Another way of calculating profits and losses was to compare the quantity of instruction with the quantity of pain to produce it, and to apply the methods that Bell raised to make work attractive.

Bentham set out a secondary school curriculum influenced by his linguistic theory and his construction of a tree of knowledge. His materialist theory of language had important psychological implications, for it determined that children should learn by direct sense-perception rather than through words which merely symbolized reality. Most interestingly, Bentham talks about what are the ends of education: instead of knowledge and the seeking for truth, the end of education is happiness. "But, would happiness be most likely to be increased or diminished by this discipline? – Call them soldiers, call them monks, call them machines: so they were but happy ones, I should not care" (Bentham 1843, vol. IV, p. 64). Besides, we should have the same suspicion with the master as with the legislator. "Be it whoever sets up an inspection-school upon the tiptop of the principle, had need to be very sure of the master; for the boy's body is no more the child of his father's, than his mind will be of the master's mind; with no other difference than what there is between command on one side and subjection on the other" (Bentham, 1843, vol. IV, p. 64). In this sense, as Bentham points out, Rousseau was a good guide and

> nor do I imagine he would have put his Emilius into an inspection-house; but I think he would have been glad of such a school for his Sophia... Dr. Priestly, would, I imagine, be altogether as averse to it, unless, perhaps, for experiment's sake, upon a small scale, just enough to furnish an appendix to Hartley upon Man... I know who would have been delighted to set up an inspection-school, if it were only for the experiment's sake, and that is Helvetius: at least, if he had been true to his principles, which he was said to be: for by that contrivance, and by that alone, he might have been enabled to give an experimental proof of the truth of his position (supposing it to be true) that anybody may be taught anything, one person as well as another. (Bentham 1843, vol. IV, p. 67)

In Bentham's educational strategy, supervision will make the case for discipline, and the powers of reward and punishment will be used, holding out dishonour for every attention a boy omits, and honour for every exertion he can bestow. Besides, Bentham also sees the disadvantage for instruction of an excessive control.

> After applying the inspection principle first to prisons, and through mad-houses bringing it down to hospitals, will the parental feelings endure my applying it at last to schools? Will the observation of its efficacy in preventing the irregular application of undue hardship even to the guilty, be sufficient to dispel the apprehension of its tendency to introduce tyranny into the abodes of innocence and youth? (Bentham 1838–1843, vol. Letter XXI)

As we have said, Bentham gave a lot of importance to the allocation of responsibility. In examining punishments, he says that "all other punishments are deficient in point of certainty" and "When the effects of punishments are thus uncertain, there is much less ground for choice, for the effects of one punishment may be the same with those of another". He includes in that corporal punishments. He talks about afflictive punishments of deformation, or punishments which alter the exterior of the person, of disablement, or punishments consisting of disabling an organ and of mutilation. Then, when he talks about punishments which affect the exterior of the person he says:

> One of these punishments, which has a greater moral than physical effect, is a mark producing only a change of colour, and the impression of a character upon the skin; but this mark is an attestation that the individual has been guilty of some act to which contempt is attached, and the effect of contempt

is to diminish goodwill... When such a mark is inflicted on account of a crime, it is essential that a character should be given to it, which shall clearly announce the intention with which it was imposed, and which cannot be confounded with cicatrices of wounds or accidental marks... A more lenient method, which may be referred to the same head, is a practice too little used, of giving to offenders a particular dress, which serves as a livery of crime. At Hanau, in Germany, persons condemned to labour on the public works were distinguished by a black sleeve in a white coat. It is an expedient which has for its object the prevention of their escape; as a mark of infamy, it is an addition to the punishment.

And he continues:

On the score of frugality, deforming punishments are not liable to any objection; disablement and mutilation are; if the effect of either is to prevent a man getting his livelihood by his own labour, and he has no sufficient income of his own, he must either be left to perish, or be supplied with the means of subsistence; if he were left to perish, the punishment would not be mere disablement or mutilation, but death. If he be supported by the labour of others, that labour must either be bestowed gratis, as would be the case if he were supported on the charity of relations and friends, or paid for, at public cost; in either case it is a charge upon the public. This consideration might of itself be viewed as a conclusive objection against the application of these modes of punishment. (Bentham 1830, The Rationale of Punishment, Book II, Of corporal punishments)

As punishment is an evil that tries to avoid some other evil, Bentham proposed a solution to the problems of insecurity, delinquency, alcoholism and idleness in England and other European countries in the eighteenth century through an economic method of surveillance (Brunon-Ernst, 2013, p. 133). Then, corporal punishment is excluded from his project of the Chrestomatic School (Bentham, 1883c).

   Bentham says that the intellectual advantages for schoolboys of more efficient learning, lesser liability to punishment and more playtime thanks to that closer supervision by the teachers is accompanied by moral costs. He reviews what children learn from free-form lessons administered by the children to one another and to themselves and doubts:

whether the liberal spirit and energy of a free citizen would not be exchanged for the mechanical discipline of a soldier, or the austerity of a monk? – and whether the result of this highly wrought contrivance might not be constructing a set of machines under the similitude of men? (Bentham 1838–1843, vol. IV, pp. 63–64, Letter XXI, Schools)

However, when considering the system of education to be developed in the pauper panopticons, Bentham spends some time describing suitable play and athletic activities, although paupers should have less time for play than the rich people. In the pauper panopticons, there should be opportunities for running, leaping, dancing, capering but, according to Bentham, they must be linked to industry and competition. In this sense, he imagines a device or structure called the "sinking stage", which can be put to use for the purposes of pleasure, productivity and profitability, all in the same moment.

> Sinking stage, for producing an up-and-down motion by the weight of children. A stage hanging at one end of a beam, with the other end connected the burthen: water (suppose), to be raised by a bucket or by a pump, whether of the lifting or forcing kind… The sport would be, which could first get into his place. Contrivance will of course be requisite to prevent the children from receiving hurt by any considerable disproportion produced suddenly between the power and the burthen; but this is no more than what any mechanist will know how to provide for. (Bentham 2010, p. 556)

So, "the aim is to provide an opportunity for play, pleasure and exercise, but also to put the energy expended by children in play to pecuniary uses. The power produced by the machinery here would presumably be directed in some way to speed up production" (Manchester, 1824). This is needed because, for Bentham, when pauper children are being educated: "no portion of time ought to be directed exclusively to the single purpose of comfort; but amusement, as well as every other modification of comfort, ought to be infused, in the largest possible dose the economy admits of, into every particle of the mass of occupations by which time it is filled" (Bentham, 2010, pp. 555–556).

Besides, as we have said, Bentham was in favour of the system proposed by the Quaker, Joseph Lancaster (1778–1838). In the Lancasterian system, abler pupils were used as "helpers" to the teacher, passing on the information they had learned to other students. It proved to be a cheap way of making primary education more inclusive. An ideal classroom is one with the master's desk in the middle of a platform, and where the master stimulates effort and rewards merit. Class lists and registers are kept (see Lancaster, 1821, pp. 7–11). As Seintrager (1977, p. 72) says, by 1817 Bentham was convinced that the Church of England had only established the National School Society in order to thwart the efforts of Joseph Lancaster and others, including Bentham himself, to establish either nonconformist or non-sectarian schools. In Bentham's eyes this was but another attempt to keep the people in subservient blindness to the corruption of the Church and the State.

Bentham is especially critical of religious institutions because he thought that the belief in the existence of an all-powerful Being, who will distribute pains and punishments to humanity, in an infinite and future condition of existence, leads to assigning to that deity a character of caprice and tyranny, of reverence. Those are beliefs "out-of-experience" that lead to censorship of pleasure and to uncertain terrors. They create religious sects and visionaries that claim to be able to interpret the supernatural interventions. It creates an anti-establishment power in the State.

Reticent about making his views about the Church known, he sought to publish an attack on the Church in 1817 under the pseudonym "Oxford Graduate". He was unsuccessful in this effort because the government was punishing publishers and booksellers of anonymous works which it considered to be libellous or blasphemous. But, in Bentham (1818), Bentham published *Church of Englandism, and its catechism examined*, in which he delineates the programme of a moral Christianity and includes an attack on the National School Society. In Bentham (1823) he publishes *Not Paul but Jesus* where he tries to demonstrate that Paul was the antichrist, a fake with a different doctrine to Jesus'. When he classifies the sciences under the consideration of their relative utility, he considers the value of the religious idea to be negative. He publishes *Analysis of the influence of the natural religion on the temporal happiness of mankind* obviating the truth or falsehood of these doctrines. If they are false and useful, it is positive to extend the idea of punishment and posthumous prize. But the moral arithmetic of these uncertain and distant expectations makes their benefits minor when compared with their prejudices, in spite of the fact that their intensity and duration are boundless. If they had influence, the result would be absolute privation and sacrifice.

6.2. Owen's educational strategy

Robert Owen had very advanced ideas on education for his time. He thought that working class children must be taught something more than to read, to write and the rules of arithmetic. For him, natural sciences, music, dance, and games were very important. He thought that education had to be natural and spontaneous, but in particular pleasant.

The New Institution and the School of Owen were rapidly completed in New Lanark and offer two of the three best surviving examples anywhere of a school erected on Lancasterian principles. However, Owen's life made him think differently to Bentham. Owen was educated in Newtown in mid-Wales by the Owens, who possessed practical retailing and administrative skills that they passed on to their offspring. Newtown was located in one of the most profoundly rural parts of southern Britain, yet beginning to be touched by economic change. It was a model for a self-contained community of its time. He evidently made such good progress at school that when he was eight or nine years old the master made him his "assistant and usher" in return for free education for the rest of his schooling. Owen seems to have played the role of monitor, in a school modelled on the ideas of educational reformers like the previously mentioned Lancaster, and the Scot, Dr Andrew Bell (1753–1832), later adopted by Owen himself in the schools at New Lanark. Really, this was mass production applied to education, where specially selected senior pupils passed on learning by heart to their juniors, sometimes in large numbers, in what became known in France as "mutual instruction". So Robert "acquired the habit of teaching others what [he] knew" (Owen, 1857, p. 3), and this experience probably gave him early responsibilities for the care, supervision and education of others. He also gained some knowledge of the elementary school curriculum, which he would revisit in his later career.

At the same time his education was carried beyond the schoolroom. "In this period", he says, "I was fond of and had a strong passion for reading everything which fell in my way", and his family's position in the community opened up to him the libraries of the learned – the clergyman, the doctor and the lawyer – "with permission to take home any volume" that he liked. His reading matter, as a result, included many classics like *The Pilgrim's Progress, Robinson Crusoe* and accounts of Captain Cook's voyages (Owen, 1857 p. 3). Robert apparently believed every word in the books to be true. Even the examples of Robinson Crusoe may have proved significant in shaping his views about enterprise. Besides reading, Owen learned to play the clarinet, and enjoyed music and dancing. Both ultimately featured strongly in his social and educational thinking and were given a prominent place in the curriculum at New Lanark and later Owenite communities in Britain and the United States (see Davidson, 2010).

Synthesizing reformist ideas from the Age of Enlightenment but drawing on his own experience as an industrialist, Owen constructed *A New View of Society* (1816) calling for a widespread social change, with education at its core. The educational Institution planned in New Lanark or in the Community of Equality at New Harmony Indiana (1824–1828) would be guided by mutual co-operation rather than profit. The new Institute for the Formation of Character was not formally opened until New Year's Day 1816. In the "Address to the Inhabitants of New Lanark" and in *A New View of Society*, Owen articulated his belief in some sort of material determinism "that the character of man is without a single exception, always formed for him". *A Statement Regarding the New Lanark Establishment* showed a detailed account of his ideas for the development of the New Institution. After these experiences, Owen arrived at the conclusion that we are affected by a certain environment or climate of gratitude and inclusion, of self confidence and love.

According to Owen, the teachers must not threaten any of the children; but were always to speak to them in a kind manner. For him, education was to be based on the play principle, no child being forced in any way (see Donnachie, 2003). However, toys were rarely seen, for to Robert Owen's mind "thirty or fifty infants, when left to themselfs, will always amuse each other without useless childish toys". When they became bored or distracted "a young active teacher will easily find and provide something they will be interested in seeing and hearing explained". Robert Owen's (1857, p. 140) description of the infants' actual instruction is worth quoting:

> The children were not to be annoyed with books; but were to be taught the uses and nature or qualities of the common things around them, by familiar conversation when the children's curiosity was excited so as to induce them to ask questions respecting them.

The schoolroom for the infants' instruction was furnished with paintings, chiefly of animals, with maps, and often supplied with natural objects from the gardens, fields and woods – the examination and explanation of which always excited their curiosity and created an animated conversation between the children and their instructors.

The children at four and above that age showed an eager desire to understand the use of maps of the four quarters of the world upon a large scale purposely hung in the room to attract their attention. Buchanan their master, was first taught their use and then how to instruct the children for their amusement – for with these infants everything was made to be amusement."

In addition to this elementary instruction, those over two years old were given dancing lessons and those aged four years and upwards were taught singing. William Davidson, writing in 1828 long after Robert Owen's departure, observed dancing being taught in the school (Donnachie, 2000, pp. 156–171).Many years later in 1903, Frank Podmore, Robert Owen's most distinguished biographer, visited New Lanark. Podmore's guide, John Melrose, told him that in his boyhood thirty years before he and the other village children still danced every morning from 7.15 to 8.00 am. Actually, what most impressed the visitors who came to New Lanark between 1815 and 1825 was the importance of dancing, music and military exercise in the school curriculum, as they were basic methodologies to achieve self command.

According to Owen, the school was attended by "every child above one year old", although some observers thought the youngest were probably two or three years old. Owen stressed the importance of character formation and, so, during the first few months of the nursery schools, he daily watched and superintended the children, expecting that if the foundation was truly laid, we can expect a satisfactory structure. Pupils are supposed to develop thanks to the interpersonal stimulus. In the Institute dancing lessons were begun at two years of age and visitors were astonished to see how "these children, standing up 70 couples at a time in the dancing room, and often surrounded by many strangers, would with the uttermost ease and natural grace go through all the dances of Europe, with so little direction from their master". "Owen", Griscom [John Griscom, noted scientist and educator] noted, "has discovered that dancing is one means of reforming vicious habits. He thinks it affects this by promoting cheerfulness and contentment, and thus diverting attention from things that are vile and degrading" (Donnachie, 2000, p. 170). The children were also taught to sing in harmony in choirs of 200 or more, performing settings of Scottish and other traditional songs, to the delight of Robert Owen and his visitors. The question is that this pedagogy seemed to work in that context and children were also equipped with basic literacy and numeracy. According to Dr Henry Macnab, who in 1819 had been sent to report on the place by the Duke of Kent, said. "The children and youth in this delightful colony are superior in point of conduct and character to all the children and youths I have ever seen. I shall not attempt to give a faithful description of the beautiful fruits of the social affections displayed in the young, innocent and fascinating countenances of these happy children" (Macnab, 1819, pp. 136–137). Yet education was only a single facet of a more powerful social gospel which preached community building on the New Lanark model as a solution to contemporary evils in the wider world.

Later, this has been extensively demonstrated, that music reinforces memory and makes it easier to recite words in a helpful order, and that it helps children learn social values such as taking turns or managing group communication. It also aids communication when the feelings are difficult to put into words (Moyles 2014, p. 205).

Most working children, however, continued their education at evening classes in the Institute. Attendance at the school for all ages was practically free. Robert Owen gave details of attendance during the Select Committee on Education of 1816. After the opening of the Institute and reduction of the working day to ten and three-quarter hours (less meal-breaks), attendance rose rapidly.

Dale Owen also left a detailed report of the school for the older children of the community. Apparently, for older children Owen adopted in part the methods of Lancaster, whereby certain boys and girls chosen to be monitors passed on lessons learned by heart to other children, so the factory system seemed to be applied to education. Great difficulty was experienced in finding suitable books for the pupils. Tales of adventure, voyages and travel were popular. Children were questioned on all they read, and encouraged to look upon books as a means to an end. In writing, copy-books were abandoned as soon as possible, and the children were encouraged to develop their own style. Arithmetic was at first taught "on the plan generally adopted at that time in Scotland" (Podmore, 1906, p. 138), but soon after, as we will see, Pestalozzi's system of mental arithmetic was introduced.

Besides these elementary studies, and forming perhaps the most notable feature of Owen's educational system in the Institute, was instruction by lecture, discussion and debate, in geography, natural science, ancient and modern history, and what we might call civics or contemporary studies. The talk was usually short, so as not to lose the attention of the young listeners and time would be allowed for questions. Contemporary prints showed the extensive use made of visual material: history time-charts or "Streams of Time" and maps, each of which were differently coloured, and represented a nation. Geography lessons played a prominent part in the education of children at New Lanark, and had a strong moral undertone, for the children were often reminded that but for an accident of birth they might have been born into a different society with values totally unlike those of their own. They were taught to respect other people's ideas and way of life and never to be uncharitable or intolerant. Field studies were important, and youngsters were encouraged to go out into the woods and fields surrounding the village.

6.3. Bentham's modernity: behaviourism

As Blake (2009, p. 55) comments, it is not usual to notice any Benthamite turning his back on questions on his/her own thinking (this critical quality was more typical of James Mill). But a self questioning spirit also depends on outside approval or disapproval. And Himmelfarb (1995) reminds us that Victorianism was an age of high intellectual, moral, and spiritual tension, in which intellectual coherence was demanded. This has counteracted a pedagogical paradigm that still continues to exist in many places, and even in the United States of the twenty-first century where corporal punishment is still authorized, often referred to as "paddling," in public schools for the purpose of disciplining students (Pollard-Sacks, 2009). However, a wealth of social science research demonstrates beyond any reasonable doubt that it is an ineffective educational tool that creates unnecessary and very serious risks to children. Fright, stress, and other strong negative feelings can interfere with cognitive functioning and result in cognitive deficits such as erroneous or limited coding of events and diminished elaboration.

In the final analysis, Bentham shows a way to obtain a conductual or behaviourist education, a change in external behaviour achieved through using reinforcement and repetition, such as the research project defended by Skinner (1838). Desired behaviour is rewarded, while the undesired behaviour is punished. Incorporating behaviourism into the classroom allows educators to assist their students in excelling both academically and personally. This has to do with involuntary behaviour or with voluntary operant behaviour that can be tested in animals, and is maintained by its consequences with reinforcement and punishment being either positive (delivered following a response), or negative (withdrawn following a response) (Skinner, 1969). Here, the teacher is the dominant person in the classroom and takes complete control. Evaluation of learning comes from him who decides what is right or wrong. The learner does not have any opportunity for evaluation or reflection within the learning process, they are simply told what is right or wrong.

However, we may also relate Bentham's doctrine of education to the creative education in schools in the late twentieth and early twenty-first centuries in the UK, whereby the teaching of creative subjects such as art, drama and music, were reinvented inside a new utilitarian paradigm and tied to outcomes such as "improving employability" of young people. According to Ken Robinson (1977) education should focus on awakening creativity through alternative didactic processes that put less emphasis on standardised testing, and give the "responsibility for defining the course of education to individual schools and teachers. Here, "creativity" is a personal capacity, linked to survival inside the increasingly uncertain and precarious labour market of the twenty-first century. Helen Nicholson (2011) has also spoken about pressures on children and teachers to "be more creative" in illuminating terms.

Obviously, this is not free, unsupervised, completely purposeless play from past and present scripts of children's education and development. Actually, the conceptualization of learning using some behaviourist approach has been considered "superficial" by some modern theorists, as the focus is on external changes in behaviour i.e. not interested in the internal processes of learning leading to behaviour change and has no place for the emotions involved in the process.

As Gallhofer and Haslam (1996) comment, also in Chrestomathia Jeremy Bentham included bookkeeping/accounting as a compulsory subject at the "final and highest stage" of the school's educational programme in a dialectical process that promises to engender progress and emancipation (see Horkheimer and Adorno, 1972). Its historical context was significant for the formation of many of today's institutions and practices, including accounting education (see Goldberg, 1957; Hume, 1970, 1981; Bahmueller, 1981; Hoskin 1979). For Owen, however, the day-to-day business is what makes accounting principles suitable. This Bentham-Owen discussion is the neverending debate in which Bentham will give precedence to theory over practice and will be very anxious about expressing some legal fictions in books with the chimerical hope of making them in transcription nearer to reality.

6.4. Owen's modernity: constructivism

The already mentioned Owen's pedagogical practice may actually be considered as a forerunner of constructivism (Piaget, 1950). Here, the instructor is a mere facilitator (Glasersfeld, 1989) and the instructor and pupils learn from each other, knowledge being subjective and objective at the same time. This creates a dynamic interaction: the learner is not a simple mirror but he constructs his own understanding through the interaction between his experiences and ideas. The learner will try to find regularity and order in the events of the world even in the absence of full or complete information and based on common sense.

Indeed, constructivism tends to focus on human development in the context of the social world (Vygotsky, 1978). Decontextualised knowledge does not give us the skills to apply or understand authentic tasks. This situated learning creates a feedback due to the assessment process that serves as a direct foundation for further development. In social constructivism, young children develop their thinking abilities by interacting with other children, adults and the physical world. This includes problem-based instruction, reciprocal teaching and, peer collaboration, which involve learning with others. For constructivism, previous knowledge is basic to construct future knowledge, which is linked in meaningful learning (Ausubel, 2000). This implies a conscious experience that emerges when potentially meaningful signs, symbols, concepts, or propositions are related to and incorporated within a given individual's cognitive structure. When individuals' experiences contradict their internal representations, they may change their perceptions of the experiences to fit their internal representations (accommodation) or they may reframe their model of the way the world works, learning from the experience of failure, or others' failure.

Owen stressed the importance of a proper education from the early years saying that

> it must be evident to those who have been in the practice of observing children with attention, that much of good or evil is taught to or acquired by a child at a very early period of its life; that much of temper or disposition is correctly or incorrectly formed before he attains his second year; and that many durable impressions are made at the termination of the first 12 or even 6 months of his existence. (Owen, 1814, p. 4, Third essay)

Actually, for those first years of life, Owen´s educational methods were specially based on the theories of the educational reformer Pestalozzi, whose conclusions were published in Paris in 1805. It is possible that Owen had known Pestalozzi and had it translated by his boys' tutor. Pestalozzi had actually founded several educational institutions both in German- and French-speaking regions of Switzerland and wrote many works explaining his modern principles of education. His motto was "Learning by head, hand and heart". By reducing knowledge to its elements and by constructing a series of psychologically ordered exercises, anybody could teach their children effectively. He emphasized that every aspect of the child's life contributed to the formation of personality, character, and reason. Pestalozzi's educational methods were child-centred and based on individual differences, sense perception, and the student's self-activity. Pestalozzi was an important influence on the theory of physical education; he developed a regimen of physical exercise and outdoor activity linked to general, moral, and intellectual education that reflected his ideal of harmony and human autonomy. Besides, Pestalozzi's philosophy of education was based on the premise that human nature was essentially good. He had a four-sphere concept of life. The first three "exterior" spheres – home and family, and state and nation – recognized the importance of the remembrance of one's past and the nurturing of individuality. It posited that education, having provided a means of satisfying one's basic needs, results in inner peace and gratitude of the world given.

Actually, as Pestalozzi lived with Charles Mayo from 1819 to 1822, he greatly influenced Charles and Elizabeth Mayo, pedagogists, who trained teachers, showing how young children could be introduced to new ideas by examining 100 objects like a wooden cube, a pin, a rubber or a piece of glass and having a dialogue with the teacher (Shepherd, 2004). Joseph Neef, who came to Philadelphia to open a model school based on Pestalozzian principles in 1806 was contacted by Robert Owen when he designed to create the utopian village on the plains of Indiana at New Harmony in 1825 (see Ruddy, 2000). Also, William Maclure introduced Pestalozzianism into the United States. "While the community was in the main an expression of the social ideals of Robert Owen, the educational interests were entrusted to William Maclure. Maclure called Joseph Neef and other Americanized Pestalozzians to his assistance in working out his educational experiment" (Monroe, 1969, pp. 109–110). "The community experiment at New Harmony collapsed after only two years, because of dissension between Maclure and Owen…" (Downs, 1975, p.120) but Owen attributed his experiment's failure to the fact that, more than Pestalozzian principles, he lacked from the Lancasterian method of teaching (Monroe, p.122) "Maclure and Owen differed rather widely in their opinions of educational practice" (Monroe, 1969, p.122).

Owen's ideas were based on an intrinsic motivation of the children to learn. Many descriptions of the Institute's arrangements survive, but the most helpful is that furnished by the young Robert Dale Owen, who following his return from Switzerland occupied himself in teaching and writing a book about the school and its curriculum, published in 1824, *Outline of the System of Education at New Lanark.* According to the younger Owen:

> The principal school-room is fitted up with desks and forms on the Lancasterian plan, having a free passage down the centre of the room… The other and smaller apartment on the second floor has the walls hung round with representations of the most striking zoological and mineralogical specimens, including quadrupeds, birds, fishes, reptiles, insects, shells, minerals etc. At one end there is a gallery, adapted for the purpose of an orchestra, and at the other end are hung very large representations of the two hemispheres; each separate country, as well as the various seas, islands etc. being differently coloured, but without any names attached to them. This room is used as a lecture- and ball-room, and it is here that the dancing and singing lessons are daily given. It is likewise occasionally used as a reading-room for some of the classes…

During the first few months of the nursery school Robert "acquired the most sincere affections of all the children" and apparently also won over the parents "who were highly delighted with the improved conduct, extraordinary progress, and continually increasing happiness of their children." Robert Owen was cautious about the selection of teachers for "it was in vain to look to any old teachers upon the old system of instruction by books". As he said, he had very little belief in books, he selected from the villagers "two persons who had a great love for and unlimited patience with infants". His unlikely choice was a former handloom weaver, James Buchanan, described as a "simple-minded, kind-hearted individual who could hardly read or write himself", but who was willing to do exactly what Robert Owen told him. Buchanan's assistant was to be Molly Young, a 17-year-old village girl. Robert Owen's instructions to his new infant master and assistant were simple as, as we have said:

> They were on no account ever to beat any one of the children or to threaten them in any word or action or to use abusive terms; but were always to speak to them with a pleasant voice and in a kind manner. They should tell the infants and children (for they had all from 1 to 6 years old under their charge) that they must on all occasions do all they could to make their playfellows happy – and that the older ones, from 4 to 6 years of age, should take especial care of younger ones, and should assist to teach them to make each other happy" (Owen, 1857, p. 139).

Much of this came indirectly from Pestalozzi, who also emphasized the importance of kindness and common sense in his teaching. Owen's practice led him, then, to open to an interpersonality philosophy, that is to say, in contradiction with utilitarianism. He found in his practice that there is a common world to be perceived, not through images and impressions, but through the appreciation of the present that allows us to be affected by a certain environment or a climate of inclusion in it.

6.5. The pleasure of movement: another relation of Owen with Adam Smith

In his educational strategy, more than with utilitarianism, Owen is linked to realism and philosophical criticism. As Levine (2015, p. 103) comments, Owen did not follow the external sense perception or the internal sentimentality options, but he was one of the founders of a psychology of social conditioning. Actually, this is the case of Adam Smith's philosophy and ethics. Smith, contrary to the traditional opinion, fiercely criticized utilitarianism trying to construct an economic theory not based on utility (Raynor, 1984).[1] *Das Adam Smith problem* of the nineteenth century (in Oncken, 1898) has been overcome in the twenty-first century, and the long and recent debate deriving from it could also help us to understand the differences between Bentham's and Owen's philosophies.

Certainly, against Hume (1964a), Smith thought that the idea of utility is a mental hallucination (Trincado, 2014b). He defined pleasure as something near to gratitude, that is to say, a natural gift that it is not necessary to bring forward or anticipate in an image. This gratitude is felt in calm events, from which pleasure can begin, "for whatever is the cause of pleasure naturally excites our gratitude" (Smith, EPS: History of Astronomy: III: 2: 48.). As we shall see, this calmness gives us a "sixth sense" without which we could not actually feel the other five senses: sight, hearing, touch, smell and taste. It is the perception of time and of depth, that is linked to a common reality that we share and means time needed to arrive where the objects are placed. This, according to Smith, is much to be developed by music and dance. Certainly, it is the case with the performers of dancing and music, in which we enjoy the pleasure of movement.[2] According to Smith, after the pleasures which arise from the gratification of the bodily appetites, there seem to be none more natural to man than music and dancing (Smith, EPS: II: 1: 187) as nothing is more graceful than habitual cheerfulness, which is always founded upon a peculiar relish for all the little pleasures, which common occurrences afford (Smith, TMS: I: ii: 5: 2: pp. 41–42.). Then, according to Smith happiness consists of and depends on tranquility and enjoyment, on the acceptance of what it is, although it may be painful, but the desire to improve its nature with your action. On the same lines, Burke was grieved by those who, as they had everything in life, they have nothing to feel in the joy of living, as they do not allow nature to continue its own process and even anticipate the desire and overcome enjoyment with pondered outlines and tricks of pleasure, so there is no interval or obstacle between desire and achievement (Burke, 1909, p. 23).

The teachings in the Owenite Institute of music and dancing were opposed by the Quakers Allen and Foster, claiming that this training was taking precedence over religion (Gordon, 1994). This led to Owen leaving the school in 1824. They thought that those bodily training sessions implied bodily pleasures that could let the children be uncontrolled. For those Quakers, self-control has to do with the avoidance of any sensation (apathia). The same as the Epicurean system, they considered the search for corporal pleasure and the avoidance of corporal pain – the body as a centre of sensations – as the only motive of action. According to Epicurus, every mental pleasure or pain is derived from one of the body and from the self-preservation principle; but mental pleasures and pains are more acute than corporal pleasures. Nevertheless, in Epicurus' system, future uncertainty is painful; so the abstention from the seeking of pleasures let man live quietly, without fears, awaiting unavoidable death.

Adam Smith refutes this need of apathy and affirms that the wise man is sensitive to whatever pleasure: all Epicurian theory is based on the seeking of prudential pleasure, not in the correction of active sensations, which are felt by leaving the mind free, accepting one's sensations and thoughts (Smith, TMS: VII: ii: 2: pp. 294–300). For Smith, the first movement is not due to self-preservation, an ex post sensation of utility, but to a desire for instinctive movement that does not depend on past experiences.

> The desire for changing our situation necessarily involves some idea of externality; or of motion into a place different from that in which we actually are; end even the desire of remaining in the same place involves some idea of at least the possibility of changing. Those sensations could not easily have answered the intention of Nature, had they not thus instinctively suggested some vague notion of external existence. (Smith 1980, pp. 167–168: Of the External Senses: 86)

In Epicurus there is a contradiction, because for Epicurus human action is passive. According to Adam Smith, active principles are possible, but depend on some free self. Smith comments that in the beginning of the formation of language, human beings must have faced the difficulty that the word "I" was very special (LRBL, Languages, 34, p. 221). The verb structure "I am" expresses an internal feeling of gratitude of existence and, in this first stage, it is inseparable from wonder and the sense of reality (Astronomy III.2, p. 49). Haakonssen (1996, pp. 135–148) points out that Smith is based on Samuel von Cocceji's theory, that asserts that the individual should understand his life to be a personal gift from God.

But, according to Smith there are two different selves: one dependent, unreal and mortal, with reactive principles of movement; the other "immortal", that may afford emotional regulation and where perception and active principles are bound to emerge (TMS VI.iii.25, p. 247; TMS III.ii.32, p. 131). The imaginary man requires an impulse 'from outside' to act; the 'I' that observes the present acts 'towards the outside' and represents an identification with ubiquity. It requires, as Ricoeur (1984, p. 53) says, being present in the passage. This implies an identification with an observer of memory – and of the present moment. It has something of what we have previously called a 'sixth sense', clearly differentiated, and made up of depth and volume. Without depth sense, the object would stay in the

area of learned concepts in the mind (see Trincado, 2003a and Huxley, 1963).
"The tangible world... has three dimensions, Length, Breadth and Depth. The
visible world... has only two, Length and Breadth. It presents to us only a flat
surface... (in the same manner as a picture does)" (External Senses, pp. 50–52,
150–152). It is thanks to movement – in time – that we can perceive the variation
of perspective (External Senses, pp. 59, 155). If at any point we have perhaps
confused flatness with depth, we only need 'time' to situate ourselves in the
intuitive position capable of understanding perspective. Smith says that, when the
blind man couched for cataracts "was just beginning to understand the strong and
distinct perspective of Nature, the faint and feeble perspective of Painting made
no impression upon him" (External Senses 67).[3] Equally, Gestalt theory speaks
of perception as something whole. 'Shapes' are perceived in an immediate, intuitive way (Marchán, 1996, pp. 239–240).

Smith's belief in the existence of a free, self-restrained 'I', immune to pleasure-
pain pulsation leads him to specially praise the virtue of self-command (Montes,
2004, pp. 101–114). And self-command does not imply negating oneself. The
passions, instead of disappearing, 'lie concealed in the breast of the sufferer'
(TMS V. ii. 11, p. 208). Actually, we feel more with present feelings that, like
music and dancing, are not self regarding. Contrary to Hume's argumentation,
Smith says that the virtues and passions we acquire by habit are not so admired,
because we find it difficult to enter into another person's habit, as we have not
acquired it by ourselves. In consequence, prudence not addressed to the care for
oneself is necessarily more admirable (Smith, TMS: VI: i: 15, p. 216). In brief,
Smith gave special importance in his moral theory to self-command, based on a
definition of freedom in positive terms. When we act guided by a moral reality
we do not listen to the applause of the real spectator. This provides us with the
tranquility of knowing that we are worthy of love. Sense of merit is made up of
a direct sympathy with the sentiments of the agent and an indirect sympathy with
the gratitude of those who receive the benefit of his actions (TMS II.i.v.2, p. 74).
This is somewhat different from Hume's account, in which sympathy consists in
feeling what others ACTUALLY feel in their circumstances. So, as Fleischacker
(2012) says, Hume's may be called a "contagion" account of sympathy, while
Smith's is a "projective" account that opens up the possibility that our feelings on
another person's behalf may often not match the feelings she herself has. A rich
discussion of Smith on sympathy can be found in Griswold (1999, ch.2).

The same as for Owen, actually, active principles, such as curiosity and
wonder, are for Adam Smith to be based on self-love that, as opposed to selfishness, is a morally positive principle, as it is the basis of the capacity to learn: the
one who does not believe in himself (or herself) shuts off his intuitive capacity,
losing one of the underpinnings of existence, that is, "attention to life". "Those
unfortunate persons, whom nature has formed a good deal below the common
level, seem sometimes to rate themselves still more below it than they really are.
This humility appears sometimes to sink them into idiotism" (TMS VI.iii.49,
p. 260). Besides, for self-love to activate itself it is fundamental that there be a
consciousness of reciprocity and that others believe in one's words. "The man

who had the misfortune to imagine that nobody believed a single word he said, would feel himself the outcast of human society" (TMS VII.iv.26, p. 336). When Smith looks in the mirror, he tries to discern self-love that is neither self-referencing nor dependent but that is grateful or friendly to reality. 'One's own face becomes then the most agreeable object which a looking-glass can represent to us…; whether handsome or ugly, whether old or young, it is the face of a friend always' (Imitative Arts I.17, p. 186).

This has much to do with the fashionable psychology of mindfulness that affords emotional regulation through the acceptance of whatever feeling attaining the awareness, appropriation and identification with the observer of the particular time of the individual. As Haynes and Feldman (2004) show, mindfulness can be seen as a strategy that stands in contrast to a strategy of avoidance of emotion on the one hand and to the strategy of emotional over engagement on the other. It is putting yourself in touch with the real present, out of time sequence. This 'living present' analysed by Husserl implies a direct perceptive contact, a 'now' that retains but also seeks the future. Time is not defined as a succession of moments, but rather it is like the identification of the subject as in the following of a narration, with a past, a present and a future (Ricoeur, 1984, p. 27). These open movements allow the mechanism of memory to be activated (see Bergson, 1911).

6.6. Conclusion and differences between Bentham and Owen

Neither Owen, nor Bentham, was personally very open minded: Owen, the same as Bentham, did not accept different ways of thinking to his own. This explains Owen's lack of readings. And, in some way, this discards the possibility of fine conclusions of their philosophy.

> A true thinker can only be justly estimated when his thoughts have worked their way into minds formed in a different school… A clear insight, indeed, into this necessity is the only rational or enduring basis of philosophical tolerance; the only condition under which liberality in matters of opinion can be anything better than a polite synonym for indifference beween one opinion and another (Mill, 1980, pp. 103–104).

In his debate with Coleridge, Owen is also shown to be somewhat utilitarian in his wording and so, Benthamite in nature, not so compromised with profound human feelings but with rationality and the progress of the human mind.

However, there is a clear difference in Bentham's and Owen's educational strategy. As we have seen, their different concepts of responsibility led Bentham to consider the determining of responsibility one of the most important elements of moral, social and political order, especially in terms of punishment, adjudication and publicity. Besides, imitation and empathy are not so important for Bentham as is the case with Owen, who wanted to substitute cooperation for competition. According to Owen, education was to be based on the play principle. In Bentham's case, there is no such awareness of the other, and rewards or punishments are just to be memorized not with an objective of being approved of or recognized by some fellow creatures, but for avoiding punishment. Owen's idea of incentives has more to do with positive rewards and recognition for participation; on the other hand, Bentham's idea of incentives has more to do with punishment for offences and sanctions denying participation. In this sense, Owen tries to empower and personalize the people, giving positive rewards that will not deny the intrinsic motivation to work. Bentham tries to depersonalize and give negative incentives through fear of isolation, making the motivation extrinsic.

Bentham considered that dancing and music cannot be found anywhere in his proposed school of Chrestomathia, or they should be deferred either to a later hour, or a later age – although for him it was important to include accountancy.[4] For Bentham, the only utility of music and dance is to exhibit them when they are extraordinary, not the ordinary feeling of freedom and reality that it renders or the simple play sensation with other children. "Talent-cultivation principle. – Natural talents of any kind, manifesting themselves in an extraordinary degree to receive appropriate culture. Examples: Musical habits principally: – viz. an extraordinary fine voice, or an extraordinary good ear, and thence affection for the pursuit. (In the instance of a natural taste for the arts of design, or of strength or comeliness adapted to dancing, or other theatrical exhibitions, superiority is less manifest, culture is less exceptionable in the eyes of a severe moralist, and the object is of inferior account.)".[5] This is especially due to the fact that music encroaches on the freedom of others and every offence needs a punishment, and not to bear other sounds needs the avoidance of musical experience: "[Admission pregnant with exclusion:] … Thus, if instruction in Music were admitted, the noise would be such, that, while it was going on, the requisite degree of attention could not be paid to any other" (footnote 94).

Bentham, then, expresses a freedom based on the harm principle that holds that individual actions should only be limited to prevent harm to other individuals. This was stated in France's *Declaration of the Rights of Man and of the Citizen* of 1789 as, "Liberty consists in the freedom to do everything which injures no one else; hence the exercise of the natural rights of each man has no limits except those which ensure to the other members of the society the enjoyment of the same rights. These limits can only be determined by law." John Stuart Mill also articulated this principle in *On Liberty,* where he argued that, "The only purpose for which power can be rightfully exercised over any member of a civilized community, against his will, is to prevent harm to others" (Mill, 1978, p. 9).

But for Bentham there are many different non-freedoms depending on the pain of not being free: "Liberty being a negative idea (exemption from obligation), it follows that the loss of liberty is a positive idea. To lose the condition of a freeman is to become a slave. But the word slave or state of slavery, has not any very definite meaning which serves to designate that condition, as existing in different countries. The pain of servitude would be different, according to the class to which the offender might be aggregated" (Bentham, 1830, Book III, Chapter V, Section V). Bentham often carried his argument quite far. Although opposed to that "civil inequality" known as slavery, as we have mentioned, he argued against its immediate abolition because to do so might threaten the security of property and he added that men "who are rendered free by... gradations, will be much more capable of being so than if you had taught them to tread justice under foot, for the sake of introducing a new social order" (Bentham, 1840b, p. 131).

Negative freedom, however, is really indefinable. It consists of not doing or doing as little as possible for dread of bothering the freedom of others. The man tries not to affect the others' "pleasures" because society is conceived as a set of atomistic desires longed for by a few individuals who look for the clear demarcation with the other. In the last analysis, the skepticism of freedom is absolute, and utilitarians tend to think that people in power know what is good, and can establish where freedom begins and ends. Bentham was aware of this, which in a certain way was questioning the idea of a progress in freedom achievements. His psychological theory where people maximize their happiness always leads us to an almost necessary best of possible worlds. Thus, it takes to relativism, something which Bentham affirms in *Essay on the Influence of Time and Place on Matters of Legislation*. For that reason, Benthamian institutions do not seek freedom, but the greatest happiness of the greatest number comparing different alternatives based on a somewhat objective measure.

> When a man feels himself favourably inclined towards a proposed institution and disposed to entertain wishes of seeing it brought into existence, a difficulty that naturally presents itself to him, and which he as naturally wishes to see removed, is – how to account for its non-existence... lest the apparent utility should turn out to be secretly overbalanced by some non-apparent inconvenience... These indications may, it would seem to be afforded by a comparative glance. (Stark 1952a, pp. 322–324: Supply without Burden)

But Owen's freedom is not negative freedom – to do whatever does no harm or does not affect others. It is positive freedom, to be free to have a personal opinion and perspective. For Owen private interests are no more than the prudence that Adam Smith disdained; educated men have a relation with common reality not in terms of property, but of gratitude. Real freedom only occurs in the heart, at least when the heart is changed and made new.

Notes

1 Haakonssen and Vivenza freed Smith from the utilitarian label in his moral and in his law theory (Haakonssen, 1981, pp. 97–100; Vivenza, 2001, p. 143). The problem of Smith's utilitarianism has also been presented, amongst other works, in Griswold, (1999, p. 540) and. Trincado (2003a).
2 Smith, EPS: Of the Nature of that Imitation which takes place in what are called the Imitative Arts: I – II: pp. 176–207.
3 See also External Senses 52, pp. 65–67, 151–152, 159–160.
4 Bentham, 1838–1843, Vol. 8.8/7/2016. http://oll.libertyfund.org/titles/2208#Bentham_0872-08_268
5 Bentham (1838–1843). Volume 8, 8/7/2016. http://oll.libertyfund.org/titles/2208#lf0872-08_label_2098.

7 Owen, Bentham and political economists

7.1. Social circles

While a cheery conversationalist, as John Stuart Mill later recalled Bentham "failed in deriving light from other minds." Because of this, Bentham was surrounded not by knowledgeable disciples but lived in a great house surrounded by some largely uncomprehending aides who copied revision after revision of his illegible prose to get it ready for eventual publication. Mackintosh said that his disciples were attracted by his charm, in spite of his writings (Mackintosh, Dissertations, p. 237, in Halévy, 1972, p. 306). In the perceptive words of William Thomas (1979, p. 25), they "looked on his work with a certain resigned skepticism as if its faults were the result of eccentricities beyond the reach of criticism or remonstrance." As Thomas continues,

> The idea that he was surrounded by a band of eager disciples who drew from his system a searching critique of every aspect of contemporary society, which they were later to apply to various institutions in need of reform, is the product of later liberal myth-making. So far as I know, Bentham's circle is quite unlike that of any other great political thinker. It consisted not so much of men who found in his work a compelling explanation of the social world around them and gathered about him to learn more of his thoughts, as of men caught in a sort of expectant bafflement at the progress of a work which they would have liked to help on to completion but which remained maddeningly elusive and obscure.

What Bentham needed desperately was sympathetic editors of his work, but his relationship with his followers precluded that from happening. "For this reason," adds Thomas, "the steadily accumulating mass of manuscripts remained largely a terra incognita, even to the intimate members of our circle." As a result, for example, such a major work in manuscript, *Of Laws in General*, astonishingly remained unedited, and unpublished, until current times.

For that reason, what Bentham writes on value, production and distribution, growth, employment or money, was not accessible to the economists of the nineteenth century, or only after Bowring's edition of 1843 (Collison Black, 1988).

According to Halévy, in the first part of the nineteenth century we can only consider Samuel Bailey as Benthamian, who in 1825 published "A Dissertation on the Nature, Measures and Causes of Value", one of the most penetrating critiques to Ricardo of the century. He was called "the Bentham of Hallamshire". He thought that the laws of political economy are an express operation of certain motives of human mind, a vision that contrasts with the physical and material theory of Ricardo. He was criticized by James Mill in the Westminster Review, January, 1826, in an anonymous article. Here, the difference between the Benthamian and the Ricardian politics, with which classical economists are identified, is made clear (Halévy, 1928, pp. 353–354).

As Rothbard (1995) says, although James Mill and David Ricardo have been considered loyal Benthamites in utilitarian philosophy and in a belief in political democracy, in economics the question is somewhat different. Bentham's ideas on economics were not taken into account, except for those of *Defence of Usury* (Collison, 1988). The classical economists favoured utilitarian ideas, but they did not use the felicific calculus to explain economic actions.[1] After his attack on usury laws, Ricardo scoffed at almost all of later Benthamite economics. As Rothbard comments, by using this inductive statistical method, Bentham was denying economics altogether – that is, the possibility of laws abstracting from particular circumstances and applying to all exchanges or actions everywhere. For instance, Bentham defended such a thing as a maximum price control on bread, a proposal clearly against the classical economics doctrine. Indeed, Bentham changes his ideas easily, and, as we have said, in *Defence of a Maximum* he reneges on his condemnation of the usury laws: a maximum rate of interest that allowed government to borrow more cheaply and he went on to admit that he now found this "advantage" decisive, so that now he would place usury laws on the governmental agenda: "I should expect to find the advantages of it in this respect predominate over its disadvantages in all others" (Stark, 1954, pp. 288–289).

Mill and Ricardo were resolute defenders of Say's law and the Turgot-Smith analysis, so they were firm in successfully discouraging the publication of the "The True Alarm." There, Bentham's major theme was that money is the cause of wealth, something that Ricardo rejected flatly. Again treating his earlier views on usury, Bentham denied that he had ever believed in any self-adjusting and equilibrating tendencies of the market, or that interest rates properly adjust saving and investment. He went on with that famous paragraph:

> I have not, I never had, nor shall have, any horror, sentimental or anarchical, of the hand of government. I leave it to Adam Smith, and the champions of the rights of man ... to talk of invasions of natural liberty, and to give as a special argument against this or that law, an argument the effect of which would be to put a negative upon all laws. The interference of government, as often as in my jumbled view of the matter the smallest balance on the side of advantage is the result, is an event I witness with altogether as much satisfaction as I should its forbearance, and with much more than I should its negligence. (Stark, 1954, pp. 257–258)

Actually, Elie Halévy thought that Bentham's adherence to the laissez faire school involved him in a fundamental contradiction with the position he had taken in legal theory where, instead of a natural identification of interests he defended the artificial identification of interests (Seintrager, 1977, pp. 64–65).

Three years later of The True Alarm, in 1804, Jeremy Bentham lost interest in economics.

Nevertheless, none of the classical economists would have objected initially to the greatest happiness of the greatest number principle. Their non-interventionism is not based on a "libertarian" philosophy where free action gives an extra incentive; the utilitarian concept of government was underlying all their political proposals. John Stuart Mill does not misinterpret the attitude of his contemporaries when he writes in 1848 that laissez faire is the general practice and that any detour from it, if it is not followed by a greatest good, is an evil, Mill (1978). But it is in the Humean sense, more than in the Benthamian sense, that we may label as utilitarian the classical economists school, as Robbins (1953, p. 178) says. With the marginalist revolution, the Benthamian definition of the *homo oeconomicus,* as well as the utilitarian concept of government, won the battle in economic science (Black, 1988). Jevons (1871) in his *Theory of Political Economy* returns to the greatest happiness principle and to the pleasure and pain as motive of action. He quotes Bentham and talks about the felicific calculus. When he goes to the question of "pleasure and pain as quantities", in chapter II, he even measures pleasures and pains for intensity, duration, certainty, propinquity, and fecundity, purity and extent, as Bentham did (see Sigot, 2002). Marshall also in his youth studied Bentham and, according to Keynes, he would never divert from utilitarian ideas. But he used them with care as he did not consider that economic problems could be solved by applying the hedonistic calculus (Keynes, 1925, p. 7). Marginalism usually accepts the feasibility of state interference in market mechanism to provide for happiness.[2]

In Owen's case, as a businessman, his circle of influence depended extensively on his seeking of new partners. As Open University (2016) claims, he naturally sought out those likely to be sympathetic and rich enough to invest in New Lanark, such as Lancaster and his rich Quaker supporters. For instance, Owen met William Godwin, the famous social philosopher and author of *An Enquiry Concerning Political Justice,* which had been published in 1793, at a dinner given for him in January 1813 by Daniel Stuart, a newspaper proprietor (Davis and O'Hagan, 2010). Godwin argued for a new social order stressing justice, freedom and equality for the individual. Education, private and public, figured prominently in Godwin's thinking, as did character formation and happiness. As Owen worked on the Second, Third and Fourth Essays, he was frequently at Godwin's house for breakfast, tea or dinner. Between January and May Owen met Godwin at least twice a week. Godwin later recorded that on one occasion he converted Owen from "self-love" to "benevolence", although the next time they met, Owen claimed that he had been too hasty in altering his opinion. Of course this does not prove that Owen's work owed much to Godwin's, but it probably exercised a great deal of influence. Owen never acknowledged a direct debt to *Political Justice,* perhaps because he never properly read it, but the influence came by his association with enlightened thinkers in Manchester, Glasgow and Edinburgh, and from discussions with visiting reformers at New Lanark. Since Godwin had fallen out of fashion, Owen could be seen as his replacement for the new century (Locke, 1980, p. 262).

Then, Godwin introduced Owen to Francis Place (1751–1854), one of the most influential of the philosophic Radicals (Thomas, 1917). Owen, Place recalled, was "a man of kind manners and good intentions, of an imperturbable temper, and an enthusiastic desire to promote the happiness of mankind". "A few interviews made us friends", said Place, "and he told me he possessed the means, and was resolved to produce a great change in the manners and habits of the whole of the people, from the exalted to the most depressed" (Wallace, 1898, 63). He told Place that most of the existing institutions were prejudiced against welfare and happiness. Owen evidently presented Place with a manuscript, asking if he would read and correct it for him, but whether this consisted of the first two essays or all four is unclear.

For his part, Owen expresses appreciation for political economists:

> My four "Essays on the Formation of Character" and my practice at New Lanark had made me well known among the leading men of that period. Among these were … William Godwin, the first Sir Robert Peel. I must not forget my friends among the political economists:- Malthus, James Mill, Ricardo, Colonel Torrens and Francis Place. I always differed from them but our discussions were maintained with great good feeling. They were friends to national education but opposed national employment for the poor and unemployed. (Owen, 1813, foot 103).

In particular, he acknowledged his disturbance by their tenacity in the defence of absurd ideas and that there was not one practical man among the party of modern political economists, the same accusation with which he charged Bentham (Owen, 1857, pp. 143–144). Owen was seen by the Whigs and the political economists as a man of one idea, which was enforced less by argument than by incessant and monotonous repetition. They disregarded him as non-intellectual (as did his son Robert Dale Owen: 1967, p. 90). According to Stephen (1900), Owen was a man of very few ideas. Besides, he was not in sympathy with any political party. Cobbett, who shared some of his views, treats him with ridicule; Southey was alienated by his religious teaching although he approved of Owen's social aims. According to Bloy (2008), Owen seems to have been regarded as a social butt whose absurdity was forgiven for his good humour. However, Owen and in particular his Grand National Consolidated Trade Union, founded in 1834, had a lot of followers – although everybody shared the idea that he was a paternalistic autocrat and that it was impossible to work with him in a non-hierarchical collective organization.

Owen's participation in the movement for factory reform was clearly much influenced by views expressed in the essays. This showed his continuing concern, first evidenced in Manchester, about the impact of industrialisation on society, a theme to which he consistently returned. His campaign for improved conditions began in 1815 with a speech to fellow cotton barons in Glasgow, and the substance was subsequently elaborated into a pamphlet, *Observations on the Effects of the Manufacturing System,* which he distributed to MPs. This contained the draft of a bill calling for a limit on working hours to 12 a day, including one and a half hours for meals; preventing the employment of children under the age of 10; limiting the hours of those aged under 12 to six hours per day; and providing basic education for children employed (Donnachie, 2000, pp. 122–6).

After lobbying senior members of the government, Owen succeeded in persuading some MPs that a bill on the lines he proposed should be introduced. Sir Robert Peel, father of the future prime minister would act as sponsor. Peel had been partly responsible for the first piece of factory legislation, the *Health and Morals of Apprentices Act,* passed in 1802. The new bill was introduced in June 1815, but with the intervention of Waterloo made no progress until 1816, when a select committee was appointed to take evidence. Owen spoke optimistically about the intentions of the country's rulers in an address delivered at the opening of the Institute at New Lanark in January that year. Before the committee met, Owen and his son Robert Dale, then just 14 years old, set off on a tour of inspection to gather evidence. Later the younger Owen was to describe the conditions they found in many mills as "utterly disgraceful to a civilised nation" (R.D. Owen, 1874, p. 101).

Appearing before the committee, Owen was closely questioned on what he had seen and what had been enacted at New Lanark. So, it was actually through his practice that he wanted to set an example. He explained that his reduction of factory hours and other reforms were partly humanitarian and partly made on the grounds of improved efficiency; he thought that they had not increased costs or reduced family income. He was able to produce school registers showing increased attendance as a result of shorter working hours. The bill after much modification became law in 1819. It brought improvements for factory children, and was the basis of more comprehensive legislation on working conditions in 1825 and 1833 (Donnachie, 2000, pp. 129–31). Recent scholarship has pointed to the fact that Bentham's followers played an important role in reforms such as the Factory Act and the Poor Law which set England on the road toward a centralized welfare state. However, there is some controversy over the exact role played by Bentham's followers in the development of the modern British welfare state (Roberts, 1960; Finlayson, 1970).

Even Bentham accepted many of Owen's ideas in his educational and religious creeds, although Bentham had no utopian objective in them. According to Brebner, Bentham turned to collectivism after 1809. But this is misleading (Brebner, 1948, p. 62 and pp. 59–73). It is true that he was not entirely a classical economist, despite all the links he had with them, especially regarding the alignment of his Westminster Review within the framework of classical economics (O'Brien, 2004, p. 16). But, actually, the defence of individual private property and the idea of laissez faire was a vital article of the utilitarian creed, as A. V. Dicey (1924, p. 198 and pp. 126–210) argued, and it went unchallenged for a long period of time.

7.2. James Mill

Jeremy Bentham created around him a set of followers thanks to his inherent ability to summon people. He wrote manuscripts in his loneliness, which he knew that the public would not read if they were not being corrected or checked by a disciple, in a language increasingly dark. For him, his friendship with the Swiss exile Etienne Dumont, diffuser of his work, which he translated into French, was of vital importance. This made him very popular in France, up to the point that he was given French citizenship. John Bowring was also an essential diffuser (Bentham, 1834, p. 11). But James Mill was the clue to the existence of the Benthamian group and of the school of the philosophical radicals. He was acquainted with Bentham in 1808. He saw in him a great man, and concentrated on giving him influence in his time and country. He knew he was the necessary intermediary between Bentham and the external world, and he became his propagator. Thanks to him, Bentham adopted the economic notions of Smith. In 1808, he was not a political radical, and James Mill made him an adept of political liberalism and philosophical radicalism (Long, 1977). Mill perceived a connection between Malthus's ideas and those of Bentham and became a Malthusian. Ricardo was another great man for James Mill, and he tried to transform him into an agent to spread the Benthamian ideas which were defended by him in the parliament (Collison Black, 1988).

James Mill, a man of abstract convictions, utilitarian rigid morality and strong believer of the doctrine of the common good, was a man without eyes for the beauty of nature or art, having systematically destroyed the impulses of feeling in himself – in short, the typical image of the utilitarian that was popular in the nineteenth century (Halévy, 1972. p 135). J. S. Mill (1986, p. 136) says that his father was a species of stoic, epicurean and cynic. He did not believe in pleasure; he was not insensitive to them, but he thought that few of them were worth the price that, at least in the current times, had to be paid for them. The majority of the mistakes in society are due to an overvaluation of pleasures. Bentham himself was also insensitive to most aesthetic pleasures (Dinwiddy, 1995).

There are certain analogies between the moral temperament of the utilitarians and that of the puritanical English sects, or of the Quakers with whom Owen was acquainted by his business deal. The radical utilitarian had something of the stoic and mechanic about him. Ethics was considered to be a laborious art based on a rational science. Bentham and his disciples were, in fact, practically monks. Bentham compared himself to the saints of the Low Church and to the Quakers. "A Methodist... what I should have been still had I not been what I am; like Alexander, if he had not been Alexander... would have been Diogenes" (Bentham 1838–1843, vol. X, p. 92).

In 1814, Bentham rented to James Mill the Ford Abbey's castle in Devonshire for four years and it was turned into a monastery where the hours of study, food and exercise were fixed for all, for Bentham and his secretaries, James Mill, his wife and children, and Francis Place in 1817–1818. After lunch, they took turns to accompany Bentham on his walks, in which they conversed. Francis Place would write to his wife: "All our days are alike, so an account of one may do for all" (Graham Wallas, *Life of Place*, p. 73, in Halévy, 1972, p. 135). Bentham turned into a solitary prisoner in his cell. Young women and foreigners asked for a hearing with the teacher, and the honor of eating with him.

Bentham was then the leader of the Utilitarians and chief of the radical philosophers but Owen did not really appreciate this. He said about Bentham that "He had little knowledge of the world, except through books" and "he spent a long life in an endeavour to amend laws, all based on a fundamental error, without ever discovering that error". However, Owen associated during 1813–1814 with James Mill (1773–1836), and, although Owen never acknowledged the fact, it was probably Place and James Mill who edited A *New View of Society* and gave the essays the clarity that is missing from some of his later works. Place was greatly offended not only by the second comprehensive edition of the essays, published in 1816, which contained material on radical political reform he had earlier read and rejected, but also by Owen's apparent arrogance in the face of some reasoned criticism.

Bentham's ideas were based on James Mill's philosophy of mind and so he considered personal identity to be a bundle of pleasures or pains (Bentham 1935). James Mill's empirical psychology consisted of neuronal attractions and repulsions producing pleasure or pain (Mill, 2001 [1829]). He admired Hobbesian nominalism and also took many ideas from Horne Tooke, who gives language a special function, that of abbreviation. We have an unlimited number of sensible impressions and we cannot designate each impression. So, we use each word to design a variety of them, with each language playing an economic role. James Mill considered that mental phenomena are reduced to their simplest elements, and the association of these into groups and successions is investigated, all association being reduced by him to one law – that of contiguity.

But Bentham also follows the associationist theory developed in 1730 by Gay, disciple of Locke: all men look for pleasure and avoid pain, a moral necessary and obligatory law to obtain happiness. The men agree in the end but not in the means, because they do not connect happiness with the same ideas. Also, David Hartley, in *Observations on Man, his Frame, his Duty, and his Expectations* (1749) tried to create a "psychology" (absent word in his English predecessors) with general deductive and synthetic laws. In 1735 he writes *The Progress of Happiness deduced from Reason* and establishes that pleasures are irreducible and differ in extension. They are a collection of simple elements associated in different ways. For Brown and James Mill, the same as Berkeley before and Erasmus and Darwin after, men experience separate and uninterrupted sensations, isolated one from the other, and with that he creates a notion of continuous space. The idea of continuity is created as a cinematographic mechanism in which we create a fiction of continuity from that discontinuism. Hartley, in contrast, presents a "theory of vibrations" which explained how the "component particles" that constitute the nerves and brain interact with the physical universe suggested by Newton – a world composed of "forces of attraction and repulsion" and having a minimum of solid matter. He offers a conceptually novel account of how we learn and perform skilled actions.

These utilitarians were sensualists; although this is not fully true for Bentham. His rationalism made Rosen defend that Bentham was not really utilitarian (Rosen, 1994). He wanted, as Hobbes did, to construct the social order as geometers. He leaves little space for free will: the laws of nature are simple and uniform.

James Mill (1829) became a follower of Benthamism in politics and government, but in economics he did not try to approach the pleasure-pain analysis of Bentham's, as his ideas were based on Ricardo's physical approach to the problems of production and distribution. His "Elements of Political Economy" (Mill 1844 [1821]) is a didactic text based on Ricardo doctrines. There, he writes that first the relative value of goods depends on supply and demand, but in the last analysis it depends on the cost of production. He even reduces the theory of value to quantity of labour. He does not defend the idea that utility is necessary, though not sufficient, for the goods to possess value. And through the Mills – the father and the son – and through McCulloch, the Ricardian ideas of value are those which dominated the English political economy until 1860. Hollander argues that "James Mill was interested in economic theory as a weapon in the service of his political program" (Hollander, 1985, p. 28). After Ricardo's death, James Mill and John R. McCulloch started popularizing a Ricardian economic doctrine that made room for the principle of population, the iron law of salaries, an anti-rent and pro-laissez-faire attitude and drastic simplifications such as a 100% labour theory of value that was never professed by Ricardo himself (Cremaschi, 2004). In some sense, Mill invented "Ricardianism", a kind of "utilitarian economics" or "economic philosophy". After, John Maynard Keynes declared that Ricardian economics "conquered England as completely as the Holy Inquisition conquered Spain" (Hollander, 1979, p. 3).

7.3. Malthus

Place was an early advocate of birth control, which he linked to the ideas of Thomas Robert Malthus (1763–1834). Precisely, Malthus wanted to refute utopianism insisting, like Machiavelli, on the principle of necessity. Malthus points to the ideas of utopians in his *An Essay on the principle of population, as it affects the future improvement of society, with remarks on the speculation of Mr Godwin, Mr Condorcet and other writers* (Malthus 1826 [1798]). So, he said that they are not human institutions, but the stinginess of nature, the base of inequality and of the principle of population: it is the instinct of multiplication that prevents progress along with the diminishing returns. In addition, if there were equality, there would be no demand for labour, and if the idle had their sustenance assured, there would not be a trend to effort, stimulating once more growth of population. Malthus's pessimistic predictions of over-population (also noted in Owen's essays) helped fuel the debate about the future of the Poor Law. The traditional system of parish relief, Malthus thought, increased the misery of the poor, encouraging procreation.

So for Malthus, the poor must feel gratitude to the rich as he lives thanks to his savings and inequality and the principle of population is not so bad at all. It takes us out of the abbies of perfectibility and excites men to action, making its faculties more acute and breaking inertia. For that reason, Carlyle will talk about economics as a dismal science and enthrone the hero against the lazy mass.

On the contrary, Bentham included equality as a subsidiary end. He feared any government-sponsored levelling tendency in respect to property, but he recognized that the condition of a body is the situation of the greater part of the individuals who compose it. According to the principle of prevention of disappointment, to take 10 pounds from A and give it to B would cause A greater pain than the pleasure which would be given to B and the result would be a diminution of overall happiness. However, according to the principle of diminishing marginal utility, that Bentham also defended, from two individuals with unequal fortunes, he who has the most wealth has the most happiness, yet the excess in happiness of the richer will not be so great as the excess of his wealth. Nonetheless, Bentham did not believe it was necessary for government to do much in the way of promoting equality since he believed, following Smith, that the working of a free market would in and of itself, go a long way toward establishing relative equality over a period of time.

Malthus never met Bentham and apparently never read any of his writings and had a rather distant and occasionally conflictive relationship with James Mill (Chremaschi 2014, p. 2). However, Malthus shared important elements with Bentham's utilitarianism. Bentham was Malthusian. He thought that the Panopticon would be ideal for establishing workhouses for paupers as it avoided procreation, as described in his extensive writing on the poor laws in the 1790s. The new "industry houses" were also based on this Panopticon design in Bentham's papers. Actually, Bentham argues for a pauper management system based on the East India Company – vanguard of free market capitalism – and here the poor were to be put to work in "industry houses" that are made profitable, primarily, via child labour! In the industry houses, all paupers work to cover the expense of their care, with the "extra-ability" – the energy, strength and talent – of poor children increasing productivity. In the time left over from labour, children will be educated, so as to be able to continue to contribute to the community when they are released (which, according to Bentham's calculations, would not be until they had reached around 20 years old, given the need to make the industry houses profitable via their productivity).

In a series of essays, some published and some not, Bentham proposed a system of agricultural communes for the south of England and a system of industry houses. Both were designed to provide care for the indigent by supplying work for them under strict supervision and, if necessary, compulsion, and encourage the beneficiaries to return to the normal labour market as soon as possible. Care must be taken to insure that the lot of those who benefited from the programmes was not superior to the lot of the poor who remained at work in the open market. To fail to do so would be to reward those able but unwilling to work. Thus the worker in the free market ought to receive higher wages than those working in the industry houses, and he ought to have the freedom to spend his wages in ways not permitted to the latter. "The demand created by indigence can never be said to extend beyond the absolute necessities of life" (UC 153, p. 24). Bentham seemed to consider that the fact that certain individuals become indigent suggests that they are imprudent. Education might be provided within the industry houses. And a Poor Mans' Bank might be established to encourage both the inhabitants of the houses and the independent poor to save. Provisions might be made to secure the indigent poor low-interest loans to aid them in times of temporary distress. Loans might be advanced to those who have nothing to pledge but their good character; they might even be granted to the independent poor to allow them to take out a mortgage on a home of their own. These proposals incorporate a great number of advanced ideas for providing assistance to the working poor, and it is very near to Owen's ideas.

Edwin Chadwick, who helped design the Poor Law Amendment Act of 1834, was Bentham's secretary for many years, and the influence of Bentham's ideas can be very clearly seen in the poor law principles and policies. And he deliberately made workhouse life as uncomfortable as possible. This also made the image of economics as a Dismal Science: in the novel of *Hard Times*, this attitude is conveyed in Bitzer's response to Gradgrind's appeal for compassion. In the 1970s, Foucault used the panopticon as a motif for describing modes of social control in contemporary society.

The new utilitarianism was a good justification for Malthus' theories. As John Stuart Mill says

> one great distinctive achievement of the Philosophic Radical consequent upon the act was, significantly, the new Poor Law, symbolic embodiment of all that was most rationally and righteously inhuman in orthodox Utilitarianism, with its implacable Malthusian logic. Utilitarianism, in fact, provided the sanction for the complacent selfishness and comfortable obtuseness of the prosperous classes in the great age of Progress: they were protected by righteous rationality from the importunities of imaginative sympathy. (Mill 1980, p. 34, introduction)

After 1820, Bentham's followers tried to bring some order into their mixed pro and anti-Malthus attitude and adopted the doctrine formulated by John Ramself McCulloch (1820) according to whom there are "Two Malthuses": the progressive one, that is, the population theorist, and the reactionary one, that is, the political economist (Chremaschi 2014, p. 4).

Malthus' economic thinking may also have had some impact on Owen. Malthus speaks in a highly respectful tone of Owen's experiment of an industrial community at Lanark run on a socially minded basis. He declares his admiration for such a man of real benevolence "a gentleman for whom I have very sincere respect" (Malthus, 1826, p. 40), and wishes him success in his campaign for an act of Parliament limiting working hours for children and preventing their employment at too early an age (Malthus 1826, vol 1, p. 334). Unlike the followers of David Ricardo, Malthus saw agriculture as intrinsically more productive than manufacturing, and Owen's later community plan placed great emphasis on intensive farming as a means of self-sufficiency. The poor law sought to compel every able person to work for a living, with access to welfare for healthy adults conditional on their performance at work. According to Owen, however, we must apply to poor children the same educational curriculum as to others. As we have said, musical performance – singing, playing an instrument, performing in an orchestra or brass band – was a core part of the curriculum for the poor child in the nineteenth century. It was seen as a means of personal and social education and a disciplinary force (a means of developing good "character", as well as of inducting the child into a collective). Learning to sing, play and march was an effective counter to the "contagion" of poverty as well as preparation for entering society as a productive worker who understood his or her place in the order of things (University of Manchester, 2014). In the report that followed – called "The Training of Pauper Children", written by James Philip Kay (1839, pp. 36–37), a poor law commissioner from Manchester – cultural activities such as gardening, singing and play are part of a programme for preparing children for a life of labour.

However, Malthus offered a dissenting opinion of Owen's work as for him the indolence engendered by equality and common property would obviate exertion and moral restraint and the pressure of numbers would soon reduce the whole community to misery (Mill, 2006, p. 376). He criticizes Owen as a representative of the systems of equality and he says that his doctrine of land "shows a great degree of ignorance" (Malthus, 1826, p. 41). In 1810, he entered in his diary, "About fifteen hundred people are employed at the cotton mill, and great debauchery prevails among them" (James, 1966, p. 223, see also Perlman, 2000, p. 292). He adds that Owen's project suffers from the difficulty of Godwin utopia, namely the fact that the natural check to population in a state of equality and community of property could only be replaced by some artificial regulation of an "unnatural" character. Although Owen was aware of population principle and cites Malthus as an authority; Malthus says that Owen's goal would not be attained but by something "unnatural, immoral or cruel to a high degree" (Malthus 1826, vol. 1, p. 338). Probably, he was referring to some rumours that Owen in Lanark had been spreading knowledge of contraceptive techniques, that is reflected in a letter from Ricardo to Malthus where the former notes that Francis Place "speaks of one of Owen's preventives to an excessive population" while commenting the doubts "whether it is right even to mention it" (Ricardo 1821, p. 118, in Cremaschi, 2014, p. 177).

7.4. David Ricardo

Bentham was a critic of the economy of David Ricardo (1772–1823). "In Ricardo's book on Rent, there is a want of logic. I wanted him to correct it in these particulars; but he was not conscious of it and Mill was not desirous. He confounded cost with value".[3] Ricardo was very clear about value in a letter to Malthus:

> M. Say has not a correct notion of what is meant by value when he contends that a commodity is valuable in proportion to its utility. This would be true if buyers only regulated the value of commodities. ... You say demand and supply regulates value [sic]; this I think is saying nothing, and for the reason I have given in the beginning of this letter: it is supply which regulates value, and supply is itself controlled by comparative cost of production. (Bonar and Hollander, 1899, pp. 173–176)

Besides, he said, if the value consisted of utility, then a lowering of price due to lesser costs of production would imply lesser utility? Obviously, he was not aware of the concept of marginal utility, already introduced by Bentham: the last unit consumed affords the consumer with lesser utility, although the total utility or consumer surplus increases. But we need to say that his arguments do not run counter to the general principle of utility posed by Bentham. Ricardo had deference to Bentham and he clearly admired his work. In the question of property, Bentham aligned with Ricardo as for him "Self-regard actually and properly [is] the universally predominant motive" (Bentham, 1983a, p. 35). Ricardo comments to Tower that "Mr. Bentham's mind and pen are employed at the present moment in elucidating the principles of Government and the safety of extending the representation" (Bonar and Hollander 1899, p. 80).

It appears that Ricardo became acquainted with Bentham through Mill in 1811, instead of with Mill through Bentham, as suggested by Bain (1882, p. 74).[4] But, according to Cremaschi (2004), there is a myth of Ricardo's dependence on Bentham through Mill, fostered by Halévy. Ricardo had already worked out his own approach to economic theory when he first met James Mill. In matters concerning political economy, Ricardo had superior knowledge of the subject, and James Mill acknowledged that fact.

Hollander (1979, pp. 109–113, 593–597) says that Ricardo was not influenced by James Mill nor Bentham. But Moses Ricardo (Ricardo, 1973, pp. 3–13) acknowledged that the relationship with Mill had been the most influential in David Ricardo's life and Halévy says that all acts in Ricardo's life have all been the result of Mill's will (Halévy, 1972). James Mill was the most important adviser Ricardo enjoyed during the last ten years of his life: his advice was partly on publication policies, partly on parliamentary politics and, during a limited phase, on readings in philosophy, history and political theory. Through this influence, Bentham says in his "Works" (vol. x, p. 45), that he took some pains to get Ricardo a seat in Parliament, although Ricardo credits himself for the merit "My efforts have been at last crowned with success, and I am now a seated member of the House of Commons" (Ricardo was elected as member for Portarlington, an Irish pocket borough, in Queen's County, on

20 February, 1819). Then, Ricardo goes on acknowledging his agreements with Bentham:

> If I could, without much trouble, get into the New Parliament, I would. I should neither be Whig nor Tory but should be anxiously desirous of promoting every measure which should give us a chance of good government. This I think [will] never be obtained without a reform in Parliament. I do not go as far as Mr. Bentham. I regret that his book is so full of invective against those from whom he differs, yet I am convinced by his arguments.[5] There is no class in the community whose interests are so clearly on the side of good government as the people; all other classes may have private interests opposed to those of the people. The great problem then is to obtain security that the representatives shall be chosen by the unbiassed good sense of the people. The suffrage must be extensive to secure the voters against corrupt influence and the voting must be by ballot for the same reason. There must be an intimate union between representatives and their constituents in order to destroy the dependence of the former on the executive government... If the suffrage is not universal there can be no danger of anarchy. A man with a very small property can have no wish for confusion if he be actuated by those motives which have always been found to influence mankind. (Bonar and Hollander 1899, N XIX Letters of Ricardo to Trower, March 1818, pp. 51–52)

But Ricardo did not encourage Bentham's economic writings. As we have said, in April 1801, Bentham gave his manuscripts *Circulating Annuities* to Étienne Dumont in Geneva for him to edit and translate for their publication in France. Dumont confessed that this was the one work of Bentham that had given him the most problems. He did not throw his scheme into the fire, but he left it in a drawer. In 1810, when the Bullion controversy had created interest in monetary circulation problems, Dumont remembered the papers, and he asked himself if their publication would be possible. He sought Mill's advice and, in January 1811, Mill sought Ricardo's advice, as he was becoming famous. It is said that Ricardo's opinion was negative, although he admitted that it contained lucid ideas. Mill told Dumont that the manuscripts were not suitable for publication and, although Dumont was at first reluctant to abandon the project, in the end the papers were not published.[6] The original manuscript, autographed, was lost, probably with the consultation between Ricardo and Mill, and it has never been found.

Not in vain, Ricardo claimed that saving is always translated into productive investment and that an increase in money supply must lead to an increase in prices, not to an increase in activity and employment. Bentham, despite being quantitativist and preoccupied about avoiding inflation effects on distributive justice, claimed that in the short run the increases in the quantity of money produces effects on the real economy. Modern economists would consider his theory valid, but Ricardo and Mill did not. Hollander (1979, p. 13) says that

Ricardo could see nothing in Bentham's doctrine, the same as he could see nothing in Malthus' ideas on effective demand and J. B. Say's ideas on utility and value. According to Viner (1949, p. 321), nor was Ricardian economy acceptable at all for Bentham, nor was Bentham's economy acceptable to Ricardo. However, as Schwartz (1982, p. 708) says, Ricardo criticized the details of *Circulating Annuities*, but not its essence. It has even been said that Ricardo made the fall of profits a consequence of shortage of land, more than of competence of capital as Smith said, due to Bentham's influence.

David Ricardo and most political economists had also shown complete disagreement with Owen's communism and his attempts to build a new society without private property. Ricardo considers Owen a visionary and he says so in his correspondence when talking about Robert Southey, a poet that contributed regularly to the first four volumes (1802–1805) of the *Annual Review* and who was connected with the *Quarterly Review* from its establishment in 1808 until 1838. "The reveries of Southey on questions of Political Economy will I hope no longer be admitted in any respectable journal. He quite mistakes his talent when he writes on such subjects, and is really no more deserving of attention than Mr. Owen or any other visionary" (Bonar and Hollander 1899, N XVIII Letters of Ricardo to Trower, 26 Jan 1818, p. 47).[7]

In the parliamentary discussion about machinery on 16 December 1819 when Owen was fighting to improve the Factory Bill before Parliament and to use a larger workforce in husbandry, Ricardo observed that he was completely at war with Owen's system, which was built upon a theory inconsistent with the principles of political economy and that "was calculated to produce infinite mischief to the community... he who was such an enemy to machinery, only proposed machinery of a different kind... namely, human arms" (Ricardo's speech on Owen's plan at a meeting held in the Freemasons' Hall on 26 June 1819, in Cannan, 1991, p. 35). We may have answered that Owen's successful entrepreneurial experience was against the consideration of workers as "hands". Ricardo understood little of business administration, but, from Owen practice, he only took into account Owen's communist proposal which was opposite to Adam's Smith individualistic vision. However, Adam Smith was not conscious of the Industrial Revolution that was beginning precisely in 1776, the date of the publication of *The Wealth of Nations*: the pin factory of which Smith speaks has 10 or 12 employees, and there is no need to manage the personnel apart from the attentive direct supervision of a capitalist or a delegate he considered trustworthy.

For Ricardo it is something different. And the true reasons for Ricardo's rejection of Owen's ideas were philosophical and utilitarian. In a letter to Trower, Ricardo asks himself:

> Can any reasonable person believe, with Owen, that a society, such as he projects, will flourish and produce more than has ever yet been produced by an equal number of men, if they are to be stimulated to exertion by a regard for the community, instead of by a regard for their private interest? Is not the experience of it against him? He can bring nothing to oppose this experience

but one or two ill authenticated cases of societies which prospered on a principle of a community of goods, but where the people were under the powerful influence of religious fanaticism. I was in hopes that Sir Wm. de Crespigny would have given me an opportunity to state my opinions shortly on this subject in the House of Commons, but he thought fit to withdraw his motion for a Committee, and therefore I was obliged to be silent. (Bonar and Hollander 1899, N 80 Letters of Ricardo to Trower)[8]

But Owen had his ideas clear. He established a wage in labour vouchers to achieve the demand growing *pari passu* with the increase in productivity, but he was never worried about the deleterious effects of machinery. He trusted that it would remedy the evils of man. After the Napoleonic wars, his proposals of self-sufficient communities meant fighting against unemployment, but Owen did not make technological innovation responsible for the crisis or for unemployment, rather the change in the productive situation with the ending of the wars. And his acceptance of technological progress was not due to its accelerating the arrival of the revolution, as Marx and Engels believed, but he was thinking as a businessman.

On another occasion, Ricardo unwillingly belonged to a committee that had to investigate and report on Mr. Owen's plan. The Committee hoped to get a large enough number of subscriptions to enable them to found something like a New Lanark in England. Owen proposed forming a new establishment in which agricultural and manufacturing employment would both be used, but of which agriculture would be the basis. He proposed to arrange the unemployed working classes into agricultural and manufacturing villages "of Unity and Mutual Co-operation" limited to a Population of from 500 to 1,500 persons. Those will cordially unite all as one good and enlightened family and will enable all rapidly to progress in knowledge and wisdom and to enjoy without interruption the highest earthly happiness to which man can attain. This plan gained a lot of publicity: "The proceedings connected with these first public meetings which I held in the City of London Tavern, were minutely and accurately narrated in all the London morning and evening newspapers, published for general news at that period" (Owen, 1857, p. 155). Owen promised to take upon himself the superintendence and repay the capital with interest, although the labourers may be placed in a state of comfort hitherto unknown to that class (Owen 1857, *Address of the Committee to the Public*, Aug. 23rd, 1819, vol. ii. pp. 21 3–4). But Ricardo says:

I am not a member of a Committee to further Mr. Owen's plans—the Committee was appointed for the purpose of examining, and not of approving those plans. I attended the meeting and had very successfully resisted all entreaties to let my name be on the Committee till attacked by the Duke of Kent and Mr. John Smith. It was in vain that I protested I differed from all the leading principles advanced by Mr. Owen,—that, I was told, was no objection, for I was not bound to approve, only to examine. With very great reluctance I at last consented, and have attended the first meeting, at which

I gave my reasons at some length for departing from all Mr. Owen's conclusions.

The question that actually moved Ricardo to this criticism was Owen's lack of knowledge of the Malthusian theories that prevented the people giving aid to the poor, as they could reproduce their numbers:

> The scheme was chiefly examined with a view to a pauper establishment or a well regulated workhouse, but even to that limited plan there are insuperable objections. Owen is himself a benevolent enthusiast, willing to make great sacrifices for a favorite object. The Duke of Kent, his great supporter, is also entitled to the praise of benevolent intentions, but he appears to me to be quite ignorant of all the principles which ought to regulate establishments for the poor—he has heard of Malthus' doctrine, and has an antipathy to it, without knowing the reasons on which it is founded or how his difficulty may be obviated. He, Mr. Preston, and Mr. Owen, appear to think nothing necessary to production, and the happiness of a crowded [sic] population, but land. We have land; it may be made more productive, and therefore, we cannot have an excess of population. (Bonar and Hollander 1899, N XXVII Letters of Ricardo to Trower, p. 79)

Finally, the Committee considered the plans practicable; but in December 1819, in view of the smallness of the subscriptions they were obliged to give up their task. After, a select Committee was appointed in June 1823, to inquire into the condition of the labouring poor in that part of the United Kingdom called Ireland. Here, Owen assured that if they gave him 8 million pounds he would make Ireland now and for ever happy. Ricardo also pleaded against.

Sauvy concludes in a rather contemptuous way for the economists, that there was a clear contrast between the world of the insensitive economists and the population that was suffering from the pains of the birth of a new society. The popular opinion, even of the middle class, was on behalf of the workers, whereas the power and the economists defended the manufacturers' interests (Sauvy, 1986, p. 46).

7. 5. John Stuart Mill

John Stuart Mill (1806–1873) was brought up on Bentham's ideals. Young Mill was kept away from children other than his siblings and was educated by his father. The latter wanted to create a genius who would continue Bentham's work. Religion was excluded from Mill's education. However, at the age of 12, he was introduced to scholastic logic. At the age of 14, Mill was sent to France to stay with the family of Samuel Bentham. During the year he stayed in France, he attended classes at the *Faculté des Sciences* in Montpellier where he was taught logic, chemistry and zoology. He was also introduced to many prominent French figures including Jean-Baptiste Say and Henry Saint-Simon.

At the age of 16, Mill refused to study at Cambridge University or Oxford. Instead, he decided to work for a living as a clerk at the East India Company. He soon began to experience problems with his mental health. When he was 20 years old, he had a nervous breakdown which he attributed to rigorous study and lack of a normal childhood. Then, in 1826, he clearly moved away from the utilitarian credo. The cause of his state he found in the education to which he had been subjected. His teachers, he said, "seemed to have trusted altogether to the old familiar instruments, praise and blame, reward and punishment," but these associations Mill now saw as artificial and mechanical, not natural. The "description so often given of a Benthamite, as a mere reasoning machine," he says, "was during two or three years of my life not altogether untrue of me." Zeal "for what I thought the good of mankind was my strongest sentiment... But my zeal was as yet little else, at that period of my life, than zeal for speculative opinions. It did not have its root in genuine benevolence, or sympathy with mankind; though these qualities held their due place in my ethical standard. Nor was it connected with any high enthusiasm for ideal nobleness." "[My] father's teachings tended to the undervaluing of feeling" – as also did Bentham's (Mill, 1985, pp. 76–77).

John Stuart Mill is, as Guillot (2016) says, the most important critic and heir of Bentham. The first movement of emancipation from the narrow mold of Benthamism was a very slight one: the rejection of Bentham's contempt for poetry. This came first through "looking into" Pope's Essay on Man, and realizing how powerfully it acted on his imagination, despite the repugnance to him of its opinions (Mill, 1985, pp. 79–80). It was from Wordsworth's poems that Mill derived "a medicine for [his] state of mind," "a source of inward joy, of sympathetic and imaginative pleasure, which could be shared in by all human beings." "From them," he says, "I seemed to learn what would be the perennial sources of happiness, when all the greater evils of life shall have been removed... I needed to be made to feel that there was real, permanent happiness in tranquil contemplation" (Mill, 1984, p. 104).

According to Mill, Bentham was blind to the different characters that imply different actions that at the same time contribute to create different characters. He claims that government and laws are the privileged instruments for the formation of character (Engelmann, 2008). As Mill (1980, p. 72) says:

> If Bentham's theory of life can do so little for the individual, what can it do for society? ... It will do nothing (except sometimes as an instrument in the hands of a higher doctrine) for the spiritual interests of society; nor does it suffice of itself even for the material interests. That which alone causes any material interests to exist, which alone enables any body of human beings to exist as a society, is natural character.

He also reproaches Bentham for his simplification of psychological life and his assessment of pleasures. Bentham denies all types of hierarchical organization of pleasures, something that John Stuart Mill criticized (Leroy, 2008).

At the same moment that he criticized Bentham, he became quite near to utopian socialism (see Losman 1971). He said that it was a most significant fact, and one from which the student in social philosophy may draw important instruction, that

> The Fourierists… believe that they have solved the great and fundamental problem of rendering labour attractive. That this is not impracticable, they contend by very strong arguments; in particular by one which they have in common with the Owenites, viz., that scarcely any labour, however severe, undergone by human beings for the sake of subsistence, exceeds in intensity that which other human beings, whose subsistence is already provided for, are found ready and even eager to undergo for pleasure. (Mill 1848, II, p. 1, 23)

According to Capaldi (2004, p. 210), what Mill objected to from Owen's scheme was the belief in environmental determinism. He criticizes Owen's belief that the workers' problems were beyond their control and that the solution to their problems lay in communal arrangements that deemphasized individuality. For that reason Mill argues in favour of autonomy and the ability of individuals to transform their lives. He replies that characters are the products, not only of education planned and carried out by others, but also of contingent experience and chance. This includes experience of the painful consequences of the character we previously had and of some feeling of admiration or aspiration incidentally aroused. And his own biography was an example of what he was trying to explain (Varouxakis and Kelly 2010, p. 41). According to Mill (1848, pp. 210–211),

> The question is, whether there would be any asylum left for individuality of character; whether public opinion would not be a tyrannical yoke; whether the absolute dependence of each on all, and surveillance of each by all, would not grind all down into a tame uniformity of thoughts, feelings, and actions. … No society in which eccentricity is a matter of reproach, can be in a wholesome state.

And Mill (1848, II, 1, 9) connected Owen with communism and uniformity and says that

> The assailants of the principle of individual property may be divided into two classes: those whose scheme implies absolute equality in the distribution of the physical means of life and enjoyment, and those who admit inequality…
> At the head of the first class, as the earliest of those belonging to the present generation, Mr. Owen and his followers must be placed. The characteristic name for this economic system is Communism.

All in all, John Stuart Mill describes the clash between Owenites and political economists in 1825:

> There was for some time in existence a society of Owenites, called the Co-operative Society, which met for weekly public discussions in Chancery

Lane... It was a lutte *corps-à-corps* between Owenites and political economists, whom the Owenites regarded as their most inveterate opponents:
but it was a perfectly friendly dispute. We who represented political economy, had the same objects in view as they had, and took pains to show it.
(Mill, 2007, p. 64)

But, according to Stephen (1900, p. 121), Owen's disciples, after some years,
came into sharp conflict with the utilitarians. In the final analysis, there is no
doubt that regarding the two sides described by John Stuart Mill – classical
economist and Owenites – Bentham belongs to the former.

7.6. Utopian socialism and others

Marx and Engels awarded the contemptuous label of "utopian" to the socialists
who appealed to the good feelings of the rich. Engels says in *Socialism: Utopian
and Scientific*[9]:

> Then came the three great Utopians: Saint-Simon...; Fourier; and Owen,
> who in the country where capitalist production was most developed, and
> under the influence of the antagonisms begotten of this, worked out his
> proposals for the removal of class distinction systematically and in direct
> relation to French materialism... Owen's communism was based upon this
> purely business foundation, the outcome, so to speak, of commercial calcu-
> lation. Throughout, it maintained this practical character. Thus, in 1823,
> Owen proposed the relief of the distress in Ireland by Communist colonies,
> and drew up complete estimates of costs of founding them, yearly
> expenditure, and probable revenue. And in his definite plan for the future,
> the technical working out of details is managed with such practical
> knowledge – ground plan, front and side and bird's-eye views all included –
> that the Owen method of social reform once accepted, there is from the
> practical point of view little to be said against the actual arrangement of
> details. (Engels, 1880, p. 7)

But what is true in this well-known label of utopian socialism? And to what
point was Owen related to Fourier and Saint Simon? It is true that the three
alleged utopian socialists were scientists and their ideas were based on facts and
observations and were considered to be leaders with obedient disciples. They
were conscious of their mutual existence but they did not mutually read each
others' works.

Utopian socialists, although they admired the organizational ability of industrial people, in general were against businessmen and the industrial class. Such is
the case of Charles Fourier (1772–1837), or state socialism of Louis Blanc
(1811–1882). But this is not true in all the cases. The anarchist Pierre Joseph

Proudhon (1809–65), who was opposed to all authority, shows a considerable admiration for industry organization (see Knowles, 2013). He says:

> It is industrial organization that we will put in place of government … In place of laws, we will put contracts … In place of political powers, we will put economic forces. In place of the ancient classes of nobles, burghers, and peasants, or of business men and working men, we will put the general titles and special departments of industry: Agriculture, Manufacture, Commerce, &c. In place of public force, we will put collective force. (Proudhon, Idée générale de la revolution [1851], in Ekelund and Hebert, 2013, p. 262)

But the one who stands out most in the defence of the "religion of industry" and in praising the role of manufacturers and their capacity of organization is undoubtedly Claude-Henri of Rouvroy, Count of Saint-Simon (1760–1825). French noble engineer, Saint-Simon may be considered utopian, but not a socialist (Santos, 1997, pp. 51–54; Denis, 1970, pp. 295–301). Society proposed by him was hierarchical, not egalitarian, it is divided into classes, depending on their skills (rational, motor and emotive). A harmonious cooperation between all men is needed. He attributed great importance to the "industrial leader" as main character of the process of production. The *Catéchisme des industriels* (Saint-Simon, 1825), the same as other Saint-Simon works (Taylor, 1975), explains how the manufacturers must proceed in order to be the most prominent class – industrial class including all the people engaged in productive work, be it business people, managers, scientists, bankers, manual workers, and others. Saint-Simon could only be called "a socialist" in his defence of power being exerted on things instead of people and the administration having the objective of improving the welfare of people. In 1817 Saint-Simon published a manifesto called the "Declaration of Principles" in his work titled "Industrie" (Taylor, 1975, pp. 158–161) that established the principles of an ideology called industrialism. Industrials are considered by Saint-Simon more qualified, and qualified for a useful purpose, and also less idle than the other classes, that he considers parasitic. In the "Declaration" Saint-Simon criticized any expansion of government intervention into the economy, saying that it can become a "tyrannical enemy of industry". Government may be replaced by the Industrial Parliament that will increase productivity for positive scientific reasons, foretelling a technocratic ideal. Saint-Simonian enthusiasm for great industry, turned by his disciples almost into a religion, was a stimulus for the growth of large banks and industrial companies.

On the other hand, Charles Fourier (1772–1837) was a prophet of decentralization and attacked Saint-Simon for being the predecessor of statism and planning and for believing in industrialization. For Fourier (1966–1968), Saint-Simon wanted to transform men with floods of words of universal love; but he – Fourier – took nature as given and wanted to give free rein to passions so as to eliminate hypocrisy and competitiveness. Fourier did not believe in progress for repression. For Fourier, the industrial and commercial world and the machinery suffocate passions. The civilized society cannot be repaired. There, men are doomed to a grey and routine existence in rivalry with their peers. Competition creates waste, there is a parasitic intermediation in the distribution of goods, an ostentation of non-lasting goods and a proliferation of useless people (soldiers, bureaucrats, attorneys, philosophers). So, we need to break the bars of the prison and make a complete industrial reform. Then, Fourier proposed to create the Phalanstères or grand hotels, where people would live and work together and law would be based on the opinion of the group. He proposed a complete social reorganization in the shape of cooperatives of voluntary formation that would work on the basis of social harmony and the satisfaction of the psychological fundamental needs. According to Fourier, the Phalanstère must be represented by 1,620 people who would represent the highest possible number of combinations of human characters. In order to make work a pleasure, there must be workgroups composed of people of both sexes and all the ages, talents, economic levels. The frequent changes of activity in meetings of less than one hour would avoid the stultifying effects of specialization without losing its advantages. There would be a friendly competition, with contests to see who works best. Nevertheless, private property would continue existing provided that different talents advise a natural inequality. Fourier only criticizes the abuse of private property, which must be transformed into participations of the common capital of the Phalanstère. As the Phalanstère would hopefully have high profits, they will be divided into 12 parts, five for work, four for capital and three for direction or capacity. That is to say, Fourier includes the organization factor in the structure of the company. Finally, a world union of Phalanstères will be created that would depend on a hierarchical structure up to the Omniarch (a position that Fourier offered to Napoleon) see Beecher (1986) and Desroche (1975).

In this context, the proposal by Robert Owen seems something quite different. It is really shocking that the historians of socialism have associated, as Engels does, Owen's practical and managerial figure with that of Fourier, a crazy dreamer. Besides, Saint-Simon, as against Owen, considered control over people unnecessary. Owen was talking about a control and influence over people, but a control that is compatible with positive freedom. Workers are motivated if they have a boss who they know, love and admire. To the practical character of Owen we need to add an industrialist, we would say capitalist, vision of the modern production that other defenders of the cooperatives were not sharing, be it for ideological reasons or simply because the majority of those who were supporting the movement were poor people.

Here there is a political element, which irritates Marx and Engels: Owen, besides putting his personal fortune in his experiments, always counted on convincing the rich and powerful to put large sums of money into his projects, and he did it quite well. Owen 1 was a successful entrepreneur who was improving the factory system from inside and put into practice his theories of incentives risking his money and prestige. His utopia was not something clearly defined in the paper: he was practising it in real life. He was based on those two theoretical principles so important for him: that environment makes character and, so, good institutions make good people and responsibility for goodness is on society, not on people; and second, the assumption that mechanization produces unemployment. As against Fourier, he was favourable to paying the capitalist a fixed interest, until they would voluntarily renounce it.

But there is a managerial element that we must not overlook either: Owen assumed that modern production needs capital, and that any community needed enough investment to grow or be competitive (Morton, 1962, pp. 38, 48, 49). Relying on his experience as an entrepreneur – Owen 1 – he constantly argued with other leaders of the cooperative movement because he thought that cooperatives or communities were not viable without an initial high capital. But the proposal of cooperative management proposed by Owen 2 was against this principle. Owen 2 considered self management, meetings and the network system the way to empower the people. Owen 2, then, overlooked the problem that self-managed firms tend to invest less in the long run as workers that leave the firm do not appropriate profits. In self-managed firms, there is no competition in the stock market or a manager market that may select the best people for administering the firm. So, entrepreneurial costs are higher than in capitalism firms (see Trincado, 2008b).

The fact that Owen 2 failed to account for the problem of capital in self-managed firms may be the reason why Marxism gained the battle, making capital the clue to the problem. But even within Marxism, a division was made between orthodoxy that considered that capitalism was doomed to failure, and revisionism, that considered that the utopia and a reform of capitalism was possible. So, they were heirs of utopianism. For assuming these revisionist ideas, however, classical economics ideas must be ruled out. For classical economists, low wages depended on unavoidable economic factors, not on human laws and the trade unions might even create an immobility that could damage the workers as a whole, although in the short run they might benefit particular workers.

Owen 2 proposes the exchange of commodities based on embodied labour so as to avoid technological unemployment. He came to the conclusion that money as an intermediary creates variations in prices not due to variations in value. Although we may sell production, we could have not paid costs of production and wages and, then, supply may not absorb all the demand. Then, Owen proposes that labour should receive all his produce so that supply and demand for goods grows *pari passu* and overproduction is avoided. In 1831 in London he founded a stock exchange to put into contact the cooperative societies and he issued a few Labour vouchers that expressed in hours the value of goods. In 1834 the Great National Consolidated Union was created based on Owen's hope of joining all the unions of any trade. But the success of affiliation made it collapse as it began to lack financing and was suppressed by the government and patrons, who obliged the workers to sign a document where they promised not to stick to the Union. Also, the stock exchange and Owen's newspaper collapsed.

In giving such great importance to productive powers, Owen was nearer to historicism than to classical economics, but he was quite far from utopianism. He considered that individualistic and atomistic method were not useful for economics, as preferences are endogenous and dependent on others' preferences. History and culture, determine individual preconceptions and, with Veblen (1899), we can say that there are dynamic institutions that foster progress, and static institutions that delay progress. More than utopian socialism, Owen's theory was much more like that of Simonde de Sismondi (1773–1842). According to Sismondi, the great productive powers of industrial revolution were not being enjoyed by workers. The traditional guilds, typical of the Middle Ages, were based on cooperation beween labour and capital; but in capitalism there was conflict of interests and competition. Then, Sismondi coins the name of proletarians. For Sismondi, capitalism creates crisis due to its own contradictions, especially the fact that production is not adapted to needs. Machines displace labour, and the increase in production creates production surplus. As machinery is expensive, it is concentrated in large businesses and small firms have to leave their business. Then, he does not admit that the increase in product creates additional opportunities of employment or an additional demand (Sismondi, 1803, 1819). However, Sismondi is not considered utopian but a critic of capitalism and, obviously, a forerunner of Marx (Sowell, 1972).

Many other socialists took ideas from Owen's concept of unionship and creativity. For instance, Owen was quite near anarchism: like Godwin, he thought that education, in Owen's case under cooperativism, would make government unnecessary as self control by individuals would emerge and good conduct would be instinctive and spontaneous. On the contrary, Bentham is clearly opposed to this utopian idea, as control from an external controller seems always necessary in his theory. For anarchists (Proudon, Bakunin, Kropotkin), as for Owen, individuals are naturally good and absence of authority is not synonymous with disorder or chaos: the problem of men is authoritative institutions such as law and private property. Owen continued with the idea of Proudhon (1809–1865) that we need to substitute property for a contractual exchange without dependence or denomination by free association. According to Proudhon (1847), however, it is more important how wealth is distributed than how it is produced, and so he defended modifying the credit system, freeing money from financial and state capital to avoid credit shortage. But Owen gave more importance to the everyday production of the workers. Owen thought that work is time devoted to production, time being the most precious gift human beings have. So, time on work also needs to be liberating and creative. In the course of time, Owen began to be nearer to Proudhon's defence of giving credit without interest and to create a reassuring system that will reflect the labour value compensating for inflationary effects.

However, in the final analysis, Owen clearly criticizes anarchist theories that talk about a constant breaking of time; that is to say, the "anti-economy". Given that for all growing creatures one part of the group must be superior to the other, to destroy any human hierarchy anarchists prefer the constant breaking of history – and, on some occasions, of human development – in order not to let the hierarchical constructions crystallize. Owen would have clearly been against this idea, proposing instead good and legitimate authority more than an absence of authority.

Finally, what were Owen's heirs? As early nineteenth century Owenism had an important role in two such different societies: Britain and America (Harrison, J. 1969). In the twentieth century, in France and many European countries, Owenism was very popular, especially after the protests of May 1968 (see Rubel 1960). In Owen's period, in Britain they largely ignored the significance of Owenism and the Owenites except insofar as they were theoretical socialists. The working class movement was based on certain narrow assumptions about the nature of social history, the relation of ideas to society and the process of social change. However, the Fabians at the end of the century took over the cooperators' view and developed it further. Fabian Society founded in 1884 was a revisionist model, and Frank Podmore (Owen's biographer), was one founding member of the Fabian Society. They found in Owen a socialist sympathetic, though misguided, reformer and in Owenism a native socialist theory which owed nothing to Marx. A second generation of Fabian historians in the interwar period integrated Owen into the history of the British working class movement (Noyes, 1870; Lockwood, 1905). This is the case with Podmore.

In America the emphasis was different. Owenism was treated as part of the communitarian tradition by historians, maybe due to their spiritualism. New Harmony exercised continuing fascination for essayists, novelists and writers (Wilson, 1964) and was used as a counter example of prejudicial unionism (Commons, 1936; Perlman, 1928). Owenism contributed to the making of the English working class, but it also related to American frontier conditions and westward expansion.

Notes

1 In the classical period there is another tendency different from Ricardian, that is subjectivism, from Say and Lloyd, to Malthus, Senior, Longfield. None of them, however, used explicitly the utilitarian philosophy of Bentham.
2 However, as Urrutia (1983) says, marginalism is not disenchanting for its state interventionism but because it produces a break between "enticement and truth".
3 Bentham Works X, 498; in Stark (1952 c: 48) introduction.
4 For his later relations with Ricardo, see Letters to Malthus, p. 55. Mill became acquainted with Ricardo on the appearance of Mill's "Commerce Defended" (1807).
5 The book, Bentham (1817), is Plan of Parliamentary Reform in the Form of a Catechism, with an Introduction, showing the necessity of Radical, and the inadequacy of Moderate Reform. The work was written in 1809, but not published until 1817.
6 These commentaries remained unpublished until the volume III of Ricardo's works, in Sraffa edition 1951 appeared.
7 His contributions to the latter journal numbered nearly one hundred in all, upon the widest range of subjects. A complete list is appended to Rev. C. C. Southey's Life and Correspondence of Robert Southey. 6 vols. London, 1849–1850.
8 The opportunity was actually presented some months later, on December 16, 1819, when Ricardo addressed the House "on Sir William de Crespigny's motion for the appointment

of a select committee to inquire into the plan of Mr. Owen for ameliorating the condition of the lower classes." See Hansard, Parliamentary Debates, vol. xli. 1206–1209; Letters to McCulloch, p. 47; Mr. Cannan on Ricardo in Parliament, Economic Journal, 1894, pp. 415–417.

9 Is a part of Anti-Düring that was published separately as a pamphlet for the first time in French by por Lafargue, 1880; and with great success, being translated into several languages.

Part IV
Conclusion

8   Some final remarks

New Lanark was for Bentham a very profitable investment. The profits obtained by the firm depended on good management, on the paternalistic authority of a man, Robert Owen, who fostered his employees' effort and work. Conversely, Bentham's own projects could be described as failures or as not appropriate for the time and place. Those are the cases of his Frigidarium, his Panopticom, his Chrestomathic school, his currency schemes, the canal through Panama or an unforgeable banknote.

In *Defence of Usury*, Bentham discussed the figure of the innovative entrepreneur. However, his investment in a firm such as New Lanark, with high returns and run under new management techniques, does not appear to have made him think of Robert Owen as a new model of entrepreneurship. It could be thought that Bentham failed to recognize Owen as a prominent entrepreneur, misguided by Owen's role as advocate of communism and his haughty and authoritarian personality. But Bentham met "Owen 1" in 1813 in his industrialist period, when he had not yet shown his communist streak. Owen promoted the welfare of the workforce, and not only did he show that this was compatible with the profits of capitalism but he also proved that it was due to those profits. There is a great difference between Owen's practice as a businessman and his later communistic proposals.

New Lanark made some remarkable achievements both in entrepreneurship, management and social reform which Bentham never acknowledged. Perhaps the fact that he did not take Owen seriously as a theorist made Bentham never write about Owen when developing his theories. To this day, this is difficult to explain. We hope that this book clarifies some of the issues. Actually, most economic historians and historians of economic thought appear to have made the same mistake: to think of Owen as a theorist, communistic social reformer, rather than as a successful entrepreneur and human resource manager, which was his main merit before 1813 and which provided him with the money and social recognition that allowed him afterwards to pursue social reform.

Owen 2, the socialist, was significantly different from Owen 1, the manager and entrepreneur; and the relevance of Owen 2 made socialist historians forget the impressive achievement of Owen 1. The transformation of Owen was due to his awareness that, at that time, the workforce did not really understand its own interests, and that an education of "false conscientiousness" was needed.

Table 8.1. Methods applied in factories to discipline hired children, 1833

Methods of punishment	Number of firms using the method	Methods of reward	Number of firms using the method
Sacking	353	Kindness	2
Threat of sacking	48		
Fines, wage deduction	101	Promotion or	
Corporal punishment	55	Higher wages	9
Complaint to parents	13	Reward	
Forbidding them to leave the factory	2		23
Humiliatingly distinctive attire	3		
Total	**575 (out of 609)**		**34 (out of 609)**

Source: Valdaliso & López (2000, p. 215), from Pollard (1987). See also, Casado (1998, p. 56), from Rule (1990)

Actually, the stubbornness of reality is evidenced when we look inside the firm. As shown in Table 8.1, it was easier for the businessmen to punish in a Benthamian way than to give positive rewards as defended by Owen. Businessmen sided with Bentham rather than with Owen in the granting of incentives. Maybe their own inability made them need simplification of the "business ethics". Owen proved that "another world is possible" and that this new world could be even more efficient than the utilitarian understanding of business, education and capitalism. But businessmen, the same as economists, preferred to leave out this intuition and they were blinded by a psychological theory of some sum of felicities, by Taylorism and by wild competition.

Acknowledging that Bentham was an original philosopher and Robert Owen a practical man, here we have seen that the differences between Bentham and Owen are the basis for two different philosophies of life, which nowadays are also a part of the different views of institutions that economists introduce in their economic models and explanations. The activity of Owen 1 was not seen as based on a much different philosophy than the one that public opinion had about Bentham's theory but, in historical terms, we see a personal evolution from classical liberalism to socialism (or social liberalism). Bentham, trying to justify the market, was a pioneer of the "black box" idea of the firm, where the firm is a place "into which resources go and out of which goods come, with little attention made to how this transformation is accomplished" (Demsetz, 1997, p. 426). Owen dealt with power inside the firm, shedding light on the black box. Owen's silent pioneering work was too ahead of his time. He disclosed the inside of non-democratic institutions in a non-democratic political government, and the questioning of power would have been a problem for the maintenance of power itself. When democracy extended worldwide, the organizing principles of power began to be unwrapped.

Owen's biographies discuss with somewhat inconclusive results whether Owen borrowed his ideas from Rousseau, Bentham and Godwin or was he influenced by his contemporaries in Manchester? But perhaps a more profitable approach is to consider Owenism as part of the whole complex of ideas of the later eighteenth and early nineteenth centuries. The first Owen, admired for being a successful businessman and an organizer of production in a technologically advanced and socially troubled sector, is quite different from the second Owen who, after being ruined with his experiments, became a communist writer, first creating a trade union, and then as a leader of the cooperative movement. We tend to admire Robert Owen for having invested his fortune in philanthropic experiments. But the opposite has been defended in this book: the fortune that Owen invested was gained as a businessman, and precisely as a businessman who dealt with the positive incentives to workers. His pioneering contribution to the practice and science of management was immense. He set up various important socialist experiments, trade union and national co-op systems, which were important steps for the history of socialism, but he also took important steps in the building of our economies and political systems.

However, Owen was wrong in his reasoning for the motivation of workers. Essential for success was Owen's own magnetic and paternal personality (Wilson 1940). He thought that his experience in New Lanark was the confirmation that, once punishments were eliminated and the lack of worker acknowledgment typical of preindustrial businesses was avoided, workers would have an aptitude to self-manage a company – especially after suitable education. The fact is that the communities that he founded failed as soon as he was not running them. His knowledge of the technologies of management, and his own charisma before the workers, were basic reasons for the success of his companies, success that he attributed to the moral improvement of workers.

Owen's theory of the entrepreneur relates to demand and consumption attitudes instead of supply and technology, challenging classical economics doctrine. He established in New Lanark an implicit but reliable unemployment insurance, which had a positive effect on the motivation and the labour environment of the firm. For Owen, the same as for Keynes (1936), inclusion of all the potential workers in a full employment economy is more important than the sum of individual happiness (a point somehow made by Piketty, 2014). Besides, Owen's paternalism meant the action of a boss whom all the workers knew by sight and whom they love and admire. Authority might be necessary for assuring some productive objectives, but authority, and esteem, must be deserved. Mere presenteeism in the workplace is the wrong policy to foster productivity when health and lack of personal life is the consequence of this organization of labour.

On the other hand, Bentham considered society as nothing but the sum of individuals. The whole force of Bentham's criticism is concentrated on the established institutions as a source of corruption and oppression, which also implies a precaution against other people, in particular the powerful ones, who are always assumed to have some "sinister interests". In politics, Bentham devised a glass prison that would reverberate to public choice theory. Bentham's theory of the entrepreneur is based on the Cantillon-Say tradition, relying on supply and technology instead of demand. Bentham's point of view was more accepted at the time because, as mentioned above, in non-democratic governments, power needed not to be questioned; when democracy was extended worldwide, the organizing principles of power began to be unwrapped.

As we have seen, both Bentham and Owen had a different philosophy of life. Owen considered progress and development the objective of happiness, the present being the time and space where we live. On the contrary, Bentham considered the accomplishment of some expectation of the future the path to happiness which is lived in a succession of time. In economics, this implies a difference between development economics that relies on objectivity and uncertainty principle, versus microeconomic analysis that relies on subjective and deterministic hypotheses. This also implies that Owen was breaking with the homo oeconomicus definition of human action based on the "homo reciprocans" moved by intrinsic motivation. Bentham considers motivation to be extrinsic and dependent on rewards and punishments. Owen's view, then, is related to William Godwin's theory of progress or to Amartya Sen's capability approach, where freedom depends on individuals' capability of achieving the kind of lives they have reason to value. On the other hand, Bentham's theory could be compared with Rawls' concept of justice: the task of justice is not to assess people's achievements, but rather to ensure the fairness of the conditions of participation in a society. In Bentham's work there is no clear concept of economic growth. His ideas are based on a static economy, as if industrial capacity was a pecuniary capital stored forever.

However, both Owen and Bentham were utopian authors: Owen's utopia is a "horizontal" one, whereas Bentham's is "vertical". In the vertical case, utopia will constitute the crowning of a linear development of history evolving to the supreme good. In the horizontal, utopia will act perpendicularly across historical process, renewing at every instant the contrast between reality and the ideal. Bentham is talking about an "aesthetic man", who values things capriciously. Owen talks about the "ethic man" who follows some principles of property in his behaviour.

With regard to their links with classical economists, Bentham was not entirely a classical economist, despite all the links he had with them. But the defence of individual private property and the idea of laissez faire were vital for him and collapsed with Owen's ideas. Both Bentham's and Owen's economics were ruled out by classical economists, who actively tried to silence different perspectives. And they managed to do so: the "visible hand" of Ricardo worked in this direction. Ricardo did not understand the concept of the marginal utility and, so he disregarded Bentham's concept of value; his disregard for Owen's activity was more due to the fact that, the same as Malthus, he was opposed to national employment for the poor and unemployed. Inequality and exclusion was not for Ricardo a problem, when for Owen inclusion is the real objective of economics and politics.

However, as we have seen, the real artificer for the extended nineteenth century English philosophy was James Mill. Like a monk, he did not need recognition for his deeds. He could even be lacking in some feeling of self regard. But he actually was the one who maintained the school of the philosophical radicals. He saw

Bentham as a great man, and concentrated on giving him influence in his time and country. He made Bentham an adept of political liberalism and philosophical radicalism. And he made him Malthusian. He managed to spread the philosophy of time as a cinematographic mechanism in which we create a fiction of continuity through imagination. But James Mill was not so successful in making Bentham a classical economist. So, as if in a casting, he sought for another main leading figure for his play: it was Ricardo who became an agent to spread the Benthamian ideas in the parliament. Bentham also tried to give Ricardo influence in his time and place, and he was successful in all of his objectives, influencing behind the scenes the future of humanity.

References

Abbott, Thomas Kingsmill (1909) *Kant's Critique of Practical Reason and other Works on the Theory of Ethics,* London, Longmans, Green and Co.

Allen Franklin, & Carletti Elena (2006) "Credit Risk Transfer and Contagion", *Journal of Monetary Economics,* 53, 89–111

Allen Franklin, Carletti Elena & Gale Douglas M. (2006) "Systemic Risk and Regulation", In Carey M. and Stulz R. (eds) *The Risks of Financial Institutions,* University of Chicago Press, Chicago, pp. 341–375

Ashworth, William J. (1994) "The calculating eye: Baily, Babbage and the business of astronomy", *British Journal for the History of Science,* 27, 409–441.

Ausubel, David P. (2000) *The Acquisition and Retention of Knowledge: A Cognitive View,* Kluwer Academic Publishers.

Bacon, Francis (1989) *New Atlantis and The Great Instauration,* Jerry Weinberger, (ed.), Wheeling, IL: Crofts Classics, pp. xxv–xxvi, xxxi [1627].

Bahmueller, Charles F. (1981) *The National Charity company: Jeremy Bentham's Silent Revolution,* Berkeley, University of California Press.

Bain, Alexander (1882) *James Mill, A Biography,* London, Longmans Green and Co.

Bartle, George F. (1991) "Benthamites and Lancasterians – The Relationship between the followers of Bentham and the British and Foreign School Society during the early years of Popular Education", *Utilitas,* 3, 2, 275–288.

Beccaria, Cesare Marchese di (1996) *De los delitos y de las penas,* Madrid, Alianza.

Beeho, Alison J. & Prentice, Richard C. (1997) "Conceptualizing the experiences of Heritage Tourists: a case study of New Lanark World Heritage Village", *Tourism Management,* 18, 2, March, 75–87.

Beecher, Jonathan (1986) *Charles Fourier: The Visionary and his World,* Berkeley, University of California Press.

Bentham, George F.M. (1997) George *Bentham: Autobiography, 1800–1834.* Toronto, University of Toronto Press.

Bentham, Jeremy (1789) *Introduction to the Principles of Morals and Legislation.* London, T. Payne.

Bentham, Jeremy (1791) *Panopticon; or, The Inspection House.* London.

Bentham, Jeremy (1817) *Plan of Parliamentary Reform, in the Form of a Catechism,* London.

Bentham, Jeremy (1818) *Defence of Usury,* Fourth edn, London: Payne and Foss, [1787].

Bentham, Jeremy (1819) *Bentham's Radical Reform Bill, with Extracts from the Reasons,* London.

Bentham, Jeremy (1821) *Principios de la Ciencia Social o de las Ciencias Morales y Políticas, Por el Jurisconsulto Inglés Jeremías Bentham, ordenados conforme al sistema del autor original y aplicados a la Constitución española por D. Toribio Nuñez*, Salamanca, Imprenta Nueva por Don Bernardo Martín.

Bentham, Jeremy (1823) *Not Paul, But Jesus*, Francis Place (ed.), London, Gamaliel Smith.

Bentham, Jeremy (1830) *The Rationale of Punishment*, London, Robert Heward.

Bentham, Jeremy (1834) *Déontologie ou Science de la Morale 2. Aplication*. Bruselas, J. P. Meline, Libraire Éditeur.

Bentham, Jeremy (1838–43) *The Works of Jeremy Bentham, Published under the superintendence of John Bowring*, 11 vols., Edinburgh, William Tait, Reimp. de Russell & Russell.

Bentham, Jeremy (1840a) *Tactique des aseemblés politiques*, en Oeuvres de Jéremie Bentham, 1, Bruselas.

Bentham, Jeremy (1840b) *Theory of legislation*, translated by Etienne Dumont. Boston, Weeks, Jordan & Company.

Bentham, Jeremy (1935) *Deontología*, Torino, Società Editrice Internazionale.

Bentham, Jeremy (1948) *A Fragment on Government and an Introduction to the Principles of Morals and Legislation*, Edited and introduced by Wilfrid Harrison, Oxford, Basil Blackwell.

Bentham, Jeremy (1968a) *The Correspondence of Jeremy Bentham, Volume 1, January 1752 to December 1776*, edited by Timothy L. S. Sprigge, London, The Athlone Press, Editor General J. H. Burns.

Bentham, Jeremy (1968b) *The Correspondence of Jeremy Bentham, Volume 2, January 1794 to December 1797*, editado por Timothy L. S. Sprigge, Londres, The Athlone Press, Editor General J. H. Burns.

Bentham, Jeremy (1970) *An Introduction to The Principles of Morals and Legislation*, Darien, Conn., Hafner Publishing Co.

Bentham, Jeremy (1971) *The Correspondence of Jeremy Bentham, Volume 3, January 1781 to December 1788*, editado por Ian R. Christie, London, The Athlone Press, Editor General J. H. Burns.

Bentham, Jeremy (1977) *A Comment on the Commentaries and a Fragment on Government*, edited by J. H. Burns and H. L. A. Hart, London, The Athlone Press.

Bentham, Jeremy (1979) *El Panóptico*, con estudios de Michel Foucault, El ojo del poder; y Maria Jesús Miranda, Bentham en España, Madrid, Colección Genealogía del Poder, Las Ediciones de la Piqueta [Bentham, Jeremy, (1791), *Panopticon; or, The Inspection House*, London].

Bentham, Jeremy (1981a) *The Correspondence of Jeremy Bentham, Volume 4, January 1789 to December 1793*, editado por Alexander Taylor Milne, Londres, The Athlone Press, Editor General J. R. Dinwiddy.

Bentham, Jeremy (1981b) *The Correspondence of Jeremy Bentham, Volume 5, January 1794 to December 1797*, editado por Alexander Taylor Milne, Londres, The Athlone Press, Editor General J. R. Dinwiddy.

Bentham, Jeremy (1981c) *Tratados de legislación civil y penal*. Clásicos para una Biblioteca Contemporanea, Edición preparada por Magdalena Rodríguez Gil, Madrid, Editora Nacional.

Bentham, Jeremy (1983a) *Constitutional Code. Volumen 1*, edited by F. Rosen and J. H. Burns, Oxford, Clarendon Press, Oxford University Press. *The Collected Works of Jeremy Bentham*. Editor General F. Rosen.

Bentham, Jeremy (1983b) *Deontology, together with a Table of the Springs of Action and Article on Utilitarianism*, edited by Amnon Goldworth, Oxford, Clarendon Press, Oxford University Press, *The Collected Works of Jeremy Bentham*. Editor General F. Rosen.

Bentham, Jeremy (1983c) *Chrestomatia*, edited by M. J., Smith and W. H. Burston, Oxford, Clarendon Press, Oxford University Press, *The Collected Works of Jeremy Bentham*, Editor General F. Rosen.

Bentham, Jeremy (1984) *The Correspondence of Jeremy Bentham, Volume 6, January 1798 to December 1801*, edited by J. R. Dinwiddy, Clarendon Press, Oxford, Editor General F. Rosen.

Bentham, Jeremy (1985) *Fragmento sobre el Gobierno*, Madrid, Sarpe.

Bentham, Jeremy (1986) *Tratado de los Sofismas políticos*, Buenos Aires, Editorial Leviatán.

Bentham, Jeremy (1988) *The Correspondence of Jeremy Bentham, Volume 8, January 1809 to December 1816*, edited by Stephen Conway, Clarendon Press, Oxford, Editor General F. Rosen.

Bentham, Jeremy (1989) *The Correspondence of Jeremy Bentham, Volume 9, January 1817 to December 1820*, edited by Stephen Conway, Clarendon Press, Oxford, Editor General F. Rosen.

Bentham, Jeremy (1989) *First Principles preparatory to Constitutional Code*, edited by Philip Schofield, Oxford, Clarendon Press, Oxford University Press. *The Collected Works of Jeremy Bentham*, Editor General F. Rosen.

Bentham, Jeremy (1990) *Securities against Misrule and other Constitutional Writings form Tripili and Greece*, edited by Philip Schofield, Oxford, Clarendon Press, Oxford University Press. *The Collected Works of Jeremy Bentham*, Editor General F. Rosen.

Bentham, Jeremy (1993) *Official Aptitude Maximised; Expense Minimized*, edited by Philip Schofield, Oxford, Clarendon Press, Oxford University Press. *The Collected Works of Jeremy Bentham*. Editor General F. Rosen.

Bentham, Jeremy (1994) *The Correspondence of Jeremy Bentham, Volume 10, January 1820 to December 1821*, edited by Stephen Conway, Clarendon Press, Oxford, Editor General F. Rosen.

Bentham, Jeremy (1995) *Colonies, Commerce, and Constitutional Law: Rid Yourselves of Ultramaria and Other Writings on Spain and Spanish America*, edited by Philip Schofield, Oxford, Clarendon Press, Oxford University Press, *The Collected Works of Jeremy Bentham*. Editor General F. Rosen.

Bentham, Jeremy (1996) *An Introduction to the Principles of Morals and Legislation*, edited by J. H. Burns and H. L. A. Hart, Oxford, Clarendon Press, Oxford University Press, *The Collected Works of Jeremy Bentham*, Editor General F. Rosen and Philip Schofield.

Bentham, Jeremy (1997) *De l'ontologie et autrestextes sur les fictions*, Texte anglais établi par Philip Schofield, Traduction et commentaires par Jean Pierre Cléro et Christian Laval, Paris, Éditions du Seuil.

Bentham, Jeremy (1998) *"Legislator of the World", Writings on Codification, Law and Education*, edited by Philip Schofield and Jonathan Harris, Oxford, Clarendon Press, Oxford University Press, *The Collected Works of Jeremy Bentham*, Editor General F. Rosen and Philip Schofield.

Bentham, Jeremy (2000) *Writings on the Poor Laws*. vol. 1, edited by Michael Quinn, Oxford, Clarendon Press.

Bentham, Jeremy (2006) Volume 12: July 1824 to June 1828, *The correspondence of Jeremy Bentham*, edited by C. Fuller, Oxford: Clarendon Press, Editor General, Philip Schofield.

Bentham, M. S. [Maria Sophia] (1862) *The life of Brigadier-General Sir Samuel Bentham,* K.S.G, London, Green, Longman and Roberts.

Berzosa, Carlos and Santos, Manuel (2000) *Los socialistas utópicos. Marx y sus discípulos,* Madrid, Editorial Síntesis.

Biernacki, R. (1995) *The Fabrication of Labor: Germany and Britain, 1640–1914.* Berkeley, University of California Press.

Black, R. D. C. (1988) "Bentham and the Political Economists of the Nineteenth Century", *Bentham Newsletter,* 12, 24–36.

Blackstone (1855 [1765]) *Commentaries on the Laws of England,* London.

Blake, Kathleen (2009) *Pleasures of Benthamism: Victorian Literature, Utility, Political Economy,* Oxford, Oxford University Press

Blamires, Cyprian (2008) *The French Revolution and the Creation of Benthamism,* New York, Palgrave.

Bloy, Marjie (2008) *The Peel web,* Retrieved July 22, 2009, http://www.historyhome.co.uk/peel/people/owen.htm.

Bonar, James and Hollander, J. H. (1899) *Letters of David Ricardo to Hutches Trower and Others 1811–1823,* Oxford, Clarendon Press.

Brandt, Richard B. (1994) *Teoría Ética,* Madrid, Alianza Editorial.

Brebner, J. Bartlet (1948) "Laissez Faire and State Internation in Nineteenth Century Britain", *The Journal of Economic History: Supplement,* vol. viii (1948), 59–73.

Brindle, Steven (2006) "Chapter 1. Father and son", *Brunel: The Man Who Built the World.* London, Hachette UK, 23 May. 2013.

Brown, Vivienne (1994) *Adam Smith's discourse. Canonicity, Commerce and Conscience,* London, Routledge.

Brunon-Ernst, Anne (2007) *Le Panoptique des Pauvres. Jeremy Bentham et la reforme de l'assistance en Angleterre,* Paris, Press Sorbonne Nouvelle.

Brunon-Ernst, Anne (2013) *Beyond Foucault: New Perspectives on Bentham's Panopticon,* Farnham, Ashgate Publishing, Ltd.

Buchanan, James M. (1999 [1962]) *Public Principles of Public Debt: A Defense and Restatement,* Indianapolis, Liberty Fund.

Buchanan, James M. (1977) *Freedom in a Constitutional Contract,* College Station, Texas, A&M University Press.

Burns, James H. (1966) *"Bentham and the French Revolution",* Transactions of the Royal Historical Society, XVI, 95–114

Burke, Edmund (1909) *On Taste. On the Sublime and Beautiful. Reflections on the French Revolution. A Letter to a Noble Lord,* New York, The Harvard Classics.

Burke, James (1978) *Connections.* BBC 10-episode documentary television series, and book based on the series. 5. The Wheel of Fortune.

Burston, W. H. (ed.) (1969) *James Mill on Education,* London, Cambridge University Press.

Burton, W. N., Chen, C. Y., Conti, D. J., Schultz, A. B., & Edington, D. W. (2006) "The association between health risk change and presenteeism change", *Journal of Occupational and Environmental Medicine,* 48, 252–263.

Butt, John (1971) "Robert Owen as a businessman", in J. Butt (ed.), *Robert Owen, Prince of Cotton Spinners,* Newton Abbot: David & Charles, pp. 168–214.

Campanella, Tomasso (1901) *City of the Sun* (text derived from Ideal Commonwealths, P.F. Collier & Son, New York) [1602].

Campos Boralevi, Lea (1984) *Bentham and the oppressed,* Berlín, Walter de Gruyter.

Cannan, Edwin (1991) "The life of David Ricardo and perspectives on his thought", in J. C. Wood (ed.), *David Ricardo. Critical Assessments,* London: Routledge, pp. 19–41.

Capaldi, Nicholas (2004) *John Stuart Mill. A Biography.* Cambridge, Cambridge University Press.

Cardoso, José Luís (1997) *Pensar A Economia em Portugal. Digressôes históricas,* Lisboa, Difusâo Editorial.

Cardoso, José Luís (coord.) (2001a) *Diccionário Histórico de economistas portugueses,* Lisboa, Temas e debates.

Cardoso, José Luís (coord.) (2001b) *A economia política e os dilemas do império luso-brasileiro (1790-1822),* Lisboa, Comissâo Nacional para as Comemoraçôes dos Descobrimentos Portugueses.

Carlisle, Y.M. and Manning, D.J. (1996) "The ideology of technology and the birth of the global economy", *Technology in Society,* 18, 1, 61–77.

Carlyle, Thomas (1853) *Occasional Discourse on the Nigger Question,* London.

Carlyle, Thomas (1956) *The French Revolution,* New York, Heritage Press.

Carlyle, Thomas (1971) *The Nigger Question,* John Stuart Mill, *The Negro Question,* edited by Eugene R. August, Appleton Century Crofts, New York.

Caruso, Sergio (2012) *Homo oeconomicus. Paradigma, critiche, revisioni,* Firenze University Press, Florence.

Casado Alonso, Hilario (1998) "La empresa en los inicios de la Revolución Industrial", en García Ruiz, José Luis (coord.) *Historia de la empresa mundial y de España,* Madrid: Síntesis, cap. 2.

Castán, Jose (1987) *Derecho civil español, comun y foral. Tomo segundo, Derecho de cosas, volumen primero, los derechos reales en general. El dominio. La posesión,* Madrid, Reus.

Chaloner, William Henry (1954) "Robert Owen, Peter Drinkwater and the Early Factory System in Manchester, 1788–1800", *Bulletin of the John Rylands Library,* 37, 1, 78–102. Reprint: *Industry and Innovation: Selected Essays of W H Chaloner.* W.H Chaloner, W.D. Farnie and W.O. Henderson (Editors). Chapter 8, pp. 135–156.

Chatterji, Monojit (2009) "New Lanark and Efficiency Wages.Economics of the New Lanark Establishment under Robert Owen's Management (1800-1825)", in *Teaching Resources for Undergraduate Economics* (TRUE). "Labour economics in a capitalist system" November 2009. Acess: 23-10-2016. http://www.economicsnetwork.ac.uk/true_showcase/labour_economics

Christie, Ian R. (1993) *The Benthams in Russia, 1780–1791,* Oxford, Berg.

Christie, Ian R. (2005) *Owenite Socialism: Pamphlets and Correspondence 1819-1825.* New York, Routledge.

Clarke, S. (1994) "Presentees: New Slaves of the Office who run in fear", *Sunday Times,* 1 October.

Coase, Ronald (1994) *Essays on Economics and Economists,* The University of Chicago Press: Chicago and London.

Cohen, David L. (1997) "Bentham's frigidarium: utilitarianism and food preservation", *Journal of Bentham Studies,* 1, 1, 1–8.

Cole, Margaret (1969) *Robert of New Lanark,* New York: Augustus M. Kelley [1953].

Collison Black, Robert Denis (1988) "Bentham and the Political Economists of the Nineteenth Century", *The Bentham Newsletter,* junio, n° 12, editor Schofield, T. P, London, University College.

Commons, John R. (1934) *Institutional Economics. Its Place in Political Economy,* Madison, The University of Wisconsin Press.

Commons, John R. et al. (1936) *History of Labour in the United States,* New York, MacMillan and co.

Condorcet, Marquis de (1795) *Sketch for a Historical Picture of the Progress of the Human Spirit,* London.

Cook, Chris (2005) *The Routledge Companion to Britain in the Nineteenth Century, 1815-1914,* London, Routledge.

Cooke, A.J. (1979) "Robert Owen and the Stanley Mills, 1802–1811", *Business History,* 21, 1, 107–111.

Cooper, Robert Alan (1979) "The English Quakers and Prison Reform 1809–23", *Quaker History,* 68, 1, Spring, 3–19.

Cremaschi, Sergio (2004) "Ricardo and the Utilitarians", *The European Journal of the History of Economic Thought,* 11, 3, 377–403.

Cremaschi, Sergio (2014) *Utilitarianism and Malthus' virtue ethics. Respectable, virtuos and happy,* Routledge, Oxford.

Cropsey, Joseph (1957) *Polity and Economy: an Interpretation of the Principles of Adam Smith,* The Hague, M. Nijhoff.

Cutler, Fred (1999) "Jeremy Bentham and the Public Opinion Tribunal", *The Public Opinion Quarterly,* 63, 3, 321–346.

Dandelion, Pink (1996) *A Sociological Analysis of the Theology of Quakers: The Silent Revolution,* London, Edwin Mellen Press Ltd.

Davidson, Lorna (2010) "A Quest for Harmony: The Role of Music in Robert Owen's New Lanark Community", *Utopian Studies,* 21, 2, 232–251.

Davis, Robert A. & O'Hagan, Frank (2010) *Robert Owen.* Bloomsbury, 3PL.

Demsetz, Harrold (1997) "The Firm in Economic Theory: A Quiet Revolution", *The American Economic Review,* 87, 2, 426–429.

Denis, Henri (1970) *Historia del pensamiento económico* [1966], Barcelona, Ariel.

Desroche, Henri (1975) *La Société festive. Du fouriérisme écrit au fouriérismes pratiqués.* Paris, Seuil.

Dicey, Albert Venn (1924) *Lectures on the Relation between Law and Public Opinion during the Nineteenth Century,* 2nd edn, London, Macmillan.

Dickens, Charles (1854) *Hard Times.* Wordsworth Printing Press.

Dinwiddy, John R. (1995) *Bentham,* Madrid, Alianza editorial [1989].

Donnachie, Ian (2000) Robert *Owen. Owen of New Lanark and New Harmony,* East Linton, Tuckwell Press.

Donnachie, Ian (2003) *Education in Robert Owen's New Society: The New Lanark Institute and Schools,* London, Not Set.

Donnachie, Ian & Hewitt, G. (1993) *Historic New Lanark. The Dale and Owen Industrial Community since 1785* (2nd edn). Edinburgh, Edinburgh University Press.

Downs, Robert B. (1975) *Heinrich Pestalozzi: Father of Modern Pedagogy,* edited by Samuel Smith, Ph.D. Boston, Twayne Publishers.

Dube, Allison (1990) "Hayek on Bentham", *Utilitas. A Journal of Utilitarian Studies,* 2, 1, May, 71–87.

Edgeworth, Francis Y., (1967 [1881]) *Mathematical Physics,* London, Augustus M. Kelley.

Ekelund, Robert B. & Hébert, Robert F. (2013) *A History of Economic Theory and Method,* Illinois, Waveland Press.

Ekelund, R. B., & Tollison, R. D. (1981) *Mercantilism as a Rent-seeking Society: Economic Regulation in Historical Perspective,* Austin, Texas University Press.

Elliott, Paul (2000) "The Derbyshire General Infirmary and the Derby Philosophers: The Application of Industrial Architecture and Technology to Medical Institutions in Early-Nineteenth-Century England", *Medical History,* 46, 65–92.

Engelmann, Stephen G (2008) "Mill, Bentham, and the Art and Science of Government", *Revue d'études benthamiennes* [En ligne], 4 2008, mis en ligne le 01 février 2008, consulté le 25 août 2016. URL: http://etudes-benthamiennes.revues.org/178

Engels, Friedrich (1880) *Socialism: Utopian and Scientific.* http://csf.colorado.edu/psn/marx/Bio/owen.html

Evans, A. 2004. Practical directions to the preservation of health. *International Journal of Epidemiology*, 33, 4, 640–649.

Evensky, Jerry (2005) *Adam Smith's Wealth of Nations: A reader's Guide*, Cambridge, Cambridge University Press.

Everett, Charles W. (1948) *The Constitutional Code of Jeremy Bentham.* London: H. K. Lewis and Co Ltd, pp. 1–29.

Everett, Charles W. (1931) *The Education of Jeremy Bentham*, New York, Columbia University Press.

Everett, Charles W. (1996) *Jeremy Bentham*, London, Weidenfeld and Nicolson.

Fassò, Guido (1982) *Historia de la Filosofía del Derecho* 2. La Edad Moderna, Madrid, Ediciones Pirámide.

Finlayson, Geoffrey (1970) *Decade of Reform: England in the Eighteen Thirties*, New York, W. W. Norton.

Fleischacker, S. (2004) *On Adam Smith's Wealth of Nations: A Philosophical Companion.* Princeton: Princeton University Press.

Fleischacker, S. (2012) "Sympathy in Hume and Smith," in *Intersubjectivity and Objectivity in Husserl and Adam Smith*, C. Fricke and D. Føllesdal (eds.), Frankfurt, Ontos Verlag, pp. 273–311.

Fleischacker, S. (2015) "Adam Smith's Moral and Political Philosophy", *The Stanford Encyclopedia of Philosophy* (Winter), edited by Edward N. Zalta, URL https://plato.stanford.edu/archives/win2015/entries/smith-moral-political.

Foucault, Michel (1984) *Vigilar y castigar, nacimiento de la prisión*, Madrid, siglo XXI editores (1977, *Discipline and Punish: The Birth of the Prison*, Penguin).

Fourier, Charles (1966–1968) *Oeuvres complètes de Charles Fourier.* 12 vols. Paris, Anthropos.

Frey, Bruno S. (1992) *Economics as a Science of Human Behaviour. Towards a New Social Science Paradigm.* London, Kluwer Academic Publishers.

Fuller, Catherine (2000) "'Primeiro e maisantigo Constitucional da Europa': El contacto de Bentham con los liberales portugeses en el perído 1820–23", *Télos*, X, 2, diciembre, 59–72.

Gabbay, Dov M. & John Woods (eds) (2008) *British Logic in the Nineteenth Century, Volume 4. Handbook of the history of logic*, Amsterdam, Elsevier.

Galbraith, John Kenneth (1998 [1958]) *The Affluent Society.* Houghton Mifflin Harcourt.

Gallhofer, Sonia and Haslam, Jim (1996) "Analysis of Betham's Chrestomathia, or towards a critique of accounting education", *Critical Perspectives on Accounting*, 7, 1, 13–31

García Ruiz, José Luis (ed.) (1994) *Historia económica de la empresa moderna*, Madrid: Istmo.

George, Claude S. (Jr) (1968) *The History of Management Thought*, New Jersey, Prentice Hall.

Ghosh, R. N. (1963) "Bentham on colonies and colonization", *Indian Economic Review*, 6, 4, 64–80.

Glasersfeld, Ernest von (1989) "Cognition, construction of knowledge, and teaching", *Synthese*, 80, 1, 121–140.

Godelier, Maurice (1999) *The Enigma of the Gift.* Chicago, University of Chicago Press.

Godwin, William (1793) *Enquiry Concerning Political Justice,* 1st edn, London, England, G.G.J. and J. Robinson.

Goldberg, Louis (1957) "Jeremy Bentham, Critic of Accounting Method", *Accounting Research,* 8, 218–245.

Goldberg, Michael (1979) "Shaw's 'Pygmalion': The Reworking of 'Great Expectations'", *The Shaw Review,* 22, 3 September, 114–122.

Goodwin, Barbara (1988) *El uso de las ideas políticas,* Barcelona, Península.

Gorb, Peter (1951) "Robert Owen as a Businessman", *Bulletin of the Business Historical Society,* 25, 3 September, 127–148. Stable URL: http://www.jstor.org/stable/3111280

Gordon, Peter (1994) "Robert Owen (1771–1858)", *Prospects: the Quarterly Review of Education* (Paris, UNESCO: International Bureau of Education), 24, 1/2, 279–296.

Gore, Charles (1997) "Irreducibly Social Goods and the Informational Basis of Amartya Sen's Capability Approach", *Journal of International Development,* 9, 2, 235–250.

Griffiths, Arthur (1884) *Memorials of Millbank and Chapters in Prison History,* 2 vols. London, Chapman & Hall.

Griswold, Charles L. (1999) *Adam Smith and the Virtues of Enlightenment,* Cambridge, CUP.

Groenewegen, Peter (1977) "Adam Smith and the Division of Labour: A Bicentenary Estimate", *Australian Economic Papers,* 161–174.

Grotius, Hugo (1625) *De Jure Belli ac Pacis, libri tres, In quibus ius naturae & Gentium: item iuris publici preciptae expilicantur,* Apud Nicalaum Buon, Paris.

Guidi, Marco (2004) "'My Own Utopia'. The economics of Bentham's Panopticon". *European Journal of the History of Economic Thought.* 11(3), 405–431.

Guillot, Armand (2016) "John Stuart Mill, héritier et critique de Jeremy Bentham", *Revue d'études benthamiennes* [En ligne], 4 2008, mis en ligne le 01 février 2008, consulté le 25 août 2016. URL: http://etudes-benthamiennes.revues.org/177

Haakonssen, Knud (1981) *The Science of a Legislator,* Cambridge: CUP.

Haakonssen, Knud (1996) *Natural Law and Moral Philosophy. From Grotius to the Scottish Enlightenment,* Cambridge: CUP.

Halévy, Elie (1972) *The Growth of Philosophic Radicalism,* with a new Preface by John Plamenatz, Chichele Professor of Social and Political Theory, London, Faber and Faber [1928].

Harris, Jonathan (1999) "Los escritos de codificación de Jeremy Bentham y su recepción en el primer liberalismo español", *Télos. Revista Iberoamericana de Estudios Utilitaristas,* Vol. VIII, n° 1, junio, Salamanca, SIEU, 9–31.

Harrison, John (1969) *Robert Owen and the Owenites in Britain and America: The Quest for a New Moral World.* London, Routledge & Kegan Paul.

Harrison, Ross (1989) "Jeremy Bentham", In *The Invisible Hand,* London, Palgrave MacMillan, pp. 53–60.

Hart, H. L. A. (1976) "Bentham and the United States of America", *The Journal of Law and Economics,* XIX, 3, October, 547–567.

Hart, H. L. A. (ed.) (1970) Of Laws in General, *The Collected works of Jeremy Bentham,* London, Athlone Press.

Harte, Negley (2005) Radical pants and the pursuit of happiness. *Times Higher Education,* 9 September

Hartley, David (1749) *Observations on Man, his Frame, his Duty, and his Expectations,* In two parts, London, Printed by S. Richardson for James Leake and Wm. Frederick.

Harvey, Rowland Hill (1949) *Robert Owen, Social Idealist*. Berkeley and Los Angeles: University of California Press.

Hayek, Friedrich A. (1932) "A note on the Development of the Doctrine of Forced Saving", *The Quarterly Journal of Economics*, vol. XLVI, Cambridge, Harvard University Press, pp. 123–133.

Hayek, Friedrich A. (1960) *Los fundamentos de la libertad*, Madrid, Unión Editorial.

Hayek, Friedrich A. (1961) "The Non Sequitur of the Dependence Effect", *Southern Economic Journal*, 27, April 1961.

Hayek, Friedrich A., (1976) *Denationalization of Money. The Argument Refined: An Analysis of the Theory and Practice of Concurrent Currencies*, London, Institute of Economic Affairs.

Hayek, Friedrich A. (1988) *The Fatal Conceit. The Errors of Socialism*, London, Routledge.

Hayek, Friedrich A. (1978) "Adam Smith's Message in Today's Language," In Hayek, *New Studies in Philosophy, Politics, Economics and the History of Ideas*, Chicago, University of Chicago Press, pp. 267–269.

Hayes, Adele M. & Feldman Greg (2004) "Clarifying the construct of mindfulness in the context of emotion regulation and the process of change in therapy", *Clinical Psychology: Science and Practice* 11 (3). doi:10.1093/clipsy/bph080.

Hazlitt, W. (1969) *The Spirit of the Age*. London: Collins Publishers [1825].

Hébert, Robert F. & Link, Albert N. (1988) *The Entrepreneur, Mainstream Views and Radical Critiques*, New York, Praeger.

Hébert, Robert F. & Link, Albert N. (2006) "The Entrepreneur as Innovator", *Journal of Technology Transfer*. 31, 589–597.

Heberton Evans Jr, G. (1949) "The entrepreneur and economic theory, a historical and analytical approach", *The American Economic Review*, Papers and Proceedings: XXXIX, May, 337–338.

Helvétius, Claude Adrien (1759) *De l'esprit or, Essays on the Mind, and its Several Faculties*, London, Albion Press.

Helvétius, Claude Adrien (1800) *Treatise on Man: His Intellectual Faculties and his Education*, transl. W. Hooper, M. D., London, Albion Press.

Hellwig, Martin F. (2009) "Systemic Risk in the Financial Sector: An Analysis of the Subprime-Mortgage Financial Crisis", *De Economist*, 157, 2, 129–207.

Hemp, Paul (2004) "Presenteeism: At work—but out of it", *Harvard Business Review*, 82, 49–58.

Herrick, James (1985) *Against the Faith: Essays on Deists, Skeptics, and Atheists*, Buffalo, NY, Prometheus Books.

Himmelfarb, Gertrude (1995) *Victorian Minds, A Study of Intellectuals in Crisis and Ideologies in Transitions*, London, Rowman & Littlefield.

Hobbes, Thomas (2012) *Leviathan*, Critical edition by Noel Malcolm in three volumes, Oxford, Oxford University Press, [1651].

Hollander, Samuel (1973) *The Economics of Adam Smith*, London, Heinemann Educational Books.

Hollander, Samuel (1979) *The Economics of David Ricardo*, Toronto and Buffalo, The University of Toronto Press.

Hollander, Samuel (1985) *The Economics of John Stuart Mill*, Toronto and Buffalo, The University of Toronto Press.

Hollander, Samuel (1999) "Jeremy Bentham and Adam Smith on the Usury Laws: A Smithian reply to Bentham and a New Problem", *European Journal History of Economic Thought*, 6, 4, 523–551.

Hollis, Patricia (1973) *Class and Conflict in Nineteenth-century England, 1815–1850, Birth of modern Britain series,* International Library of Sociology and Social Reconstruction, Routledge, London.

Holyoake, George Jacob (1896) *The Origin and Nature of Secularism: Showing that where Free Thought Commonly Ends Secularism Begins,* Wisconsin, Watts.

Horkheimer, Max & Adorno, Theodor (1972) *Dialectic of Enlightenment,* New York, Herder and Herder.

Hoskin, Keith, (1979) "The Examination, Disciplinary Power and Rational Schooling", *History of Education,* 8, 2, 135–146.

Hoskin, Keith & Macve, Richard (1986) "Accounting and the examination: A genealogy of disciplinary power", *Accounting, Organizations and Society,* 11, 105–136.

Huerta De Soto, Jesús (2000) *La escuela Austriaca, mercado y creatividad empresarial,* Madrid, Editorial Síntesis.

Hume, David (1964a) *The Philosophical Works,* Volume 1, edited by Thomas Hill Green and Thomas Hodge Grose. London, Scientia Verlag.

Hume, David (1964b) *The Philosophical Works,* Volume 2, edited by Thomas Hill Green and Thomas Hodge Grose. London, ScientiaVerlag.

Hume, David (1964c) *The Philosophical Works. Essays Moral, Political and Literary,* Volume 1, edited by T. H. Green and T. H. Grose, London, Scientia Verlag Aalen.

Hume, David (1964d) *The Philosophical works. Essays Moral, Political and Literary,* Volume 2, edited by T. H. Green and T. H. Grose, London, Scientia Verlag Aalen.

Hume, L. J. (1970a) "The Development of Industrial Accounting: The Benthams' Contribution", *Journal of Accounting Research,* Spring, 21–33.

Hume, L. J. (1970b) "Jeremy Bentham on Industrial Management", *Yorkshire Bulletin of Economic and Social Research,* 22, 1, May, 3–15.

Hume, L. J. (1981) *Bentham and Bureaucracy,* Cambridge, Cambridge University Press.

Hutchison, T. (1956) "Bentham as an Economist", *The Economic Journal,* 66, 262, 288–306.

Huxley, Aldous (1963) *The Doors of Perception,* New York, Harper & Row Publishers.

Ignatieff, Michael (1978) *A Just Measure of Pain: The Penitentiary in the Industrial Revolution, 1750–1850,* London, Macmillan.

Ippolito, Richard A. (1977) "The Division of Labour in the Firm", *Economic Inquiry,* 15, 469–492.

James, P. (1966) *The Travel Diaries of Thomas Robert Malthus,* Cambridge, Cambridge University Press.

Janis M. W. (2010) Blackstone and Bentham: The Law of Nations and International Law. In: *America and the Law of Nations 1776-1939,* Oxford, Oxford University Press.

Jevons, William Stanley (1871) *The Theory of Political Economy,* London, Macmillan and Co.

Kant, Immanuel (1996) *The Metaphysics of Morals.* Translated by Mary J. Gregor. Cambridge, Cambridge University Press [1689].

Kant, Immanuel (1997) *Groundwork of the Metaphysics of Morals,* Cambridge, Cambridge University Press.

Kay, James Phillips (1839) *The Training of Pauper Children,* London, William Clowes and sons.

Keynes, John Maynard (1925) "Alfred Marshall", *Memorials of Alfred Marshall,* edited by A. C. Pigou. London, Palgrave Macmillan.

Keynes, John Maynard (1936) *The General Theory of Employment, Interest and Money,* London, Palgrave Macmillan.

Kierkegaard, Soren (1965) *Obras y papeles de S. Kierkegaard*, Madrid, Guadarrama.

Kirzner, Israel M. (1973) *Competencia y empresarialidad*, 2ª edición, Madrid, Unión Editorial, [1998].

Knight, Frank H. (1921) *Riesgo, Incertidumbre y Beneficio*, Madrid, Aguilar [1947].

Knowles, Rob (2013) *Political Economy from Below: Economic Thought in Communitarian Anarchism 1840–1914*, London, Routledge.

Koopman, C. et al. (2002) "Stanford presenteeism scale: Health status and employee productivity", *Journal of Occupational and Environmental Medicine*, 44, 14–20.

Lafargue, Paul (1880) *Socialisme utopique et socialisme scientifique*, Paris.

Lancaster, Joseph (1821) *The Lancasterian System of Education, with Improvements*, London, Ogden Miles Printer.

Lapidus, André and Sigot, Nathalie (2000) "Individual utility in a context of asymmetric sensitivity to pleasure and pain: an interpretation of Bentham's felicific calculus", *European Journal for the History of Economic Thought*, 7, 1, 45–78.

Lees, Lynn Hollen (1998) *The Solidarities of Strangers: The English Poor Laws and the People, 1700–1948*, Cambridge, Cambridge University Press.

Leibenstein, Harvey (1966) "Allocative Efficiency vs. 'X-Efficiency'", *The American Economic Review*, Vol. LVI., June.

Leloup, Sandrine (2002) "El liberalismo económico, a prueba en Bentham: Panóptico y mercado de crédito", *Télos. Revista Iberoamericana de Estudios utilitaristas:* X: 2: 2001, 7–20.

Leroy, Marie-Laure (2008) "Quantité et qualité des plaisirs chez Bentham", *Revue d'études benthamiennes*, URL: http://etudes-benthamiennes.revues.org/180

Leslie, Stephen (1900) *The English Utilitarians*, L. S. E. and Political Science Series of Reprints of Scarce Works on Political Economy, n° 9–11, 3 vols., L.S.E. and P.S. Gloucester, Mass.

Levin, David Michael (1997) "Keeping Foucault and Derrida in sight: Panopticism and the politics of subversion", in *Sites of vision: The discursive construction of sight in the history of philosophy*, edited by D. M. Levin, Cambridge, MA, MIT Press, pp. 397–465.

Levine, Norman (2015) *Marx's Rebellion against Lenin*, Springer.

Levy, David M. (1999) *Economic Texts as Apocrypha*, Center for Study of Public Choice, George Mason University.

Levy, David M. (2000) *Hard Times & the Moral Equivalence of Markets and Slavery*, Center for Study of Public Choice, George Mason University.

Locke, John (1689) *Two Treatises of Government*, London, Awnsham Churchill.

Locke, Don (1980) *A Fantasy of Reason: The Life and Thought of William Godwin*, London, Routledge & Kegan Paul.

Lockwood, George B. (1905) *The New Harmony Movement*, New York, Appleton.

Long, Douglas G. (1977) *Bentham on Liberty: Jeremy Bentham's Idea of Liberty in Relation to his Utilitarianism*, Toronto, University of Toronto Press.

Long, Douglas G. (1988) "Censorial Jurisprudence and Political Radicalism: a Reconsideration of the Early Bentham", The Bentham Newsletter, June, n° 12, editor Schofield, T. P, London, University College.

Long, Douglas G. (1990) "La 'utilidad' y el 'principio de utilidad'. Hume, Smith, Bentham, Mill", *Utilitas. A Journal of Utilitarian Studies*, 2, 1, 12–39.

Losman, Donald L. (1971) "J. S. Mill on Alternative Economic Systems", *American Journal of Economics and Sociology*, 30, 85–103.

Luxemburg, Rosa (1904) *Rosa Luxemburg. Selected Political Writings*, London, The Chaucer Press, 1972.

Mackay, S. (1820) *Settler Letters: Stephen Bourne and Joseph Purnells's letters, Settler Emigration Letters*, London, National Archives in Kew.

Mack, Mary P. (1962) *Jeremy Bentham. An Odyssey of Ideas 1748–1792*, London, Melbourne, Toronto, Heinemann.

Macnab, Henry Gray (1819, *The New Views of Mr. Owen of Lanark Impartially Examined*, London, H. Hatchard and Son.

Malthus, Thomas Robert (1826) *An Essay on the Principle of Population*, London, John Murray.

Manning, D. J. (1968) *The Mind of Jeremy Bentham*, London, Longmans, Green.

Marchán, Simon (1996) *La estética en la cultura moderna*, Madrid, Alianza Editorial.

Marshall, Peter H. (1984) *William Godwin*, New Haven and London, Yale University Press.

Mata, Maria Eugénia (1988) "As Três Fases do Fontismo: Projectos e Realizaçoes", en *Estudos e Ensais en homenagem a Vitorino Magalhâes Godinho*, Lisboa, Livraria da Costa Editora.

Mata, Maria Eugénia (2001) "Economic Ideas and Policies in Nineteenth-Century Portugal", *Luzo-Brazilian Review*, XXXVIII II.

Mccabe, J. (1920) *Robert Owen*. London, Watts.

Mcculloch, John M. R. (1820) "Review of Malthus's Principles of Political Economy", *The Scotsman or Edinburgh Political and Literary Journal*, April, 171.

Mckinlay, Alan (2006) "Managing Foucault: Genealogies of management", *Management & Organizational History*, 1, 87–100.

Mclaren, David J. (1983) *David Dale of New Lanark: A Bright Luminary to Scotland*. Heatherbank Press; 1st edition (Feb. 1983).

Mcwilliam, Neil (1993) *Dreams of Happiness: Social Art and the French Left, 1830–1850*, Princeton, NJ, Princeton University Press.

Menger, Carl (1984) *Investigations into the Method of the Social Sciences with Special Reference to Economics*, New York, New York University Press [1883].

Menudo, José María and O'Kean, José María (2006) "The French Tradition: an Alternative Theoretical Framework", *Working papers series*, WP ECON 06.24, Department of Economics, UPO.

Middaugh, D. J. (2006) "Presenteeism: Sick and tired at work", *Medsurg Nursing*, 15, 103–105.

Mill, James (1844 [1821]) *Elements of Political Economy*, London, Henry G. Bohn.

Mill, James (1955 [1823]) *An Essay on Government*, edited with an introduction by Currin V. Shields, New York, Bobbs Merrill.

Mill, James (2001) *Analysis of the Phenomena of the Human Mind*, Bristol, Thoemmes Press [1829].

Mill, John Stuart (1838) "Bentham", *London and Westminster Review*, 1.

Mill, John Stuart (1978 [1848]) *Principios de Economía Política*, México, Fondo de Cultura Económica.

Mill, John Stuart (1978) *On Liberty*, Indianapolis, Hackett Publishing.

Mill, John Stuart (1980) *Mill on Bentham and Coleridge*, with an introduction by F. R. Leavis, Cambridge, Cambridge University Press.

Mill, John Stuart (1986) *Autobiografía*, Madrid, El Libro de Bolsillo, Alianza Editorial.

Mill, John Stuart (1997) *Ensayos sobre algunas cuestiones disputadas en economía política*, edición de Rodríguez Braun, Madrid, Alianza [1844].

Mill, John Stuart (2007) *The Autobiography of John Stuart Mill*. Sioux Falls (D.S.), Nuvision Publications [1864].

Mill, John Stuart (1985) *The Collected Works of John Stuart Mill*, Volume X Essays on Ethics, Religion, and Society, edited by John M. Robson, Introduction by F.E.L. Priestley, Toronto: University of Toronto Press, London: Routledge and Kegan Paul. http://oll.libertyfund.org/titles/241

Miller, Peter & O'Leary Ted (1987) "Accounting and the construction of the governable person", *Accounting, Organizations and Society*, 12, 235–66.

Miller, Peter N. (ed.) (1993) *Priestley: Political Writings*. Cambridge, Cambridge University Press.

Mises, Ludwig von (1949) *La acción humana. Tratado de Economía*, Unión Editorial, Madrid [2001].

Mitchell, Wesley C. (1918) "Bentham's Felicific Calculus", *Political Science Quarterly*, 33, 2, 161–183.

Monroe, Will S. (1969) *History of the Pestalozzian Movement in the United States*. New York, Arno Press & The New York Times

Montefiore, Simon Sebag (2001) *Prince of Princes: The Life of Potemkin*, Phoenix Press.

Montes, L. (2004) *Adam Smith in Context: A Critical Reassessment of Some Central Components of his Thought*, New York, Palgrave Macmillan.

Montesquieu, Charles de Secondat, Baron de (1748) *De L'Esprit des loix*, Geneve, Barrillot and Fils.

Morris, Clarence (1997) *The Great Legal Philosophers. Selected Readings in Jurisprudence*, Philadelphia, University of Pennsylvania Press.

Morton, A.L. (1962) *The Life and Ideas of Robert Owen*, New York, International Publishers.

Moyles, Janet, (2014) *The Excellence Of Play*, Maidenhead, McGraw-Hill Education.

Murphy, Antoin E. (ed.) (1984) "Francis Ysidro Edgeworth," *Economists and the Irish Economy. From the 18th century to the present*, Dublin, Irish Academic.

Muthu, Sankar (2008) "Adam Smith's Critique of International Trading Companies: Theorizing 'Globalization' in the Age of Enlightenment," *Political Theory*, 36, 2, 185–212.

Nelson, Richard R., and Sydney, Winter G. (1982) *An Evolutionary Theory of Economic Change*, Cambridge, The Belknap Press of Harvard University Press.

Neusüss, A. (ed.) (1968) *Utopie*. Begriff und Phänomen des Utopischen, Neuwied.

Newlyn, Lucy (2002) *The Cambridge Companion to Coleridge*, Cambridge, Cambridge University Press.

Nicholson, Helen (2011) *Theatre, Education and Performance*, London, Palgrave Macmillan.

Norris, John (1963) *Shelburne and Reform*, London, Macmillan.

Noyes, John Humphrey (1870) *History of American Socialism*, New York, repr 1961.

Nozick, Robert (1974) *Anarchy, State and Utopia*, Nueva York, Basic Books.

Nussbaum. Martha (2011) *Creating Capabilities: The Human Development Approach*, Cambridge, MA, Harvard University Press.

Oakeshott, Michael (1962) *Rationalism in Politics and Other Essays*, London, Methuen.

O'Brien, Denis P. (2004) *The Classical Economists Revisited*, Princeton, New Jersey: Princeton University Press.

Ogden, C. L. (1932) *Bentham's Theory of Fictions*, London, Kegan Paul, Trench, Trubner.

O'Hagan, F.J. (2005) "Robert Owen and The Development Of Good Citizenship In 19th Century New Lanark. *Enlightened Reform Or Social Control?" Global Citizenship Education*, 1–11.

Oliver, W. H. (1964) "The Consolidated Trades' Union of 1834", *The Economic History Review*, New Series, 17, 1, 77–95.

Oncken, August (1898) "Das Adam Smith Problem", *Zeitschrift fur Sozialwissenschaft,* 1.

Owen, Robert (1970) *Report to the County of New Lanark. A New View of Society,* Penguin Books (Introduction" by V. A. C. Gatrell, pp.7–81).

Owen, Robert (1857) *The Life of Robert Owen, by Himself,* Effingham Wilson, London.

Owen, Robert Dale (1967) *Threading my Way. An Autobiography* [1874], New York: Augustus M. Shelley. Extractos, in <http://athena.louisville.edu/a-s/english/subcultures/colors/red/jtrieb01/RDO3.html>

Owen, Robert (1812) *Statement Regarding the New Lanark Establishment.* Edinburgh: John Moir.

Owen, Robert (1813) *A New View of Society; or Essays on the Principle of the Formation of the Human Character* [essays 1 and 2]. London: Cadell& Davies, 1813; [essays 3 and 4]. London: R. & A. Taylor, 1814; [essays 1-4]. New York: E. Bliss & E. White, 1825.

Owen, Robert (1816) *An Address to the Inhabitants of New Lanark,* London.

Owen, Robert (1818–1823) *Letters to Jeremy Bentham.* British Museum, Additional Manuscripts, Vols. 7,952-44,389 "Robert Owen Papers", 33,545 (9) 1818–1823. Robert Owen to Jeremy Bentham.

Owen, Robert (1821) *Report to the County of Lanark of a Plan for Relieving Public Distress, and Removing Discontent by Giving Permanent Productive Employment to the Poor and Working Classes.* Glasgow, Glasgow University Press.

Owen, Robert (1849) *The Revolution in Mind and Practice of the Human Race or the Coming Change from Irrationality to Rationality,* London, Effingham Wilson.

Owen, Robert (1857) *The Life of Robert Owen: Written by Himself.* Vol. I. London, Effingham Wilson.

Owen, Robert Dale (1824) *An Outline of the System of Education at New Lanark,* Glasgow, University Press.

Owen, Robert Dale (1967) *Threading my Way, Twenty-seven Years of Autobiography,* London: Augustus M. Kelley [1874].

Pack, S. J. (1991) *Capitalism as a Moral System: Adam Smith's Critique of the Free Market Economy,* Aldershot, Hants, England; Brookfield, USA: Edward Elgar.

Pack, S. J. (1995) "Theological (and Hence Economic) Implications of Adam Smith's "Principles which Lead and Direct Philosophical Enquiries", *History of Political Economy,* 27, 2, 289–307.

Pack, S. J. & Schliesser, E. (2006) "Smith's Humean Criticism of Hume's Account of the Origin of Justice", *Journal History of Philosophy,* 44, 1, 47–63.

Paley, Gregory (2002) *Citizens and Saints: Politics and Anti-Politics in Early British Socialism,* Cambridge, Cambridge University Press.

Parekh, Bhikhu (1974) *Jeremy Bentham. Ten Critical Essays,* London, Frank Cass.

Passmore, John A., (ed.) (1964) *Priestley's Writings on Philosophy, Science and Politics.* New York: Collier Books.

Pease, Catherine (2002) "Jeremy and Samuel Bentham – The Private and the Public". *Journal of Bentham Studies* (5).

Perdices De Blas, L. (ed.) (2003) *Historia del Pensamiento Económico,* Madrid, Editorial Síntesis.

Perdices De Blas, L. & Reeder, J. (1988) *El mercantilismo: política económica y Estado Nacional,* Madrid, Síntesis.

Perlman, Selig (1928) *Theory of the Labour Movement,* New York, repr. 1948.

Persky, Joseph (1995) "Retrospectives: The Ethology of Homo Economicus." *The Journal of Economic Perspectives,* 9, 2 (Spring), 221–231.

Pesciarelli, E. (1989) "Smith, Bentham and the development of contrasting ideas on entre-preneurship", *History of Political Economy*, 21, 3, 521–536.

Pesciarelli, E. (1990) "The emergence of a vision: the development of Schumpeter's theory of entrepreneurship". *History of Political Economy*, 22, 677–696.

Piaget, Jean (1950) *The Psychology of Intelligence*. New York: Routledge.

Piketty, Thomas (2014) *Capital in the Twenty-First Century*. Cambridge, MA, Belknap Press.

Podmore, F. (1906) *Robert Owen: A Biography*. London, George Allen and Unwin.

Pollard, S. (1987) *La génesis de la dirección de empresa moderna*, Madrid: Ministerio de Trabajo y Seguridad Social. [1965].

Pollard-Sacks, Deana (2009) "State Actors Beating Children: A Call for Judicial Relief" *UC DAVIS LAW REVIEW*, 42, Available at SSRN: http://ssrn.com/abstract=1242622

Posner, Richard A. (1976) "Blackstone and Bentham", *The Journal of Law and Economics*, XIX, 3, October, 569–606.

Postema, G. J. (1986) *Bentham and the Common Law Tradition*, Oxford, Oxford University Press.

Proudhon, Pierre Joseph (2010) *System of Economical Contradictions: or, The Philosophy of Poverty*, Kessinger Publishing [1847].

Pufendorf, Samuel von (1927) *The Two Books On The Duty of Man And Citizen According to the Natural Law* [De Officio Hominis et Civis Juxta Legem Naturalem Libri Duo], Carnegie Institution of Washington, Washington DC [1673].

Putterman, Louis (ed.) (1994) *La naturaleza económica de la empresa* [1986], Madrid: Alianza.

Quarter, Jack (2000) *Beyond the Bottom Line: Socially Innovative Business Owners*, Praeger (September 30).

Quigley, William, P. (1996) "Five Hundred Years of English Poor Laws, 1349–1834: Regulating the Working and Nonworking Poor", *Akron Law Review*, 1, 73–128.

Quinn, Michael, (1994) "Jeremy Bentham on the Relief of Indigence: AnExercise in Applied Philosophy", *Utilitas. A Journal of Utilitarian Studies*, 6, 1, May, Oxford, Oxford University Press, pp. 81–96.

Quinn, Michael (1997) "The fallacy of non interference: the poor panopticon and equality of opportunity", *Journal of Bentham Studies*, 1

Rae, John (1895) *Life of Adam Smith*, London, Macmillan.

Rawls, John (1971) *A Theory of Justice*, Cambridge, MA, The Belknap Press of Harvard University Press.

Raynor, David R. (1984) "Hume's Abstract of Adam Smith's 'Theory of Moral Sentiments'", *Journal of History of Philosophy*, 22, 51–80.

Reay, Barry (1985) *The Quakers and the English Revolution*, London, Palgrave Macmillan.

Ricardo, David (1899) *Letters Of David Ricardo To Hutches Trower And Others*, 1811–1823, Oxford: Oxford Clarendon Press.

Ricardo, David (1966) *The Works and Correspondence of David Ricardo, Vol.2, Notes on Malthus's Principles of Political Economy*, edited by Piero Sraffa with the collaboration of M.H. Dobb, Cambridge, Cambridge University Press.

Ricardo, David (1973) *The Works and Correspondence of David Ricardo, Vol.10*, edited by Piero Sraffa with the collaboration of M.H. Dobb, Cambridge, Cambridge University Press.

Ricardo, David (2005) *The Works of David Ricardo*. Indianapolis, Liberty Fund.

Ricoeur, Paul (1984) *Time and Narrative Vol. I*, Chicago, The University of Chicago Press.

Riley, Patrick (2006) "The Social Contract and Its Critics", in *The Cambridge History of Eighteenth-Century Political Thought*, edited by Mark Goldie and Robert Wokler,

Vol 4 of *The Cambridge History of Political Thought*, Cambridge University Press, pp. 347–375.

Roberts, A. (1997) Social Science and the 1834 Poor Law [web edition]. Available at http://studymore.org.uk/sshhome.htm

Roberts, David (1960) *Victorian Origins of the British Welfare State*, New Haven, Yale University Press.

Robertson, Alex J. (1971) "Robert Owen, Cotton Spinner: New Lanark, 1800–1825" In S. Pollard & J. Salt (eds) *Robert Owen: Prophet of the Poor.* London, Macmillan, pp. 145–165.

Robbins, C. Lionel (1953) *The Theory of Economic Policy in English Classical Political Economy*, London, MacMillan.

Robinson, Ken (1977) *Learning through Drama: Report of The Schools Council Drama Teaching Project* con Lynn McGregor and Maggie Tate. UCL

Rocker, Rudolf (2004) *Anarcho-Syndicalism Theory and Practice.* Oakland, Edinburgh: AK Press.

Rodríguez Braun, Carlos (1986) "Entrevista con Friedrich A. Hayek", *Revista de Occidente*, marzo, nº 58, Madrid, pp. 124–135.

Rodríguez Braun, Carlos (1992) "Pownall on Smith on Colonies", *Storia del Pensiero Economico*, 23, bolletino di informazionesse mestrale, Firenze, pp. 3–10.

Roll, Eric (1939) *History of Economic Thought*, New York, Prentice Hall Inc.

Romilly, S. (1840) *Memoirs of the Life of Sir Samuel Romilly written by himself, with a selection from his Correspondence*, edited by his sons (3 vols.), London, J. Murray.

Roncaglia, Alessandro (1997) "Reseña del libro de John Bonner, Economic Efficiency and Social Justice", *Journal of the History of Economic Thought*, 19, 2, 319.

Rosen, Frederick (1983) *Jeremy Bentham and Representative Democracy. A Study of the Constitutional Code*, Oxford, Clarendon Press.

Rosen, Frederick (1992) *Bentham, Byron and Greece: Constitutionalism, Nationalism, and Early Liberal Political Thought*, Oxford, Oxford University Press.

Rosen, Frederick (1994) "¿Es Bentham utilitarista?", *Télos. Revista Iberoamericana de Estudios Utilitaristas*, Vol. III, nº 1, junio, Salamanca, SIEU, pp. 11–26.

Rosen, Frederick (2003) CLASSICAL UTILITARIANISM FROM HUME TO MILL. London, Routledge.

Rosenberg, Nathan (1965) "Adam Smith on the Division of Labour: Two Views or One", *Economica*, 32, 127–139.

Rosenberg, Nathan (1976) "Another Advantage of the Division of Labour", *Journal of Political Economy*, 84, 4, 861–868.

Rosenberg, Nathan (1982) *Inside the Black Box: Technology and Economics,* Cambridge, Cambridge University Press.

Ross, Ian Simpson (1995) *The Life of Adam Smith*, Oxford, Clarendon Press.

Rothbard, Murray N. (1995) *An Austrian Perspective on the History of Economic Thought,* Alabama, Ludwig Von Mises Institute.

Rothbard, Murray N. (2000) *Historia del Pensamiento Económico, Volumen II. La economía clásica*, Madrid, Unión Editorial [1995].

Rousseau, Jean-Jacques (1762a) *Du contrat social ou Principes du droit politique*, Amsterdam, Marc Michel Rey.

Rousseau, Jean-Jacques (1762b) *Emile ou de l'éducation*, Jean Néaulme, La Haye.

Royle, Edward (1998) *Robert Owen and the Commencement of the Millennium: The Harmony Community at Queenwood Farm, Hampshire, 1839–1845*, Manchester, Manchester University Press.

Rubel, Maximilien (1960) "Robert Owen a Paris en 1848". *L'Actualité de l'histoire*, No. 30 (Jan–Mar), pp. 1–12. https://bsstock.files.wordpress.com/2014/03/rubel_owen1848.pdf

Ruddy, Michael (2000) "Pestalozzi and The Oswego Movement" (PDF). Retrieved 28 June 2015.

Rule, John (1990) *Clase obrera e industrialización. Historia social de la revolución industrial británica, 1750–1850*, Editorial Crítica, Barcelona.

Saint-Simon, Conde de (1825) *Nouveau christianisme* (New Christianity). Paris, France.

Salas Fumás, Vicente (1993) "La empresa en el análisis económico", *Papeles de Economía Española*, 57, 126–170.

Santos, Manuel, y Ramos, Jose Luis (2000) "Los socialistas utópicos", en Berzosa, Carlos, *et al, Los socialistas utópicos. Marx y sus dicípulos*, Madrid, Síntesis.

Santos Redondo, Manuel (1997) *Los economistas y la empresa. Empresa y empresario en la historia del pensamiento económico*, Madrid: Alianza.

Santos Redondo, Manuel (2002) "Robert Owen, pionero del management", *Sociología del trabajo*. 45, 97–124.

Santos Redondo, Manuel (2003) "Robert Owen, empresario", *Revista Empresa y Humanismo*, 6, 1, 179–198.

Santos Redondo, Manuel (1994) "La fábrica de alfileres y la mano invisible", *Cuadernos de relaciones laborales*, 5, 183–196.

Santos Redondo, Manuel (2000) "La teoría neo-institucionalista de la empresa como metodología". *Argumentos de Razón Técnica*, 3, 189–205, http://institucional.us.es/revistas/argumentos/3/art_7.pdf

Sauvy, Alfred (1986) *La máquina y el paro. Empleo y progreso tecnológico*, Madrid, Espasa Calpe [1980].

Scarpe, Geoffrey (1996) *Utilitarianism. The Problems of Philosophy*, London and New York, Routledge.

Schlossberger, E. (2008) A *Holistic Approach to Rights:* Lanham, Maryland: University Press of America.

Schneewind, J. B. (1990) "The Misfortunes of Virtue," *Ethics*, 101, 42–63.

Schofield, Philip (1990) "Bentham on Public Opinion and the Press" *Economical with the Truth: The Law and the Media in a Democratic Society*, ed. Kingsford-Smith and Oliver, Oxford, pp. 95–108.

Schofield, Philip (1996) "Bentham on the Identification of Interests", *Utilitas. A Journal of Utilitarian Studies,* 8, 2, 223–234.

Schofield, Philip (1998) "Jeremy Bentham: Legal Philosopher and Political Radical", in *The Old Radical: Representations of Jeremy Bentham*, edited by C. Fuller, London, pp. 2–3.

Schultz, Alyssa B. and Edington, Dee W. (2007) "Employee Health and Presenteeism: A Systematic Review", *Journal of Occupational Rehabilitation*, September, 17, 3, 547–579.

Schumpeter, J. (1934) *Theory of Economic Development*. Harvard University Press. Reprint: Transaction Publishers, 31 dic. 2011

Schumpeter, J. (1954a) *Economic Doctrine and Method: An Historical Sketch*. New York, Oxford University Press [1914].

Schumpeter, J. (1954b) *History of Economic Analysis,* Oxford, Oxford University Press.

Schwartz, Pedro (1976) "La influencia de Bentham en España", Información Comercial Española, 517, septiembre, 52–56.

Schwartz, Pedro (1982) "El monopolio del Banco Central", *Homenaje a Lucas Beltrán*, Madrid: Moneda y Crédito.

Schwartz, Pedro (1986) "Jeremy Bentham's democratic despotism", *Ideas in Economics*, edited by R. D. Collison Black, Basingstoke, Macmillan Press, pp. 74–103.

Schwartz Pedro (1988) "El despotismo democrático de Jeremy Bentham", *Información Comercial Española, ICE: Revista de economía*, n° 656, pp. 53–70.

Schwartz, Pedro y Rodríguez Braun, Carlos (1986) "Las relaciones entre Jeremy Bentham y Simón Bolivar", Alberto Filippi (editor), *Bolivar y Europa en las crónicas, el pensamiento político y la historiografía*, Caracas Ediciones de la Presidencia de la República, Comité Efecutivo del Bicentenario de Simón Bolivar, pp. 445–460.

Schwartz, Pedro, y Rodríguez Braun, Carlos (1992) "Bentham on Spanish Protectionism", *Utilitas*, 4, 1, may, 122–132.

Semple, Janet (1993) *Bentham's Prison: A Study of the Panopticon Penitentiary*, Oxford, Clarendon Press.

Sen, Amartya (1989) "Development as Capability Expansion," *Journal of Development Planning*, 19, 41–58.

Shepherd, Janet (2004) "Mayo, Elizabeth (1793–1865)", *Oxford Dictionary of National Biography*, Oxford, Oxford University Press.

Sigot, Nathalie (1996) "Jeremy Bentham on private and public wages and employment", In L.S. Moss, *Joseph A. Schumpeter, historian of economics*. London, Routledge, pp. 195–213.

Sigot, Nathalie (2002) "Jevons's Debt to Bentham: Mathematical Economy, Morals and Psychology". *The Manchester School*, 70, 262–278.

Skinner, Burrhus Frederic (1938) *The Behavior of Organisms*. New York: Appleton-Century-Crofts.

Skinner, Burrhus Frederic (1969) *Contingencies of Reinforcement: A Theoretical Analysis*, New York, Appleton-Century-Crofts.

Sismondi, Jean Charles Leonard de (1803) *De la richesse comercial*, Geneve, J. J. Paschoud.

Sismondi, Jean Charles Leonard de (1819) *Nouveaux principles d'économie politique, ou de la richesse dans ses rapports avec la population*, Paris, Chez Delaunay.

Smith, Adam (1976a) The Theory of Moral Sentiments, *The Glasgow Edition of the Works and Correspondence of Adam Smith, vol. 1*, edited by D. D. Raphael and A. L. Macfie, Oxford, Oxford University Press. (TMS) [1759].

Smith, Adam (1976b) An Inquiry into the Nature and Causes of the Wealth of Nations, *The Glasgow Edition of the Works and Correspondence of Adam Smith, vol II*, Volume 1 and 2, Edited by R. H. Campbell and A. S. Skinner. Textual editor W. B. Todd., Liberty Classics, Indianapolis, Oxford University Press [1776]: (WN)

Smith, Adam (1978) Lectures on Jurisprudence, *The Glasgow Edition of the Works and Correspondence of Adam Smith. Vol. V*, edited by R. L. Meek, D. D. Raphael and P. G. Stein, Clarendon Press, Oxford, Oxford University Press [1896]: (LJ: LJ (A) 1762–3; LJ (B) 1766).

Smith, Adam (1980) Essays on Philosophical Subjects, edited by W. P. D. Wightman y J. C. Bryce, with Dugald Stewart's Account of Adam Smith, *The Glasgow Edition of the Works and Correspondence of Adam Smith. Vol. III*, edited byr I. S. Ross. General editors, D. D. Raphael y A. S. Skinner, Clarendon Press, Indianapolis, Oxford University Press [1795, London, ed. Cadell and Davies with Dugald Stewart in 1797]: (EPS).

Smith, Adam (1983) Lectures on Rhetoric and belles lettres (with Consideration concerning the First Formation of Languages), *The Glasgow Edition of the Works and Correspondence of Adam Smith. Vol. IV*, Edited by J. C. Bryce, General Editor A.S. Skinner, Oxford, Clarendon Press, [1958] (LRBL).

Smith, Adam (1987) The Correspondence of Adam Smith, edited by Ernest Campbell Mossner and Ian Simpson Ross, *The Glasgow Edition of the Works and Correspondence of Adam Smith, vol VI*, edited by Ernest Campbell Mossner and Ian Simpson Ross, Indianapolis, Oxford University Press, Liberty Classics.

Smith, Craig (2013) "Adam Smith and the New Right," in *The Oxford Handbook of Adam Smith,* edited by C. J. Berry, M. Paganelli & C. Smith, Oxford, Oxford University Press, pp. 539–558.

Southey, Robert (1929) *Journal of a tour in Scotland in 1819,* London: John Murray.

Sowell, Thomas (1972) "Sismondi, a neglected pioneer", *History of Political Economy*, 4, 1, 62–88.

Spengler, Joseph J. (1975) "Adam Smith and society's decision-makers", *Essays on Adam Smith*, edited by A. S. Skinner and T. Wilson, Oxford, pp. 397–400.

Spiegel, Henry W. (1999) *El desarrollo del pensamiento económico, Historia del pensamiento económico desde los tiempos bíblicos hasta nuestros días,* Barcelona, Ediciones Omega.

Stark, W. (1952a) *Jeremy Bentham's Economic Writings.* Critical Edition Based in his printed Works and unprinted Manuscripts, volume 1, London, Published for The Royal Economic Society by George Allen & Unwin LTD.

Stark, W. (1952b) *Jeremy Bentham's Economic Writings.* Critical Edition Based in his printed Works and unprinted Manuscripts, volume 2, London, Published for The Royal Economic Society by George Allen & Unwin LTD.

Stark, W. (1954) *Jeremy Bentham's Economic Writings.* Critical Edition Based on his printed Works and unprinted Manuscripts, volume 3, London, Published for The Royal Economic Society by George Allen & Unwin LTD.

Steintrager, James (1977) *Bentham*, London, George Allen & Unwin Ltd.

Stephen, Leslie (1900) *The English Utilitarians*, London, Duchworth.

Steven, Kreis (1996–2014) The History Guide. Lectures on Modern European Intellectual History: Abelard to Nietzsche. "Lecture 22. The Utopian Socialists: Robert Owen and Saint-Simon (2)". http://www.historyguide.org/intellect/lecture22a.html (Access: 10-12-2016)

Stevens, Peter F. (2003) "George Bentham (1800–1884): the life of a botanist's botanist", *Archives of Natural History*, 30, 2, 189–202.

Storey, Mark (1997) *Robert Southey: A Life.* Oxford, Oxford University Press.

Tasset, José Luis (1994) "Utilitarismo y teoría del desarrollo moral", *Télos. Revista Iberoamericana de Estudios Utilitaristas*, Vol. III, n° 1, junio, pp. 49–83.

Tasset, José Luis (1999) *La ética y las pasiones*, La Coruña, Servicio de Publicacións de Universidade da Coruña.

Taylor, W. L. (1955) "Bentham as Economist: A Review Article", *South African Journal of Economics,* 23, 1, 66–74.

Taylor, Keith (ed, tr.) (1975) *Henri de Saint Simon, 1760-1825: Selected writings on science, industry and social organization.* New York, USA: Holmes and Meier Publishers, Inc.

Taylor, Keith (2013) *Political Ideas of the Utopian Socialists*, Routledge, London.

Taylor, Anne (1987) *Visions of Harmony. A Study in Nineteenth-Century Milleniarism.* Oxford: Clarendon Press.

The Open University (2016) Robert *Owen and New Lanark,* see http://www.open.edu/openlearn/history-the-arts/history/history-art/robert-owen-and-new-lanark/content-section-0

Thomas, William E. C. (1917) *The Philosophic Radicals: Nine Studies in Theory and Practice 1817–1841,* Oxford: The Clarendon Press.

Thornton, Henry (2000) *Credito papel*, con estudio preliminar de Fernando Méndez Ibisate, Madrid, ediciones Pirámide.

Trincado, Estrella (2003a) *Crítica a la doctrina de la Utilidad y Revisión de las teorías de Hume, Smith y Bentham*, E-Prints UCM, Madrid.

Trincado, Estrella (2003b) "Adam Smith: crítico del utilitarismo", *Télos. Revista Iberoamericana de Estudios Utilitaristas*, XII, 1, 43–62.

Trincado, Estrella (2004a) "Equity, utility and transaction costs: on the origin of the judicial power in Adam Smith", *Storia del Pensiero Economico*, July, 1, 33–51.

Trincado, Estrella (2004b) "Bentham. Precursor de los Austriacos", Procesos *de Mercado. Revista Europea de Economía Política*, 2, 2, 119–149.

Trincado, Estrella (2005a) "Utility, Money and transaction costs: Authoritarian vs libertarian monetary policies", *History of Economic Ideas*. XIII, 1, 57–77.

Trincado, Estrella (2005b) "Las constituciones utilitaristas", *Télos*, 14,1, 145–180.

Trincado, Estrella (2006) "Adam Smith criticism of the doctrine of utility: a theory of the Creative Present", in Montes, Leonidas and Schliesser, Eric (eds.), *New Voices on Adam Smith*, New York and London, Routledge, pp. 313–327.

Trincado, Estrella (2008a) "Economía del desarrollo vs Economía del bienestar: distintas filosofías de la vida", *Revista de Economía Mundial*, 18, 141–154

Trincado, Estrella (2008b) "Autogestión y universidad: la historia de un sistema corporativo", *Revista empresa y humanismo,*Vol. 11, 1, 273–312.

Trincado, Estrella (2009) *Crítica del utilitarismo. Utilidad frente a realidad presente*, Maia Ediciones, Madrid.

Trincado, Estrella (2013) "Time as a milestone in economic thought", *Filosofía de la Economía*, 1, 2, 247–273

Trincado, Estrella (2014a) "Socialistas utópicos, Karl Marx y los historicistas" en David Sanz (coord.), *Historia del pensamiento económico*, UCAV, Ávila.

Trincado, Estrella (2014b) "On Smith's notion of pleasure", *Filosofía de la Economía*, 3, 49–58

Trincado, Estrella (2015) "Silencios Que Hacen Ruido: De Cómo Se Sobrepuso John Stuart Mill De Los Estados Melancólicos Del Utilitarismo", *Telos. Revista Iberoamericana de Estudios Utilitaristas*, XX/1: 27–50.

Trincado, Estrella & Santos, Manuel (2014) "Bentham and Owen on entrepreneurship and social reform", *The European Journal Of The History Of Economic Thought*, 21, 2, 252–277.

Tumim, Judge Stephen (1994) "Janet Semple. Bentham's Prison: A Study of the Panopticon Penitentiary", Oxford Clarendon Press, 1993, pp. 344", *Utilitas. A journal of Utilitarian Studies*, 6, 1, p. 137.

Turgot, Anne Robert Jacquess (1769–70) *Reflections on the Formation and Distribution of Wealth*, London, E. Spragg.

Tusseau, Guillaume (ed.) (2014) *The Legal Philosophy and Influence of Jeremy Bentham. Essays on 'Of the Limits of the Penal Branch of Jurisprudence*, Routledge, Research in Constitutional Law.

Tuttle, Charles A. (1927) "The entrepreneur function in economic literature", *Journal of Political Economy*, August, 504–505.

UNESCO (2001) New Lanark, Date of Inscription: 16th December 2001, UK, Excerpt from the Report of the 25th Session of the World Heritage Committee, Retrieved March 10, 2009 from http://whc.unesco.org/en/list/429/.

University College London (UCL) 'London University, Manuscripts Room: The Bentham Papers'. Access http://www.a2a.org.uk/

University of Manchester (2014) "Training the pauper child – musical performance", @ PoorTheatres By ADMIN-POOR IN BLOG, EDUCATION, PAUPER CHILDREN, POOR LAW ON JUNE 23, 2014

Urrutia, Juan (1983) *Economía Neoclásica. Seducción y verdad*, Madrid: Pirámide.

Valdaliso, Jesús Mª, y López, Santiago (2000) *Historia económica de la empresa*, Barcelona, Crítica.

Varouxakis, Georgios & Kelly, Paul (2010) *John Stuart Mill: Thought and Influence: The Saint of Rationalism*, London and New York, Routledge.

Veblen, Thorstein (1899) *The Theory of the Leisure Class*. New York: MacMillan.

Vygotsky, L.S. (1978) *Mind in Society: The Development of Higher Psychological Processes*, Cambridge, MA, Harvard University Press

Viner, Jacob (1949) "Bentham and J. S. Mill: the utilitarian Background", *American Economic Review*, XXXIX, 321.

Vivenza, Gloria (2001) *Adam Smith and Classics. The Classical Heritage in Adam Smith's Thought*, Oxford, OUP.

Wallace, Graham (1898) *The Life of Francis Place*, London, New York, Longmans, Green.

Walsh, Eamonn J. and Stewart, Ross (1993) "Accounting and the construction of institutions: The case of a factory", *Accounting, Organizations and Society*, 18, 783–800.

Warke, Tom (2000) "Classical Utilitarianism and the methodology of determinate choice, in economics and in ethics", *Journal of Economic Methodology*, 7, 3, 373–394.

Wells, Thomas (2016) *Sen's Capability Approach, The Internet Encyclopedia of Philosophy* (IEP), "http://www.iep.utm.edu/sen-cap/

Williams, Robert B. (1997) *Accounting for Steam and Cotton: Two Eighteenth Century Case Studies*, New York, Garland.

Wilson, Edmund (1940) *To the Finland Station: A Study in the Writing and Acting of History*, Garden City, NY, Doubleday.

Wilson, William E. (1964) *The Angel and the Serpent*, Bloomington.

Williford, Miriam (1980) *Jeremy Bentham on Spanish America, An Account of his Letters and Proposals to the New World*, Louisiana, Louisiana State University Press.

Winch, Donald (1997) "Bentham on colonies and Empire", *Utilitas*, 9, 1, March, 147–154.

Whitehouse, David (2005) "Workplace presenteeism: How behavioral professionals can make a difference". *Behavioral Healthcare Tomorrow*, 14, 32–35.

Wolff, Jonathan (1993) "Hume, Bentham and the Social Contract", *Utilitas. A Journal of Utilitarian Studies*, 5, 1, 87–90.

Index

For Product Safety Concerns and Information please contact our EU
representative GPSR@taylorandfrancis.com
Taylor & Francis Verlag GmbH, Kaufingerstraße 24, 80331 München, Germany

www.ingramcontent.com/pod-product-compliance
Ingram Content Group UK Ltd.
Pitfield, Milton Keynes, MK11 3LW, UK
UKHW020953180425
457613UK00019B/660